World
Agriculture
and the GATT

International Political Economy Yearbook, Volume 7

William P. Avery and David P. Rapkin, Series Editors

World Agriculture and the GATT

edited by
William P. Avery

Lynne Rienner Publishers   •   Boulder & London

Published in the United States of America in 1993 by
Lynne Rienner Publishers, Inc.
1800 30th Street, Boulder, Colorado 80301

and in the United Kingdom by
Lynne Rienner Publishers, Inc.
3 Henrietta Street, Covent Garden, London WC2E 8LU

Library of Congress Cataloging-in-Publication Data
World agriculture and the GATT / edited by William P. Avery
      p.   cm. — (International political economy yearbook : v. 7)
   Includes bibliographical references and index.
   ISBN 1-55587-309-X (alk. paper)
   1. Agriculture and state. 2. Produce trade. 3. General Agreement
on Tariffs and Trade (Organization) 4. Uruguay Round (1987–)
I. Avery, William P. II. Series.
HF1410.I579   1992 vol. 7
[HD1415]
337'.05 s—dc20
[382'.41]   92-28186
                                              CIP

British Cataloguing in Publication Data
A Cataloguing in Publication record for this book
is available from the British Library.

Printed and bound in the United States of America

The paper used in this publication meets the requirements
of the American National Standard for Permanence of
Paper for Printed Library Materials Z39.48-1984.

Contents

Tables and Figures

FIGURES

The Contributors

William P. Avery is professor of political science at the University of Nebraska–Lincoln. He has published a variety of articles on international political economy and has edited several books, including (with David Rapkin) *Markets, Politics, and Change in the Global Political Economy* and *America in a Changing World Political Economy.*

Theodore H. Cohn is professor of political science at Simon Fraser University, British Columbia. He has written extensively on global and Canadian agricultural topics and is author of the recent book, *The International Politics of Agricultural Trade: Canadian-American Relations in a Global Agricultural Context.*

Andrew F. Cooper is associate professor of political science and director of the International Studies Program at the University of Waterloo, Ontario. He has been a visiting scholar at Harvard University and the Australian National University. His recent research focuses on the role of middle powers in the international political economy.

Aurelia George is senior lecturer at the Australian Defence Force Academy, University of New South Wales. Her research and writings have dealt with the agricultural policy, interest groups, and foreign policy of Japan. She is presently working on a book on Japanese agricultural policy.

Ulrich Hausner is a research assistant and Ph.D. student in the Department of Agricultural and Applied Economics at the University of Minnesota. He previously studied at the University of Bonn. His research interests are in the area of agricultural and trade policy, as well as production economics and natural resources economics.

Richard Higgott is reader in international relations and public policy and director of studies in foreign affairs and trade at the Research School of Pacific Studies, Australian National University. Among his extensive publications is a recent coedited volume entitled *Pacific Economic Relations in the 1990s: Cooperation or Conflict?*

Raymond F. Hopkins is professor of political science at Swarthmore College. He is author of several books and articles on food policy and international politics, dealing largely with less developed countries. He has been consultant to various organizations, including the World Bank and the World Food Program.

H. Wayne Moyer is Rosenfield Professor and director of the Rosenfield Program in Public Affairs, International Relations, and Human Rights at Grinnell College. He has been a visiting scholar at Stanford University and the University of London and resident fellow at Resources for the Future. He is coauthor (with Tim Josling) of the book *Agricultural Policy Reform: Politics and Process in the EC and USA.*

Robert L. Paarlberg is professor of political science at Wellesley College and associate at the Harvard Center for International Affairs. He is widely published in the area of U.S. agricultural trade policy. His most recent book is *Fixing Farm Trade*, sponsored by the New York Council on Foreign Relations. A frequent consultant on food policy to government agencies, his current research is supported by the Ford Foundation and the Overseas Development Council.

David P. Rapkin is associate professor of political science at the University of Nebraska–Lincoln. His research on international political economy has recently focused on Japan and world leadership. He is author or editor of a number of publications, including the recent book, *World Leadership and Hegemony*. He spent 1988 and 1990 as Foreign Scholar at the University of Tsukuba, Japan.

C. Ford Runge is associate professor in the Department of Agricultural and Applied Economics at the University of Minnesota, where he also holds appointments in the Hubert H. Humphrey Institute of Public Affairs and the Department of Forest Resources. Recipient of numerous awards and fellowships, he was special assistant to the U.S. Ambassador to the GATT in 1988. He has published a wide variety of books and articles on agricultural policy and natural resources policy. His most recent book (with Willard W. Cochrane) is entitled *Reforming Farm Policy: Toward a National Agenda.*

Harald von Witzke is associate professor in the Department of Agricultural and Applied Economics, University of Minnesota, where he serves as director of the Center for International Food and Agricultural Policy. He has served with the Ministry of Agriculture in Germany and taught at the University of Bonn. He is author of several books and numerous articles on international agricultural development, policy, and trade.

Acknowledgments

Most of the chapters in this book were originally presented at the Twelfth Hendricks Symposium, "American Trade Policy in a Changed World Political Economy," sponsored by the Department of Political Science, University of Nebraska–Lincoln, April 5–6, 1991. The symposium, organized by the editor of this volume, was part of the Nebraska Lectures in American Government and Politics made possible through the generosity of G. E. Hendricks, an alumnus of the University of Nebraska and later a Colorado attorney. Mr. Hendricks had a lively interest in American politics and was especially concerned about the limitation of public discussion during the early 1950s. Therefore, during the period 1949 to 1957, he gave to the University of Nebraska Foundation a substantial sum of money to be used to deal with "current controversial political questions . . . in a non-partisan, unbiased manner." Mr. Hendricks believed that a more intelligent examination and consideration of political questions would lead to better government and public policy. The symposium, sponsored with his gift, and this volume were designed to promote these aims.

In addition to the Hendricks Fund, several others at the University of Nebraska contributed generously to the funding of the symposium: the Montgomery Lecture Series, the University Research Council, and the College of Arts and Sciences. Valuable staff assistance was provided by the Department of Political Science, in particular by Helen Sexton, Jan Edwards, and Royce Ammon. The support of John Peters, dean of the College of Arts and Sciences, is especially noteworthy. Not only has he provided financial support for various Hendricks symposia, but he has consistently supported the editorial activities of the *IPE Yearbook* and its editors.

The volume also benefited from the cooperation and assistance of a great many other individuals and institutions. My thanks to the *Yearbook* board of editors and all those colleagues who assisted in the evaluation of the manuscripts. William Browne is due special thanks for reading and commenting on the entire volume. It no doubt would be a better book had I heeded all his advice. Andrew Cooper's work on Chapter 6 was supported by the Social Sciences and Humanities Research Council of Canada. He and Richard Higgott are also grateful to Kim Nossal, Robert Young, T. K. Warley, Robert Solfe, and Stuart Harris for helpful comments on earlier drafts of their chapter. The research of Raymond Hopkins in Chapter 7 was supported by the U.S. Agency for International Development, and additional assistance was provided by Nien-he Hsieh and Mark Hopkins. Harald von Witzke and Ulrich Hausner conducted the research for Chapter 8 with the assistance of a grant from the Agricultural Experiment Station, University of Minnesota, and the North Central Experiment Station Regional Project NC-194. Ford Runge's research (Chapter 9) is based in part on his work with the 1991 State of Food and Agriculture Report issued by the Food and Agriculture Organization in Rome.

Finally, my thanks to my colleague and *Yearbook* coeditor, David Rapkin, for his assistance, encouragement, and intellectual inspiration throughout the life of this project; and to Gia Hamilton, project editor at Lynne Rienner Publishers, with whom it is always a joy to work.

William P. Avery

William P. Avery 1

Agriculture and Free Trade

One would be hard pressed to identify an area of economic policy that causes more problems for world trade than agriculture. Agriculture is central to the interests of both the rich industrialized countries, in which it is heavily subsidized, and the poor nonindustrialized countries, in which it is often the principal source of export earnings. In most instances, farm interests are disproportionately represented in international trade policy processes. Particularly in the industrialized countries, political leaders are subjected to the push and pull of powerful and often contradictory political pressures so intense that international agreement on agricultural trade issues is nearly impossible. Leaders are exposed to strong domestic agricultural interests, on the one hand, and equally strong international interests of the state, on the other. The resulting dilemma frequently leads to paralysis in trade policymaking.

Although all the contributions to this volume deal directly or indirectly with this dilemma, the primary purpose is to broaden our understanding of the range of issues involving agriculture in the global trade regime and to explain how and why free trade in agriculture has proved so intractable in world trade negotiations. The particular focus is on the multilateral trade negotiations (MTNs) currently under way, known as the Uruguay Round.

THE GATT AND AGRICULTURE

Since the end of World War II, the world trading system has operated under the auspices of the General Agreement on Tariffs and Trade (GATT). Negotiated under the leadership of the United States in 1947, the agreement was based on broad principles of free trade and provided a framework for negotiating multilateral reductions in trade barriers. Since that time, through seven "rounds" of negotiations, GATT signatory nations have succeeded in lowering tariffs, mostly on manufactured goods, from an average exceeding 40 percent to about 5 percent today.

In stark contrast to the industrial sector, agriculture has been largely exempted from tariff-lowering rules throughout the existence of the GATT. Just as the United States can take much of the credit for leading the way toward freer trade in manufactured products, as frequently noted in this volume, it also must take the blame for blocking the extension of GATT rules to agriculture. Facing stiff opposition from domestic farm interests, the United States "used its international political muscle in 1955 to obtain a waiver of most of its GATT obligations with respect to agriculture" (Palmeter, 1989: 47). This waiver extended broad discretion to the United States to insulate its domestic agricultural market from foreign competition.

U.S. insistence on the exemption of agriculture from GATT discipline led to the development of a special relationship of agriculture to GATT rules. In virtually all other areas of trade, GATT rules were established to instruct countries on what they could and could not do to intervene in domestic markets and industries. However, in agriculture, the reverse was true. Instead of governments bringing their domestic practices into line with GATT rules, "GATT rules were written to fit the agricultural programs then in existence, especially in the United States" (Hathaway, 1987: 104). Subsequently, GATT rules have been "fitted" to the domestic agricultural programs of a variety of other countries.

Efforts in previous rounds of multilateral trade negotiations to bring agricultural trade more fully under GATT rules proved unsuccessful. During the earliest MTNs, agriculture was a back-burner issue as negotiators concentrated mainly on trade in manufactures. It was not until the Dillon Round (1960–1961) that agricultural trade issues began to receive greater attention. This was spurred by the developing tensions between the United States and the newly formed European Community (EC) over the discriminatory and trade-distorting effects of its Common Agricultural Policy (CAP). During the Kennedy Round (1963–1967), nontariff barriers and the effects of domestic agricultural policies were put on the table, although little progress was made. Again, the conflicting positions of the EC and the United States dominated the agriculture portion of the round. The Tokyo Round (1973–1979) included consideration of nontariff barriers to agricultural trade, but it too foundered on the opposing positions of the EC and the United States.

Then a crisis hit world agriculture in the 1980s. Prices fell, exports declined, and general economic distress in agriculture forced large numbers of farmers to give up farming altogether. Under these conditions, both direct and indirect import barriers spread and export subsidies soared. Among industrialized countries, agricultural support costs rose to nearly $300 billion in 1988, almost 3 percent of total consumption and 10 percent of savings for these countries in that year (Junz and Boonekamp, 1991: 12).

An international group of twenty-nine agricultural experts meeting in Ottawa, Canada, in May 1988, concluded that "the programs governments have developed to assist farmers, maintain farm income, and stabilize market prices are a major factor contributing to global problems." Such programs, they argued, "have continued to encourage rapid increases in output in many countries at a time when the growth in world demand has slackened" (Bergsten, 1988: 3). The result was that agricultural commodity prices fell to their lowest levels since the economic crisis of the 1930s.

In addition to the crisis in agriculture, other problems had developed in the world trading system by the early 1980s, which combined to create a sense of urgency in the need for reform. The liberal trade regime established after World War II had suffered serious erosion. Demands for protection had erupted throughout the system, as states were faced with heightened competition and resulting problems of labor adjustment. The amount of world trade covered by GATT rules was shrinking. Trade tensions were growing, and more and more trading partners were turning toward bilateral agreements to deal with them. U.S. economic dominance had declined as the world economy grew more interdependent. In addition to the remarkable postwar economic expansion of Europe and Japan, new aggressive exporters had emerged in some parts of the developing world. Faced with these changes and its own decline, the United States demonstrated a diminished ability and willingness to defend an open trade regime. The result was a trading system moving toward fragmentation.

Against this background of mounting disarray, the finance ministers of GATT member countries met in Punta del Este, Uruguay, during September 1986. At that meeting, the ministers issued the Punta del Este Declaration, which called for a new round of multilateral trade negotiations, the Uruguay Round, to begin in January 1987. The declaration, the culmination of several years of hard and complex bargaining, specified new trade sectors to be negotiated into the GATT and a strengthening of GATT rules and discipline. The United States, which had been a prime mover in this and previous rounds, was particularly committed to bringing agriculture and other previously excluded sectors into liberalized trade.

The Uruguay Round began with a remarkably broad and ambitious negotiating agenda, which was to be concluded in its entirety in 1990. Even before the deadline arrived, however, it was clear that failure to reach agreement on agriculture would block completion of the round. The United States had been pushing for the elimination of all farm subsidies and price supports by the year 2000, a position the EC flatly rejected and one that many U.S. farmers likewise did not support. Although the EC was willing to make some concessions on domestic farm programs, there was almost no chance that its member countries (especially France) could resist the fierce opposition of their farm constituencies and agree to remove all subsidies and price supports, even if larger EC international trade interests ultimately might benefit. In fact, there was then—and there continues to be—virtually no support in Europe for a completely free market in agriculture.

TWO-LEVEL BARGAINING

The bargaining dilemma facing the EC and virtually all of the industrialized countries in the Uruguay Round, in which trade negotiators must try to reconcile powerful and well-established domestic interests with the often conflicting larger international interests of the state, can be conceptualized by what Putnam (1988) referred to as "two-level games." At the international level (Level I), bargaining takes place among representatives of states in order to forge an agreement. Level II bargaining involves attempts to gain ratification of the agreement by those domestic constituencies whose concurrence is needed to implement the agreement. Quite often, what may be in the interests of the state at Level I collides head-on with opposing interests of entrenched domestic interests at Level II.

Obviously, the two levels are highly interactive. Level II interests usually mold the bargaining positions and strategies of negotiators at Level I. Expectations about prospects for ratification also determine the parameters within which potential agreements are considered. Conversely, Level I developments can affect politics at Level II, sometimes increasing prospects for ratification and at other times diminishing them.

One difficulty of such two-level bargaining is that failure to gain acceptance of the agreement at Level II can doom the agreement altogether. This is because the agreement cannot be amended at Level II without reopening the negotiations at Level I. Negotiators thus must always be aware of the constraints imposed on them in Level I deliberations by Level II constituencies. However, Level II constraints can work to the advantage of negotiators at Level I. When these constraints are perceived to be especially restrictive, one's negotiating counterparts may extend an additional degree of bargaining latitude.

Game theorists speak of such interaction between the two levels in terms of "win-sets." A win-set consists of the set of all possible Level I agreements that would win ratification at Level II. Wider win-sets enhance the prospects for ratification because the win-sets of each side are more likely to overlap. Ratification is impossible if no overlap exists. Just as negotiators with narrow win-sets may garner some bargaining space from their counterparts, negotiators whose win-sets are perceived to be large will be pressed to make concessions. Rational bargaining strategies, of course, would refrain from pressing the latter to make concessions that threaten ratification (i.e., restrict or eliminate the overlap between win-sets).

Putnam's framework of two-level games in international bargaining is especially useful in analyzing agricultural trade negotiations. Whether applied to the United States or the European Community, representatives of any country with strong domestic farm preferences and coalitions must grapple with this bargaining problem. The contributions to this volume bring this problem into sharp focus through a comprehensive analysis of the role of agriculture in the Uruguay Round of trade negotiations and in the global trade regime more generally.

THE CONTRIBUTIONS

The book's analysis begins with a detailed survey of the evolution of the global agricultural trade regime. This chapter provides the necessary substantive background for subsequent discussion of the specific actors in the Uruguay Round. In sequence, those chapters deal first with the main antagonists in the round—the United States, Japan, and the EC—followed by discussion of the respective roles of the Cairns Group and the less developed countries (LDCs). The focus then shifts to a formal study of the determinants of agricultural policy intervention in developed countries and the implications of such intervention for a liberal trade regime. The final chapter looks beyond the Uruguay Round to emerging issues in agricultural trade policy.

Theodore H. Cohn provides a comprehensive discussion in Chapter 2 of the changing and dominant role of the United States in shaping the global agricultural trade regime. Building on previous work by Finlayson and Zacher (1981), he identifies two sets of contrasting principles that have prevailed in world trade throughout the post–World War II period. The first set embraces interdependence principles such as liberalization, multilateralism, economic development, and nondiscrimination. Adherence to these principles promotes general welfare through collaboration and tends to strengthen the liberal trade regime. Sovereignty principles make up the second set, emphasizing exemptionalism, major state interests, and reciprocity, all of which work to weaken the regime.

Cohn argues that agricultural trade comprises an identifiable and analytically distinct regime "nested" within the more general international trade regime. The United States has been the main architect of both regimes and, as previously noted, is largely responsible for the illiberal treatment of agriculture. Cohn traces the U.S. negotiating position on agriculture from full-fledged defense of sovereignty principles during the 1950s to insistence on complete interdependence in the Uruguay Round. His analysis captures the tension often prevalent in two-level game bargaining, demonstrating the ongoing struggle between multilateralism and sovereign interests in shaping the U.S. position on agriculture.

In Chapter 3, Robert L. Paarlberg directly employs Putnam's two-level game approach to explain how agriculture came to dominate the Uruguay Round and why differences concerning agriculture ultimately deadlocked the negotiations. Market-oriented appointees of the Reagan administration, seeking to end costly domestic farm support programs and having met stiff bipartisan opposition to such proposals in Congress, devised a clever plan. Their plan, Paarlberg contends, was to transfer the debate to a different arena, one in which the administration might have more leverage. Hence, a strategy was launched to pursue the domestic agricultural "reform" agenda through an international negotiation—the Uruguay Round. The round became the collective focus of top U.S. officials, who sensed an opportunity to "internationalize" this thorny domestic issue. Domestic farm price supports thus became a priority subject in the agricultural negotiations of the round.

One of the presumed and major advantages of this strategy, from the standpoint of U.S. agricultural officials, was the opportunity to circumvent the powerful and highly effective domestic farm lobby. These officials believed that the only way to defeat this lobby was to take the farm policy process out of traditional channels. Negotiations would be conducted among like-minded trade ministers and specialists abroad, with ratification by the whole Congress and not just the powerful agriculture committees. Moreover, congressional ratification would be conducted under special "fast-track" authority, whose rules—including no amendments, limited debate, and a single up-or-down vote on the entire agreement—greatly favored ratification. As Paarlberg points out, U.S. negotiators were hoping this strategy would expand their win-set in the negotiations.

Domestic farm interests, however, had little trouble devising their own two-level game strategy. Ironically, the administration provided the farm lobby its greatest tactical advantage by comparing agricultural negotiations to arms control negotiations. Farm interests were quick to seize the arms control metaphor and use it to make several demands from the negotiations. They resisted farm subsidy cuts by arguing against "unilateral disarmament while negotiations are under way." And they even called for more subsidies as "bargaining chips" that could be later traded away to achieve a better deal in the round.

Congress, all too eager to portray the domestic farm problem as a global one, joined the farm lobby in casting the U.S. farmer as victim in a global environment of unfair subsidized foreign competition. The result, Paarlberg argues, is that domestic farm interests succeeded in narrowing the win-set of Level I negotiators, making agreement less likely in the MTNs. The two-level game strategy of the farm lobby thus proved to be effective in blocking the round and in bolstering arguments for even greater agricultural subsidies at home.

Paarlberg concludes with a pessimistic assessment of the prospects for a breakthrough in agricultural negotiations. Instead, he suggests that farm policy reform, although difficult, might be possible one country at a time. For this to happen, however, he believes that the approach must change from a "contest against foreigners" to internal reform outside the GATT. Budgetary crises in both the United States and the EC suggest that this may well be the ultimate outcome.

The Japanese debate over rice liberalization provides David P. Rapkin and Aurelia George (Chapter 4) with excellent case material for systematic application of the two-level game framework. They contend that the "interests underlying rice protection run directly counter to the economic interests of Japan's urban consumers, its world class manufacturing industries, and its cosmopolitan interests in an open world trading order." Japan has benefited enormously from the liberal trade regime constructed under the GATT and should be expected, through enlightened self-interest, to play a leadership role in successfully concluding the Uruguay Round. Rapkin and George believe that, whereas the main sticking point in the negotiations is the conflict between the EC and the United States, Japan's opening of its rice market could be just the initiative that would spawn agreement in the round and thus preserve Japan's larger Level I interests. Nonetheless, Japan has remained firm in its no-concessions policy on rice liberalization.

Why Japanese policymakers have chosen to adhere so stubbornly to this policy is the central analytic task of Chapter 4. The authors' carefully crafted use of the two-level game framework greatly facilitates this task and demonstrates the particular utility of the framework in analyzing international bargaining in agricultural trade. They examine separately three sets of factors, suggested by Putnam, that affect the size of a country's win-set: the preferences and coalitions of Level II constituents; Level II political institutions involved in ratification; and the strategies used by Level I participants in the negotiations.

Two coalitions of interests have formed in Japan: one around preferences for the status quo and another for opening the rice market. The status quo is preferred by the government, agricultural bureaucrats, farm organizations, some consumers, and the major political parties, including opposition parties that covet the rural vote that has traditionally supported the ruling party, the Liberal Democratic Party (LDP). However, the authors note that the status quo coalition has undergone some degree of erosion in the past year or so, particularly as the LDP, a core member of the coalition, has slowly begun to reconcile itself to the need for some form of market opening in order to expand Japan's win-set in the Uruguay Round.

The market-opening coalition, as might be expected, includes primarily private business organizations and government ministries that represent business (especially export) interests. This obviously reflects their realization that it is Japan's competitive manufacturers that stand to benefit the most from successful completion of the round. GATT reform would increase their access to world markets, strengthen GATT rules for such things as dispute settlement, and probably also curb U.S. tendencies toward unilateralism in its trade dealings with Japan.

Even if Japan's trade negotiators are able to forge a winning coalition for market opening, the particular Japanese ratification process could still make approval difficult. Putnam (1988: 449) argued that "the Japanese propensity for seeking the broadest possible domestic consensus before acting constricts the Japanese win-set, as contrasted with majoritarian political cultures." The reverse is true as well. States with greater autonomy from their Level II constituencies are better able to engineer wider win-sets. Rapkin and George contend that although Japan apparently has acquired some measure of autonomy in its industrial policies, its autonomy in agricultural trade policy is much more limited.

The interaction of the two bargaining levels is further demonstrated by the manner in which Japan's Level II preferences, coalitions, and ratification processes combine to shape its negotiating position in the round. Japan has clung to a rigid domestic food security strategy, pressing for exceptionalist treatment of its rice production, even to the point of linking rice to its national culture and identity. The authors discuss various ways in which Japanese negotiators could have widened their Level I win-set as well as minimize the impact on Level II constituencies. They show, however, that at each turn Japan chose to stick to its most extreme protectionist position. The result, they conclude, is that ultimately, if the EC and the United States reach agreement, Japan likely will be forced to liberalize along lines dictated by others. More broadly, the authors argue that the peculiar nature of Japan's state-society relationship in agriculture has blocked an opportunity for Japan to exercise constructive leadership in the world political economy.

The European Community's defense of price support mechanisms of the Common Agricultural Policy bears resemblance to Japan's obstinacy toward rice liberalization. Although the EC position has not been as extreme as the no-concessions stand of the Japanese, the EC refusal to accommodate U.S. demands caused the trade talks to break down in December 1990. Despite significant changes in the EC negotiating position, which allowed negotiations to restart in 1991, the continuing pressure from national farm constituencies to maintain the CAP has made further movement difficult. H. Wayne Moyer explains these developments in the EC negotiating process in Chapter 5.

Trade policy formulation within the EC is arguably more complex than it is for any of the other participants in the Uruguay Round. As Moyer demonstrates, policy is made through a multitiered, compartmentalized, consensus-driven process that favors agriculture. Just as Putnam's bargaining game logic proved useful in the previous analyses of the United States and Japan, Moyer finds that a modified form of the framework also provides insight into the dynamics of EC negotiations. Because EC bargaining takes place at the regional level, as well as within national governments and within the GATT, it is necessary to conceptualize the bargaining as a three-level game. The three levels examined are the EC negotiators in the GATT talks (Level I), the EC regional bargaining process (Level II), and the bargaining of national governments (Level III).

Moyer begins his analysis with Level II, where trade policy decisions are reached in the regional European Commission and the Council of Ministers. He observes that agricultural interests have important advantages at this level because the agriculture commissioner is backed by the full resources of the Commission's largest bureaucratic unit, the Directorate General for Agriculture. Moreover, the agriculture commissioner has the implied support of powerful national farm lobbies, causing other commissioners to defer to him or her in agricultural deliberations. National farm interests are additionally represented at this level, in that the Council of Ministers includes representatives from the national ministries of agriculture, who take the initiative in protecting national agricultural interests. Hence, any proposal to weaken the CAP is met with stiff opposition.

At the level of national governments (Level III), agricultural interests enjoy similar advantages. Moyer argues that even though national cabinets may be able to balance agricultural interests with other priorities, the agriculture ministers are still the ones who represent their respective national cabinet's position in the regional Council of Ministers. That the agriculture ministers have strong incentives to interpret their individual tasks in a way most favorable to their country's domestic agricultural interests should be no surprise.

The bargaining processes at Levels II and III have a significant impact on bargaining strategies of the EC negotiating team in the GATT talks (Level I). Whereas the EC Commission has sole authority to negotiate international trade agreements, within the Commission agriculture is accorded special negotiating authority. The Commission's Directorate General for External Affairs has authority to negotiate for the Commission in every trade sector except agriculture, which is given to the Directorate General for Agriculture. The implications of these procedures for the Uruguay Round are profound. As Moyer states, "The organization with the strongest interest in maintaining the CAP is placed in the driver's seat for the actual conduct of negotiations." The larger interests of trade policy reform are thus submerged under the national interests of CAP preservation.

Moyer concludes that, up to this point in the negotiating process, the EC win-set in the Uruguay Round had been reduced by the bargaining dynamics occurring at the national and regional levels. After the collapse of negotiations in December 1990, however, a budget crisis emerged in the EC in which spending on agricultural support programs played a dominant role. This crisis, induced largely by rising costs of agricultural subsidies, led agricultural interests within the EC Commission to propose transforming the CAP in such a way as to save its crucial elements while meeting many of the demands being made by the United States. The proposal contemplated sharp reductions in export subsidies and import restrictions while retaining income support that was not production oriented.

These changes in the EC policy environment altered the previous balance among the bargaining levels and widened the EC win-set in the GATT negotiations. Resumption of negotiations thus began with the opposing positions of the EC and the United States much closer together. However,

Moyer cautions against premature optimism. A serious obstacle remaining is the rigid opposition of France to CAP reform. French farmers produce most of the EC agricultural surplus and would suffer most from reduced export subsidies. And because farm exports comprise a sizable portion of France's export earnings, the net effect of an agreement that includes agricultural reform may be worse than no agreement at all. Whether the EC win-set can be broadened enough to produce a ratifiable agreement may well depend on how the French position evolves. In the end, Moyer speculates that France may allow the negotiations to go forward, telling its domestic farm constituencies that it held out as long as possible, got the best deal it could, but finally went along in the name of European unity.

Throughout much of the agricultural negotiations in the Uruguay Round, the main ally of the United States has been a group of agricultural exporters known as the Cairns Group. From both sides of the North-South divide in the international political economy, the Cairns Group represents a broad cross-cutting coalition of developed middle powers and smaller less developed countries. As might be expected, given the makeup of the coalition, different perspectives on trade policy and divergent interests rendered unity difficult to maintain. Surprisingly, however, it was tension between the two most developed members of the group, usually like-minded Australia and Canada, that caused the most problems. In Chapter 6, Andrew F. Cooper and Richard Higgott examine the role of the Cairns Group in the multilateral trade negotiations, with specific attention given to the respective leadership roles of Australia and Canada.

Although both of these countries are middle powers and familiar with the problems and opportunities offered by middle-power statecraft, Canada traditionally has taken the lead. Cooper and Higgott argue, however, that within the Cairns Group their leadership roles have been reversed. Canada, apparently unwilling to assume the costs of leadership, came increasingly to be viewed as a backslider within the group. Australia, on the other hand, increasingly took on the managerial responsibilities and intellectual leadership of the group. To help explain this shift in the leadership positions of the two countries, the authors join with other contributors to this volume by drawing upon the two-level game framework.

The importance of agriculture for the economy of Australia is considerably greater than it is for Canada. Australia's smaller manufacturing sector and greater dependence on agricultural exports have made it far more sensitive to issues of market access and trade-distorting effects of domestic farm support programs. A rapidly escalating rural crisis in the early 1980s greatly sharpened Australia's sensitivity to the impact of foreign agricultural practices on its domestic farm economy. The ruling Labor party became especially concerned that deteriorating economic conditions in the countryside would threaten its rural legislative seats, without which Labor might not retain its legislative majority.

Cooper and Higgott contend that the Labor government responded to the domestic farm crisis with an international strategy. The strategy called for waging battle with the EC and the United States on their trade-distorting illiberal practices in agriculture as a means of shifting the debate from domestic causes of the crisis to international causes. Australia thus eagerly supported liberalization of agricultural trade as a means to secure benefits for its very efficient rural sector and to counter the view that it was doing too little to ease the farm crisis. In this sense, the Australian response was similar to the "contest against foreigners" employed by U.S. farm interests in their two-level game strategy with the U.S. government (see Chapter 3).

Australia's Level I strategy of asserting leadership in the Cairns Group, although prompted by its Level II farm problem, proved beneficial to the group's effectiveness in the Uruguay Round. The authors describe the group's role in the round as one of conflict-mitigating, agenda-moving, and proposal-building coalitions, rather than the traditional power-based negotiating capabilities that characterize the role of major powers. They suggest that the activities of the Cairns Group "represent an important exercise in complex coalitional diplomacy of a kind that will likely be increasingly important in the future."

With respect to Canada's handling of the agricultural issue, Cooper and Higgott observe that it originally pursued a Level I strategy not unlike that of Australia. However, over time it was forced to adopt a defensive and less aggressive inward-oriented approach. This was necessary because of a sharp division among its farm constituencies, pitting export-oriented farm groups against import-sensitive ones. Needing farm electoral support to survive, the government of Prime Minister Mulroney opted to put off making a clear choice between the two opposing camps. Such an ambiguous policy, stressing the least harmful option, undermined Canada's credibility in the Cairns Group. It also had the effect, the authors note, of fully internalizing foreign economic policymaking so that every diplomatic move was carefully scrutinized by adjusters (export-oriented farmers) and resisters (import-sensitive farmers) as a test of the government's goodwill. Although the authors do not make the point directly, these developments imply that the Level II dispute reduced Canada's win-set in the Level I negotiations.

The discussion of developing countries in Chapter 7 completes the analysis of the participants in the Uruguay Round. Raymond F. Hopkins argues that developing countries have behaved very differently in this round than in previous ones, especially the Tokyo Round of the 1970s. Less developed countries played a very vocal role in that round, pressing a unified position on a new economic order for the world system. In the current round, however, LDCs have constituted a distinctly weak force. They have neither produced a consistent negotiating position nor fashioned the coalition to promote one.

Why LDCs have failed to forge proposals and coalitions from which to bargain with greater power is the central question Hopkins seeks to answer. He acknowledges that domestic farm groups often distort or block larger economic interests of LDCs, but he departs from the arguments advanced in this volume's preceding chapters. In his view, LDC behavior in the trade talks is better explained by three factors: (1) uncertainty among LDCs that makes it difficult to identify and pursue their interests; (2) ineffectiveness that stems from having few concessions to offer; and (3) difficulty establishing "compensatory measures," even when participants may favor doing so.

LDCs have been unable to exert any meaningful degree of influence in the agricultural deliberations because their bargaining position is in disarray. Their behavior has been essentially reactive, permitting other parties to define the issues and establish the alternatives. Hopkins claims that such behavior can be traced partly to LDCs' uncertainty about what their interests are and how best to pursue them. This, combined with political disorganization, means that they are unable even to thwart developments that are clearly "unsatisfactory" for them.

Hopkins provides evidence, for example, showing that failure to achieve liberalization in agriculture would harm the welfare interests of food producers in most LDCs. Yet, only the few developing countries in the Cairns Group apparently understand this. Most other LDCs oppose liberalizing agriculture, at least not without compensatory guarantees, which, of course, are themselves inconsistent with the principles of open markets. All LDCs realize, however, that freer trade in agricultural products will probably cause some prices to rise, which would hurt consumers in the poorest of the LDC food importers. Despite this knowledge, only five of the dozens of countries likely to be affected joined together to formulate a position. And when they produced a proposal for compensation under the GATT, none of the other affected countries agreed to cosponsor it.

Chapter 7 concludes with case studies of five developing countries that illustrate and provide support for the argument that the high degree of uncertainty produces risk-averse behavior among most LDCs. Agricultural trade liberalization certainly will affect LDCs. The problem for them has been how to determine, with any degree of confidence, the magnitude and timing of those effects, and then how to work within the MTNs to influence the reform process to their advantage.

One of the most distinguishing features of world agriculture is the difference between policies of LDCs toward the farm sector and those of their counterparts in developed countries. Countries with low levels of economic development tend to tax agriculture, and the producer price of farm products is below world prices. As countries acquire greater wealth, however, they usually switch from taxing to subsidizing agriculture, and farm prices generally exceed international levels. Explaining this phenomenon is one of the tasks of agricultural economists Harald von Witzke and Ulrich Hausner in Chapter 8.

The authors employ public choice theory to explain the relationship between economic development and agricultural price supports. They argue that for countries at low levels of development the marginal political economic benefits of supporting farm prices above world levels are low compared to the high costs of doing so. The marginal benefits of farm price support are low, they reason, because the urban population tends to be small, geographically concentrated, better educated, and have access to a better infrastructure. The costs of organizing urban dwellers for political economic purposes are thus relatively low. The incentive to do so is a strong interest in low food prices because personal incomes are low at these early stages of development, and the share of income spent on food is high.

By contrast, the farm population is geographically dispersed, has poor infrastructure, and lacks sufficient education to enable them to comprehend the relationship of government agricultural policies to their own economic well-being. Hence, organizing for political economic purposes tends to be more costly than it is for urban people. The result of low marginal benefits of farm price support compared to its high costs is equilibrium in which producer prices are kept below world prices.

In the course of economic development, the relationship between marginal costs and benefits of supporting agriculture reverses. The costs of organizing a farm lobby are reduced as the farm population declines and becomes better educated, and as the rural infrastructure improves. As the urban population grows, the cost of political organization becomes more expensive. The share of income spent on food decreases as urban incomes increase, making the price of food less important. This leads to a decline in the marginal costs of supporting agriculture and an increase in the benefits of doing so. Countries thus shift from taxing agriculture to subsidizing it.

This relationship between agricultural policy and economic development occurs over long periods of time and provides the context for the authors' examination of shorter term determinants of price support policy in developed countries. Using empirical evidence from wheat and corn policies in the United States, von Witzke and Hausner find that relatively low (high) expected agricultural income or low (high) expected budgetary expenditures result in high (low) producer support prices.

The implications of these findings for world agriculture are significant. As more and more countries switch from taxing agriculture to subsidizing it, world prices of farm commodities become more depressed compared to what they would be in a free-trade environment. One country's attempt to support its farmers resonates across world agricultural markets, reducing prices. Other countries, in turn, adjust their price support levels upward, further depressing world prices. Von Witzke and Hausner argue, therefore, that the farm income problem in developed countries cannot be solved by unilateral long-term subsidies. Because of the interdependence of world agriculture and the high cost of support programs, "policymakers can no longer provide political

economic rents to farmers via distortionary agricultural and trade policies."
What is needed is a liberal agricultural trade regime in the international
political economy. Such a regime, they conclude, "represents an international
public good."

In the final chapter, C. Ford Runge looks beyond the Uruguay Round to
three issues that are likely to dominate agricultural trade policy in the years
ahead. The first is the role of LDCs in the world trading system. Second is
the emerging North American free trade bloc that Runge expects, in
microcosm, to define many of the issues that will divide rich and poor
countries in future global trade policy. Third, nontariff barriers—in the form
of environmental, health, and safety (EHS) regulations—will likely become a
critical problem in agricultural trade for all countries.

With respect to LDCs in world agricultural trade, Runge makes a strong
case for net welfare benefits accruing to most developing countries from full
participation in trade reform. The future economic interests of LDCs, he
argues, largely depend on the outcome of three key elements in the
agricultural negotiations of the Uruguay Round. First, greater access to the
markets of developed countries will depend heavily on discussions bearing on
EHS barriers to LDC farm exports. If such access is achieved, Runge sees
maximum export gains for developing countries in several key commodities.
Second, a substantial reduction in the farm export subsidies wars of the major
traders would greatly benefit many LDCs, especially agricultural exporters
such as Argentina and Brazil. Third, appropriate LDC adjustment policies
must allow the gains from higher food prices to be passed along to farmers.
This will create incentives to expand output and eventually reduce import
dependency. Although special and differential treatment will remain necessary
for many LDCs within the GATT, these must not be used as excuses for
insulating their economies from world markets. As Runge puts it, often
"adjustments are put off that, once made, would allow . . . [LDCs] to share
in opportunities for growth."

Many of the issues of agricultural trade between LDCs and developed
countries in the Uruguay Round have also surfaced in the negotiations to
create a North American Free Trade Agreement (NAFTA). Concern has been
expressed in the United States over the Mexican use of pesticides and other
U.S.-banned chemicals in agricultural production. Environmental groups
protest the opening of U.S. markets to such products. Various farm groups
in the United States, such as sugar growers, oppose the agreement because of
threats to import quotas, whereas others, such as grain producers, are strong
supporters because of likely gains from larger markets.

The movement toward a North American free trade bloc has been
interpreted by some analysts as an alternative to broader trade liberalization
within the GATT. However, Runge contends that the two will likely be
pursued in tandem. Simultaneous bilateral and multilateral negotiations, he
argues, allow for diversification of the risk of failure on either front.

Moreover, simultaneous talks serve as implied mutual threats against each other: stalled progress in one can be offset by moving ahead in the other. Pressure from Congress and other domestic sources for unilateral trade actions, Runge believes, will prompt the president to push both sets of negotiations in order to blunt protectionist and retaliatory appeals at home. To be sure, NAFTA is only one in a set of trade blocs likely to emerge as issues beyond the Uruguay Round.

Looming on the horizon is a sticky trade issue involving the use of EHS standards as disguised forms of protectionism. Existing rules, designed to prevent such standards from creating "unnecessary obstacles to international trade," have proved ineffective. And fundamental differences exist in the views of developed and less developed countries over appropriate EHS regulations. Such differences are rooted in the differential income levels of developed countries compared to LDCs. In low-income countries, where "the share of national resources devoted to food and agriculture remains large, environmental quality and occupational health risks are widely perceived as concerns of the rich."

The income levels of LDCs prohibit the development and maintenance of EHS regulations comparable to those in wealthy countries. What has developed are contrasting systems of regulations, one in developed countries that preserves relatively strict standards and another in LDCs that is lax or nonexistent. The trade implications of this structure have not been lost on LDCs or developed countries. Developing countries anticipate growing consumer concerns within developed countries over the impact of EHS standards on food safety. Such concerns can create powerful constituencies for nontariff barriers to LDC farm exports, all justified as health and saftey measures. Runge is not optimistic about the prospects for agreement on a single set of international EHS standards. Instead, he calls for a negotiated mechanism "to accommodate differences in national priorities linked to levels of economic development and cultural factors."

SUMMARY

The chapters in this volume together illustrate the ongoing problem that agriculture has posed for the world trading system. Integrating agriculture into the liberal trade regime has proved to be one of the most intractable issues in the world economy since the GATT was established in 1947. Domestic farm preferences and coalitions have become well entrenched in developed countries, forming powerful constituencies for preservation of existing illiberal price and export support programs. As the authors demonstrate, overcoming these obstacles is one of the most formidable trade challenges of the century.

One of the most important contributions of this book is the deliberate and sustained use of Putnam's two-level approach to international bargaining. This approach is an especially powerful analytic tool for explaining the dilemma created by tensions inherent in the often conflicting interests of national groups and the larger international interests of states. How successful policymakers are in resolving this dilemma depends on their ability to manipulate the two-level bargaining game.

This book also has shown that both systemic and national levels of analysis are necessary for understanding the agriculture debate in world trade. Knowledge of the many domestic factors that shape the process and content of that debate is inadequate without some understanding of the larger trade system and the role of agriculture in it. Admittedly, however, the bulk of the emphasis has been on the political dynamics of agricultural trade policy formation at the national level. The editor is convinced that this emphasis is justified in view of the preponderance of literature analyzing the processes and issues of trade at the systemic level. It is hoped that this volume will promote greater awareness of and attention to domestic political processes in trade policymaking and the interaction of these processes with those at the systemic level.

One final note: The authors of this volume do not display much optimism for the prospects of successful inclusion of agriculture in the global free trade regime. And ample evidence suggests that without its inclusion the trade negotiations may fail altogether. Questions are thus raised as to what will follow in the wake of failed negotiations. Will the GATT continue its slow deterioration over time to a point of irrelevance? Or will it "crash and burn" in a massive and sudden departure of states convinced that the GATT has outlived its usefulness? Will the trading system evolve into one of competing trading hierarchies, or trade blocs, and what would this mean for world trade, economic growth, and welfare gains or losses? These are questions that must occupy the attention of scholars and policymakers now and for the foreseeable future.

Theodore H. Cohn 2

The Changing Role of the United States in the Global Agricultural Trade Regime

The United States as the predominant power in the postwar period was the main force directing the global trade regime. According to hegemonic stability theory, this U.S. dominance contributed to trade liberalization and stability after the war, and the loss of U.S. hegemonic status by the mid-1970s resulted in a reversion to trade protectionism and instability (see Webb and Krasner, 1989: 183). Some analysts have pointed out that the hegemonic model cannot adequately account for several features of the global trade regime, including differences among various trade sectors within the regime (Lipson, 1982: 453). Agricultural trade is a prime example of the need to consider sectoral differentiation because it seems to operate according to different rules than those applied to other sectors. As one of the guiding forces in the agricultural trade regime, the United States has also followed policies in agriculture that often diverge rather widely from its trade policies in other areas.

The main purpose of this chapter is to examine the changing role of the United States in the agricultural trade regime and the implications of these changes for global trading relations. This chapter also draws comparisons between the agricultural trade regime and the more general trade regime of which it is a part, and assesses the usefulness of the regime concept for examining agricultural trade issues. Furthermore, some observations are provided about the applicability of two theories of regime change to agricultural trade issues—the theories of hegemonic stability and surplus capacity. It is first necessary to outline some of the characteristics of the regime regulating agricultural trade.

THE AGRICULTURAL TRADE REGIME

International regimes may be defined as "sets of implicit or explicit principles, norms, rules, and decision-making procedures around which actors' expectations converge in a given area of international relations"

(Krasner, 1982: 186). Some regimes encompass only one sector or issue; others are broader in scope and have specific regimes "nested" within more diffuse regimes (Puchala and Hopkins, 1982: 248; Aggarwal, 1981, 1985).[1] Principles are general guidelines relating to the behavior of states, and the principles of specific regimes are derived from the principles of more diffuse regimes. Norms are "the most general prescriptions and proscriptions" of a specific regime, and rules and decisionmaking procedures are established to reflect or implement regime norms (Zacher, 1987: 175–176).

This chapter examines agricultural trade as a specific regime nested within the more diffuse global trade regime (see Cohn, forthcoming). As a result, the principles of the agricultural trade regime are drawn from the more general international trade principles of liberalization, nondiscrimination, reciprocity, exemptionalism, special treatment for developing countries, multilateralism, and the role of major interests in negotiations.[2] An additional principle that implicitly underlies all of the above is the maintenance of a certain degree of stability in the international trade regime. As Table 2.1 shows, the trade regime principles can be divided into two general categories, sovereignty and interdependence. Whereas the sovereignty principles derive "from the traditional structure of international politics" and serve to weaken a regime, the interdependence principles "incline states to maximize welfare through collaboration" and normally strengthen a regime (Finlayson and Zacher, 1981: 564).

The weakness of the agricultural trade regime stems from the importance attached to its sovereignty principles of exemptionalism, major interests, and reciprocity. As defined here, exemptionalism is an agreement to release a sector of trade or a state from an obligation required of other sectors or states, either on a temporary or long-term basis.[3] The exemptionalism principle has a definite role in the general trade regime because states would not agree to concessions without assurances of a limited right to escape from import disruption (Lipson, 1982: 426). However, these escape hatches have been more dominant and long term in agriculture than in most other trade sectors. This chapter discusses several major instances of exemptionalism in agriculture, including the special provisions in GATT Articles XI and XVI and the U.S. waiver of 1955.

Table 2.1
Principles in the Global Trade Regime

Interdependence Principles	Sovereignty Principles
Liberalization	Exemptionalism
Multilateralism	Major interests
Economic development	Reciprocity
Nondiscrimination	

Source: Derived from Finlayson and Zacher (1981: 595–596).

Finlayson and Zacher (1981: 593) have noted that there is an "ongoing battle between the . . . [principles] of multilateralism and major interests." Whereas multilateralism involves a commitment to genuine multilateral rule-making and surveillance processes, the major interests principle has often legitimated the dominance of these processes by the three most powerful actors—the United States, the European Community, and Japan. In the agricultural trade regime, the major interests principle has been especially prominent—in earlier years through the dominance of the United States, and more recently through the dominance of the United States and the European Community. The reciprocity principle "owes little to economic liberal theory, which stresses the benefits accruing to the country that lowers barriers, even unilaterally" (Finlayson and Zacher, 1981: 576). Reciprocity in agricultural trade has been especially important in recent years, with the escalation of the U.S.-EC export subsidy "war" and the refusal of either side to retreat from this contest on a unilateral basis.

The prominence of sovereignty principles in the agricultural trade regime stems largely from the unwillingness of governments to revamp their domestic programs so that international agreements can function (Hathaway, 1983: 451). Agriculture shares many characteristics with other product groupings for which there are strong protectionist pressures, such as steel, textiles, clothing, and shoes. In general, these industries are involved with "wage-sensitive, produce standardized, price-competitive products, use relatively standard technologies, and are under the direction of national firms" (Lipson, 1982: 443). Protectionism also results from the special characteristics of agriculture, including the unpredictable fluctuations in supply and demand, the chronic problem of food surpluses in relation to effective demand, the threat of serious social problems resulting from structural change in rural areas, the political influence of farmer and agribusiness groups, and the importance countries attach to food self-sufficiency (Warley, 1976: 293–294).

Not surprisingly, all of these characteristics contribute to yet another feature of the agricultural trade regime: it is highly conflictual in nature. Because "the word 'agriculture' is nearly synonymous with the word 'subsidy' in the context of international trade," agricultural products are at the center of many major trade disputes (Palmeter, 1989: 59). For example, although agriculture accounts for only about 4 percent of total U.S.-Canada trade, a majority of the recent antidumping and countervailing duty (CVD) investigations between the two states have involved agricultural products (Steger, 1988: 161). Some of these cases have also been especially significant in establishing precedents. Canada's imposition of a countervailing duty on U.S. grain corn imports in the late 1980s marked the first time a foreign country had levied a CVD against U.S. producers. Furthermore, a U.S. CVD on Canadian pork imports resulted in the first use of the extraordinary challenge procedures under the bilateral Free Trade Agreement (FTA). The countervail mechanism for dealing with "unfair" trade has been especially unsuited to agriculture, however, because GATT rules for this sector are so inadequate. Thus, only 27 percent of the countervail petitions made against agricultural products have resulted in affirmative outcomes, compared with 58 percent for all industries (Nam, 1987: 738).

The agricultural trade regime is so weak that some analysts question whether the regime concept even applies to it. The authors of one book, for example, opted for a regional approach to food politics, warning that "the analyst can fall into the trap of discussing a 'world food regime' which has yet to materialize" (Carey, 1981: 4). Nevertheless, Jackson (1989: 44) has noted that some writers and practitioners "have made the error of stating that GATT does not legally apply to agricultural goods." Agricultural trade is guided partly by the principles that regulate the overall trade regime, but in this case the sovereignty principles are far more prominent. The GATT Uruguay Round experience has demonstrated that the interdependence principles of liberalization, nondiscrimination, multilateralism, and economic development must be more rigorously applied in the case of agriculture, and that failure to do so could jeopardize the entire set of negotiations. Thus, a statement by Aggarwal (1985: 186) regarding the textile trade regime is also applicable in the case of agriculture:

> Regimes may be preferred in subsystems if higher-level system arrangements are undermined by particular national actions (e.g., when national actions in textiles undermine the overall trade regime). In such a case, a regime that is at least partially in accord with rule systems at higher levels will be preferred to unrestrained national actions.

Any discussion of the agricultural trade regime would be incomplete without examining the central role played by the United States, which has consistently been the world's single most important food exporter and the largest or second largest single food importer. However, the predominance of the United States has declined in certain respects, especially in relation to the European Community. From 1973 to 1987, the U.S. share of global food exports fell by 7.9 percent, whereas the EC countries in the "top ten" increased their share by 11.1 percent.[4] U.S. wheat exports, in particular, fell from 47.4 percent of the world total in 1975–1976 to 29.6 percent in 1985–1986, whereas the EC share rose from 11.6 to 17.1 percent, respectively (Canadian Wheat Board: various years). The following discussion examines the changing U.S. role in greater detail.

U.S. PREDOMINANCE IN THE POSTWAR AGRICULTURAL TRADE REGIME: THE 1950s TO EARLY 1960s

Some analysts have pointed to inconsistencies in the U.S. commitment to trade liberalization, even when its hegemonic status was unquestioned after

World War II (see Strange, 1987: 559–563; Grunberg, 1990: 437–439). There is no area where these inconsistencies were greater than in agriculture. The U.S. propensity to opt for exemptionalism over liberalization in agricultural trade was evident during the negotiation of the Havana Charter. A 1935 amendment (Section 32) to the U.S. Agricultural Adjustment Act had permitted the Department of Agriculture to use export subsidies, and the U.S. delegation resisted pressures from Great Britain, Canada, and Brazil to prohibit them in the charter. This contributed to the addition of escape clauses and exceptions that weakened the charter provisions (Porter and Bowers, 1989: 3). In the end, the Truman administration decided not to submit the charter to Congress for approval because of opposition from many sources (including U.S. farm organizations). The proposed International Trade Organization (ITO) was thus never established.

The General Agreement on Tariffs and Trade, designed to be temporary but replacing the ill-fated ITO, contains two agricultural exemptions, which were included largely to conform to provisions in the U.S. farm program. GATT Article XI calls for the elimination of quantitative restrictions on imports, but permits such restrictions for agriculture when they are needed to enforce governmental measures that limit the quantities or "remove a temporary surplus of the like domestic product." Article XVI (Section B) prohibits export subsidies for manufactured goods, but an exception is provided for agricultural and other primary products. The only limitation on agricultural export subsidies is an ambiguous provision (in Article XVI:3) that they should not permit a country to gain "more than an equitable share of world export trade" (GATT, 1986).

Article XI was patterned partly after Section 22 of the U.S. Agricultural Adjustment Act, which sanctioned the use of import quotas for commodities under price support programs. In contrast to Article XI, however, Section 22 permitted import restrictions even when there were no restraints on domestic production. This difference eventually led to a major conflict between the United States and the GATT. Two actions taken by the U.S. Congress in response to the development of agricultural surpluses (especially in dairy products) were the main precipitating factors.

First, starting in 1948, "members of Congress repeatedly chided the executive branch for being too backward in its use of Section 22" to limit agricultural imports (Evans, 1971: 72). Congress then amended Section 22 to permit the imposition of farm import quotas regardless of any international agreement. President Truman opposed this amendment, but Congress ensured its passage by attaching it to the 1951 extension of the reciprocal trade agreements authority (Porter and Bowers, 1989: 8). Second, Congress attached a rider (Section 104) to a bill extending the 1950 Defense Production Act, which virtually required the secretary of agriculture to impose quantitative restrictions on a wide range of agricultural goods for which there were no production controls. President Truman opposed the rider because it was contrary to GATT provisions, but he could not veto the entire Defense Act and therefore signed it into law. When import quotas were imposed for a number of commodities, including dairy products, a protracted struggle ensued between the president and Congress, and also between the United States and the GATT. The dairy quotas were criticized in a number of GATT proceedings, and the Netherlands (with GATT approval) retaliated by imposing a quota on U.S. wheat flour imports. However, Congress was largely unphased by these actions, and in 1955 the United States sought and received an unusually broad waiver—which has no time limit—from its Article XI obligations (Hudec, 1975: ch. 16).

The dispute over Article XI demonstrates a major shortcoming of the hegemonic stability model. In positing that "regime strength depends on the international distribution of state power," it ignores not only sectoral differentiation but also domestic politics (Lipson, 1982: 442). Because domestic politics is so important in agricultural trade policy, this is a serious oversight. In the 1952 congressional committee hearings on the agricultural import quotas, Executive Branch officials argued that such quotas threatened damage to European economic recovery and to U.S. leadership. However, Congress was focusing more narrowly on the plight of U.S. dairy farmers, and because of congressional authority over international trade matters, its view carried the day (Hudec, 1975: 172).

In addition to the GATT exceptions, some matters relating to agricultural trade were largely excluded from the GATT determinations. At the end of the Korean War in 1953, the demand for food grains declined, but production in the major exporting countries was increasing to record levels. The problem was especially severe in the United States, where Congress approved the Agricultural Trade Development and Assistance Act (PL 480) to dispose of food surpluses through concessional transactions.[5] Some GATT members were extremely concerned that PL 480 and other U.S. surplus disposal mechanisms would infringe upon their commercial agricultural exports. At the 1954–1955 GATT review session, Australia therefore proposed that a new article on concessional sales be added to the General Agreement, calling for mandatory prior consultations and compulsory arbitration to protect competing exporters. However, the United States was unwilling to accept a major GATT role in this area (Warley, 1976: 350).

Although the United States called for severe limits to the GATT's jurisdiction, it did agree to a role for less demanding international organizations in regulating some aspects of agricultural trade. Thus, the issues of concessional food exports and surplus disposal were passed on to the Food and Agriculture Organization (FAO). The major trading nations adopted the FAO Principles of Surplus Disposal to ensure that concessional exports did not interfere with normal trading patterns, and the FAO's Committee on Commodity Problems established a Consultative Sub-committee on Surplus Disposal to assist it in monitoring adherence to the principles. However, the legal status of the FAO principles is unclear because (unlike the GATT) they do not represent "a binding instrument" on signatory countries (FAO, 1980: 2).

Although the United States was ambivalent about agricultural trade liberalization, it did perform an important regime-maintenance role in the early postwar period: it was willing to assume some disproportionate costs to promote stability in this area (see Webb and Krasner, 1989: 184–186). For example, during the 1950s–1960s, the United States was by far the largest food aid donor. Despite competitors' complaints about price-cutting, the diversion of U.S. surpluses through concessional channels often provided a protective "umbrella" over the commercial markets of other agricultural exporters (Shefrin, 1966: 47). The United States also joined with a smaller partner (Canada) in a duopolistic arrangement in the 1950s to control agricultural surpluses and support commercial prices. The two countries agreed to hold substantial wheat reserves off the commercial market, and they endorsed a series of international wheat agreements with pricing provisions. McLin (1979: 35–55) has described this duopoly as a form of "surrogate international organization," which promoted price stability for commercial exporters and food security for less-developed countries.

The United States also promoted stability as leader of the Western alliance in accordance with "the security version" of the hegemonic stability thesis (Webb and Krasner, 1989: 183–198). In the 1950s and 1960s, the United States normally did not sell grain to the Soviet Union and China primarily for political-security reasons.[6] This policy was followed even though U.S. exporters were at a disadvantage relative to competitors that faced fewer restrictions in their trade with the Communist states. In some respects, this policy contributed to stability and to U.S. cooperation with its allies. For example, the United States and Canada had a tacit division of markets, with Canada's increased grain sales to the Communist states partly compensating for its losses to the United States elsewhere. The United States also "accepted western European and Japanese departures from international economic liberalization" to ensure that they remained within its sphere of influence (Webb and Krasner, 1989: 185). Thus, the political-security objective tempered the U.S. response to the development of the EC's protectionist agricultural policies.

In summary, the United States was largely responsible for the agricultural exemptions from GATT liberalization measures in the 1950s and 1960s. The United States did contribute to stability in the agricultural trade regime, but it tended to rely on extra-GATT mechanisms rather than to support the interdependence principle of multilateralism. Not surprisingly, the Canada-U.S. duopoly could not serve as an adequate substitute for a strong GATT-based regime in agriculture. Because the duopoly functioned in the absence of a global arrangement with explicit multilateral obligations, the decision to terminate it depended on only two states—primarily the

United States—which became less supportive when cooperation in international wheat trade declined in the mid-1960s (McLin, 1979: 54–55; Cohn, 1979–1980: 132–149).

A major factor accounting for U.S. ambivalence toward GATT regulation of agriculture was the primacy of domestic politics. In formulating agricultural policy, the U.S. government often "found the pressures of special-interest groups . . . so strong that it did not behave in a manner consistent with its hegemonic interests" (Cowhey and Long, 1983: 161). Even those U.S. policies that helped to stabilize the agricultural trade regime could be viewed as an unintended result of domestic factors. Indeed, Paarlberg (1982: 127) has maintained that U.S. grain policy in earlier years

> was never closely tied to the pursuit of external objectives. The stabilization of the world grain market made possible by U.S. policy prior to 1972 was mostly an unintended effect of that policy. A large grain surplus was accumulated by the United States not for the purpose of promoting stability or security in the world market but to satisfy internal political demands for high and stable farm income.

In their article on the auto trade, Cowhey and Long (1983) found that "surplus capacity" as well as hegemony was required to explain regime change, and the present study adds support to their findings. Surplus capacity exists when "for a sustained period of time and a large percentage of all producers, demand is not sufficient to absorb enough output for prices to sustain substantial employment and adequate returns on investment in a sector" (Cowhey and Long, 1983: 162; see also Strange, 1979: 303–334). It is a sad irony that surplus capacity has been a chronic problem in North American agriculture while many less-developed countries have suffered from serious food shortages. Although poorer peoples are often the most in need of foodstuffs, they are also those most lacking in effective demand backed by purchasing power. Foodgrain shortages were a salient issue for major exporters only in the early 1970s; at other times surpluses were the primary problem. Thus, even when the United States was an undisputed hegemony in the agricultural trade regime, the existence of surplus capacity ran counter to the forces of trade liberalization.

THE EMERGENCE OF OTHER MAJOR ACTORS:
THE MID-1960s TO LATE 1970s

Despite its early contribution to agricultural protectionism, the United States became increasingly concerned about the financial costs of its agricultural programs as well as about the protectionist policies of others. The United States obtained a major concession from the European Community in the 1960–1962 GATT Dillon Round—the agreement to zero duty bindings on EC oilseed imports. However, after the Dillon Round the EC introduced the main elements of its highly protectionist Common Agricultural Policy, which included high support prices for major crops, a variable levy system for imports, and the use of export subsidies (referred to as export refunds or restitutions) to deal with surplus production. The variable levies ensured that foreign agricultural goods would always be more expensive than those produced in the EC, and they were therefore more akin to quantitative restrictions than to genuine fixed tariffs. The United States strongly opposed the variable levies; however, its own 1955 waiver provided (and still provides) some legitimacy for the EC's more protectionist policies.

In subsequent GATT rounds the United States became more committed to the interdependence principle of agricultural trade liberalization. The 1962 U.S. Trade Expansion Act required that any new negotiations give equal emphasis to agricultural and industrial tariff reductions, and President Lyndon Johnson even promised U.S. farmers that there would be no Kennedy Round agreement "unless progress is registered toward trade liberalization on the products of our farms as well as our factories" (Curtis and Vastine, 1971: 26; Paarlberg, 1988: 48). The United States viewed the Kennedy Round as a vehicle for maintaining its agricultural export markets and for limiting the growth of EC trade barriers. However, the European Community insisted that its agricultural policy was an essential—and still evolving—element binding the EC together, and that it was not subject to negotiation. The Kennedy Round gains in agriculture were therefore limited to tariff cuts, and even these were excluded from the linear (as opposed to item-by-item) tariff-cutting approach used for industrial goods. Furthermore, although tariffs accounted for only a small part of agricultural protectionism, no agreement was reached on limiting subsidies, EC variable levies, and other nontariff measures (see Schnittker Associates, 1979: 8–11).

Between the Kennedy and Tokyo Rounds, the deteriorating U.S. economic condition contributed to more vigorous liberalization efforts in agriculture. The costs of domestic programs and the Vietnam War had undermined U.S. efforts to improve its balance-of-payments, and deficits seemed to be chronic by the end of the 1960s. The United States had a disastrous balance of payments deficit in 1971, which included a trade deficit for the first time since 1893. This led some analysts to maintain that the hegemonic decline of the United States was more evident in its changing trade patterns than in any other area (Goldstein, 1988: 179). In responding to the deficits, U.S. policies were characterized increasingly by the "use of aggressive reciprocity and by the use of trade measures to force access in foreign markets" (Whalley, 1986: 93). During the 1970s the United States also became more aware of its comparative advantage in agriculture, and more dependent on agricultural trade. Farm output increased by 54 percent between 1950 and 1975, but U.S. agricultural exports almost quadrupled. Exports accounted for only 10 percent of farm cash receipts in 1950, and for 24 percent by the mid-1970s (Houck, 1980: 268). Most important, agriculture was one of the few areas where the United States continued to have a positive trade balance, and its farm exports were viewed as one means of redressing unfavorable balances elsewhere.

U.S. participation in the Tokyo Round was authorized under the Trade Act of 1974, which indicated (in Section 103) that "to the maximum extent feasible, the harmonization, reduction, or elimination of agricultural trade barriers and distortions shall be undertaken in conjunction with the harmonization, reduction, or elimination of industrial trade barriers and distortions." The president's special representative for trade also warned that "progress in agriculture is the sine qua non of progress in normalizing the international economic situation and improving our trade relations" (Warley, 1976: 289–290). To give practical effect to these efforts, the United States wanted agriculture to be treated the same as other sectors in the negotiation; for example, negotiation on subsidies would deal with trade in agricultural as well as nonagricultural products. However, the EC insisted on a separate negotiation for agriculture, because it was unwilling to bargain away any elements of its Common Agricultural Policy in exchange for concessions in other areas. This issue resulted in a standoff that blocked further progress in the Tokyo Round from 1974 to 1977, not only in agriculture but also generally. After the election of President Jimmy Carter in November 1976, the United States was more conciliatory, and the logjam was broken in July 1977 when the United States accepted the EC demand for separate agricultural negotiations (Winham, 1986: 156–167; Warley, 1989: 8–13).

The results for agriculture in the Tokyo Round, as in the Kennedy Round, were disappointing. The United States agreed to some mutual tariff concessions and easing of quotas with the EC and Japan. However, the new Tokyo Round subsidies code did not resolve the major agricultural subsidy issues under dispute, and other nontariff barriers in agriculture were unaffected by the negotiation. Both the Kennedy Round and the Tokyo Round demonstrated that the United States wanted the interdependence principles of liberalization and multilateralism to be applied more rigorously in the case of agriculture. However, a variety of factors related to changes in hegemony and surplus capacity limited the degree to which the United States had the determination and the ability to influence EC policies.

During the Kennedy Round, the United States, as a hegemon in the security sphere, continued to be preoccupied with East-West issues. U.S. demands that the EC liberalize its agricultural policies were therefore tempered by U.S. strategic interests in promoting European integration. The economic ability of the United States to alter the agricultural trade regime it had done so much to create was also becoming more circumscribed. As Warley (1976: 387) has noted, hegemonic decline was one factor limiting U.S. influence:

> The Kennedy Round agricultural negotiations marked the shift in political power which had occurred in the postwar world. The United States had long dictated the course and form of international economic

relationships. But in . . . [the Kennedy Round] it was defeated on ground of its own choosing. It was unable to prevent the European countries from persisting with, and indeed extending even whilst negotiations proceeded, a system and level of agricultural support of which it disapproved.

In the 1970s, U.S. determination to alter EC policies was moderated by agricultural shortages and the rising demand for imports. Indeed, world agricultural trade increased by 41 percent in volume during the 1970s, and by more than ten times in value (Porter and Bowers, 1989: 16). Conditions were particularly favorable for the United States, due to the devaluation of its dollar and the ability of its farmers to respond to the demand with excess supplies. The United States captured a larger share of the world wheat market during this period through a combination of "supply availability, assured delivery and aggressive selling by the U.S. private grain trade" (Hill, 1977: 30). The surplus capacity variable therefore eased the pressures to liberalize agriculture in the Tokyo Round. The U.S. ability to influence the EC had also become more circumscribed by the late 1970s. Thus, the Tokyo Round could be completed only when the United States dropped its demand that negotiations for agricultural and nonagricultural products should occur together. The price of this concession was the agreement to continue treating agriculture as an exception.

In addition to the factors of hegemony and surplus capacity, domestic issues (in both the United States and the European Community) also played a role in limiting U.S. influence. The EC was so preoccupied with domestic changes and disputes over agricultural policies that it was unwilling to cede to U.S. pressures in this area. In the first few years of the Kennedy Round, for example, EC representatives lacked the authority to even consider offering agricultural concessions because a dispute was raging between France and the EC over financing and voting issues. The dispute was eventually resolved with an agreement that did not bode well for the GATT negotiations: France, a country with a major stake in agricultural protectionism, would continue to have a de facto veto over major EC decisions (Evans, 1971: 215–217; Paarlberg, 1988: 48). In the Tokyo Round this preoccupation with domestic issues continued, to the point that the Europeans "wanted the CAP more than they wanted a successful negotiation" (Winham, 1986: 164).

Efforts of the U.S. Executive Branch to pressure strongly for liberalization were also thwarted by differences with Congress, which was more attuned to protectionist interests. Although Congress delegated wide-ranging tariff-cutting authority to the Kennedy Round negotiators, it was reluctant to delegate authority to deal with the more important nontariff measures, which were closely tied to domestic agricultural programs. In the Tokyo Round, a procedure for "fast track" approval was developed to ensure that Congress would vote on agreements in a timely fashion without amendment. Nevertheless, "the anticipated need to win positive

Congressional approval for NTB [Non-Tariff Barrier] agreements helped to undermine the administration's bold negotiating strategy for agriculture" (Paarlberg, 1988: 49–51).

Furthermore, although the United States opposed the idea of separate negotiations for agriculture, in some respects it remained committed to the exemptionalism principle. This ambivalent behavior resulted largely from domestic divisions involving the Executive Branch, Congress, and special interests. When the Kennedy Round negotiations were at a critical stage, the U.S. case for liberalization was weakened by its approval of import restrictions for beef, veal, and lamb (Johnson, 1984: 737). The United States also refused to relinquish its 1955 waiver, which continued to give some measure of legitimacy to the EC's policies.

There were numerous instances in which the United States demonstrated its resolve to retain its special privileges. During the Kennedy Round, a working party indicated that "the disinvocation of the . . . [U.S.] waiver . . . would be of particular significance at a time when the contracting parties were engaged in trade negotiations" (Warley, 1976: 347–348). However, the U.S. representative refused even to consider the working party's suggestion. In two GATT lawsuits during the mid-1970s, the United States maintained that European agricultural trade policies violated GATT regulations, despite its own waiver from the same obligations. The United States "defended its arguably two-faced posture by claiming that, if the EC wanted the same legal freedoms as the United States, it too should seek a waiver" (Hudec, 1988: 150). Whereas the U.S. Executive Branch was pushing more aggressively for agricultural trade liberalization, protectionist farm interests and their congressional supporters were doing their best to ensure that agriculture still received special treatment.

It should be mentioned that there were also domestic pressures for liberalization in both the United States and the European Community. As discussed, U.S. liberalization pressures related to the high cost of agricultural programs, the chronic balance-of-payments problems, and the desire to benefit from the country's comparative advantage in agriculture. In the European Community, market imbalances and increased costs of support for the CAP led to successive efforts to remedy the situation. The major importing countries, Great Britain and West Germany, reacted negatively to the fact that they were paying high prices for food and were also paying to support those prices. In the 1970s, the European Community therefore moved toward implementing several policies, such as coresponsibility levies for producers, which seemed to accord with U.S. positions. Nevertheless, a number of EC members strongly resisted any major structural changes, and the word "reform" continued to be politically taboo for the CAP until the 1980s (Tracy, 1989: 303; Porter and Bowers, 1989: 12–14).

In summary, despite U.S. government efforts to liberalize agricultural trade in the Kennedy and Tokyo Rounds, a configuration of factors related to hegemonic, surplus capacity, and domestic variables precluded any major change in the global agricultural trade regime. The sovereignty principle of exemptionalism therefore continued to hold sway over the interdependence principle of trade liberalization. GATT agricultural negotiations also were dominated increasingly by disputes between the United States and the European Community. Thus, the negotiating process was being guided by the sovereignty principles of special interests and reciprocity rather than the interdependence principle of multilateralism.

A CRISIS PERIOD IN GLOBAL AGRICULTURAL TRADING RELATIONSHIPS: THE 1980s TO THE EARLY 1990s

Although U.S.-EC differences emerged over agricultural trade issues in the 1960s, conflict was limited during much of the 1970s because the major grain exporters benefited from short supplies and an expansion of trade. A variety of global and domestic factors, however, contributed to a return to surplus conditions in the 1980s (see Cohn, 1990). Unlike the period of surplus capacity in the 1950s and 1960s, U.S. hegemony had now declined and the European Community had emerged as a formidable competitor. The stage was therefore set for a major confrontation. Although a number of agricultural exporters were adversely affected by excess capacity in the early 1980s, the problems were particularly severe for the United States, whose share of global wheat exports fell sharply, from 45.0 percent in 1980–1981 to 29.6 percent in 1985–1986. This loss resulted largely from the relatively high U.S. wheat prices, which stemmed from the rising value of the dollar, high domestic support levels, and shrinking technological advantages. However, another factor in the loss of U.S. competitiveness (which was of considerable salience to U.S. policymakers) was the EC's export subsidies.

The agricultural trade surplus of the United States with the European Community fell from $7.5 billion in 1980 to $2.5 billion in 1986, but the United States was even more concerned about growing EC competition for third-country markets. Although Western Europe had traditionally been a net agricultural importer, the EC dependence on food imports declined with the postwar recovery and the creation of the CAP. By 1980, imports were largely limited to commodities such as hard wheat, corn, oilseeds, and tropical products, which West European countries could not produce in sufficient amounts. Surplus production also became increasingly important; according to one study that compared the 1961–1965 and 1978–1980 periods, "West European exports of agricultural products appear to have increased faster than for any other region of the world" (Moore, 1985: 242). In the 1980s the EC became a net exporter of grains, and it benefited greatly from the rising value of the U.S. dollar.

The United States at first attempted to work mainly through the GATT to produce a change in EC agricultural policies. In March 1975, a U.S. representative at the GATT subgroup on subsidies and countervailing duties proposed that direct export subsidies on all products be prohibited. However, the EC refused to recognize the jurisdiction of this subgroup, and to acknowledge that its export restitutions were in fact export subsidies. The United States also tried to use the Tokyo Round's Subsidy Code to delegitimize the EC's agricultural subsidy practices, but a 1983 GATT panel failed to provide a definitive decision on this issue (Porter and Bowers, 1989: 14; Paarlberg, 1988: 52).

Frustrated with its GATT efforts, the United States then moved to engage the European Community more directly in an export subsidy contest. The United States had export subsidy programs in the 1950s and 1960s when government price supports were far above international levels. However, these programs were discontinued during the period of grain shortages in 1973 and did not re-emerge as a policy instrument until 1983. The U.S. Department of Agriculture opposed export subsidies in principle, and the Reagan administration tended to view them as unfair trade practices. Nevertheless, under pressure from the Senate leadership and the director of the Office of Management and Budget (OMB), the United States established an Export Enhancement Program (EEP) in May 1985 to regain its lost market share and to force the EC to the bargaining table (U.S. GAO, 1987: 16). The EEP authorizes the Commodity Credit Corporation (CCC) to offer government-owned commodities as bonuses to U.S. exporters to expand sales of agricultural products. The bonuses are, in fact, a form of export subsidy because exporters can sell commodities at prices that are well below domestic levels. The EEP contributed to a U.S.-EC export subsidy "war," which lowered world grain prices, and smaller exporters found it difficult to compete.

The U.S. government indicated that the EEP would target only European Community markets, and initially its policies were consistent with these assurances. However, smaller exporters felt that U.S. statements were belied by its actions when (in August 1986) it extended the EEP to the Soviet Union, where 48 percent of the market was served by "nonsubsidizing" competitors. A diverse coalition of fourteen so-called fair trading countries therefore formed the Cairns Group in 1986, with the joint goal of pressuring for an end to the U.S.-EC export subsidy war.[7]

The United States defended itself against Cairns Group criticisms by pointing out that it was also a victim of EC policies, and to demonstrate its resolve for reform, the United States submitted broad-ranging agricultural proposals to the GATT Uruguay Round in July 1987. Its proposals regarding import barriers and export subsidies marked a complete turnaround from the 1940s–1950s, when the United States had viewed agriculture as an exception. The United States proposed that all nontariff barriers be converted to tariffs that would be gradually reduced; this would end the GATT Article XI exception, which permitted quantitative restrictions for agriculture to protect supply management programs. The United States also called for a complete phasing out of trade-distorting subsidies, which would eliminate the GATT exception for agriculture under Article XVI. In essence, the U.S. government was calling for a full integration of the global trade principles of liberalization and multilateralism into the agricultural trade regime. The U.S. proposal also gave limited recognition to the trade regime principle of special and differential treatment for less-developed countries, permitting some deviations from the implementation plan but no permanent exceptions for these countries (U.S. GAO, 1988: 17–19; McDonald, 1990: 304–305).

Although the U.S. proposal was considered in some circles (including the Cairns Group) to be a good first negotiating step, many groups in the United States and elsewhere felt that the U.S. demands were unrealistic and certain to promote instability in the agricultural trade regime. In particular, the U.S. government could be faulted for failing to fully appreciate the significance of agriculture in a European context. Some European countries, such as France and Ireland, are more protectionist in agricultural trade, whereas others, such as Great Britain, Denmark, and the Netherlands, are more free-trade oriented. There are some compelling reasons why protectionist forces are strong in much of European agriculture. About 8 percent of the EC population lives on farms, compared with only 3 percent in the United States. In the twelve countries of the European Community there are more than 10 million farmers, compared with only 2 million in the United States. European farm policies also place considerable emphasis on social and ecological as well as economic objectives. Furthermore, some major EC agricultural products (such as wheat in France) would be far less competitive under free-market conditions. The U.S. government, therefore, underestimated European resistance to any basic changes in domestic farm programs.

The United States also underestimated the degree to which its hegemonic position—and thus its ability to force changes upon the EC—had declined. A 1989 report of the U.S. Department of Agriculture's Office of the Inspector General found that the Export Enhancement Program had little impact on the EC's market share (Mendelowitz, 1989: 19–23). To continue its sales, the European Community had to spend somewhat more on export restitutions, but the payment by U.S. taxpayers to finance the EEP has been far greater. Although the EEP was one of the factors that brought the European Community to the negotiating table, the EC has continued to resist external pressures for change, and it is uncertain that there will be a meaningful agreement to liberalize agricultural trade. Thus, Paarlberg has argued that "as bargaining chips go, the EEP isn't weighty enough to threaten the Community, or to be traded away against EC export subsidies, which dwarf the EEP in size by a margin of roughly 10 to 1" (Paarlberg, 1990a: 20).

The U.S.-EC differences over agriculture have delayed the completion of the Uruguay Round, and have posed a threat to the viability of the GATT itself. Although originally scheduled for completion in December 1990, negotiators failed to reach agreement and were forced to postpone completion until 1992. If the EC does eventually agree to compromise on agricultural subsidies, it is likely that motivating factors other than the U.S. Export Enhancement Program will be primary. The European Community is more likely to alter its policies because farm programs regularly absorb about 60 percent of the entire EC budget and because the EC does not wish to jeopardize trade agreements in other areas such as services and intellectual property.

Yet another source of instability in the agricultural trade regime has been changing U.S. policies on political-security issues. In the 1970s, the United States began to sell to the major Communist countries, largely for economic reasons. Thus, the Soviet Union became eligible for Commodity Credit Corporation export credits in 1971, and China was offered CCC credit beginning in February 1972. The United States was no longer willing to remove itself from the major Communist markets, and this provided a new source of competition in agricultural trade. However, U.S. concerns with political-security issues quickly revived when the Soviet Union invaded Afghanistan in 1979, and the United States expected its export competitors to cooperate in an embargo on grain sales to the Soviets. The U.S. approach to political-security issues had nevertheless changed since the 1950s and 1960s, and the United States did not hesitate in seeking to recoup its embargo losses by turning to the China market. This infuriated Canada, and a few weeks later that country's participation in the Soviet embargo was formally ended. In the mid-1980s the United States initially excluded the major Communist states from its Export Enhancement Program, and Argentina, Australia, and Canada strongly criticized the United States when it extended the EEP to the Soviet Union in August 1986 and to China in January 1987.

The strong U.S. stance against EC policies in the Uruguay Round was yet another indication that the United States had changed its position on political-security issues. In the Kennedy and Tokyo Rounds the United States had agreed to expanding market opportunities for trade in manufactures, despite the EC's unwillingness to make the desired agricultural concessions. One factor in the U.S. flexibility was its reluctance "to risk the political consequences of a failure of the trade negotiations as a whole given their relationship to broad security policy" (Warley, 1976: 390–391). In the Uruguay Round, by contrast, the United States was far more adamant in linking the outcome of the agricultural negotiations with the results of the entire round. The United States, it seemed, had become less willing to make economic sacrifices for strategic-security reasons, largely because of changing cold war relationships and growing U.S. economic problems. Despite the far-reaching U.S. proposals for agricultural reform, it also remained uncertain as to whether the United States would really be willing to sacrifice the "exemptionalism" principle. Cairns Group critics, for example, have pointed to the irony that the United States has continued to increase its own export subsidies while advocating their elimination. As in earlier years, the United States also refused to relinquish its 1955 waiver, and it continued to insist that other GATT members abide by regulations from which the United States itself was exempt. In December 1988, for example, the United States requested that a dispute settlement panel be formed to determine whether Canadian quotas on ice cream and yogurt were inconsistent with the GATT. U.S. officials argued that these were processed foods, which were not covered by the Article XI exception. In September 1989, a GATT panel decided in favor of the U.S. complainant that the Canadian import restrictions did not conform with Article XI. Although Canada accepted the decision, it maintained that implementation would be premature pending the outcome of the Uruguay Round. Canada's agriculture minister also argued that the decision was unfair because the U.S. waiver had given it "an exemption from the GATT for its import quotas since 1955" (Government of Canada, 1989: 1).[8]

Some U.S. farm groups would also be unwilling to accept the U.S. GATT proposals, even if they were endorsed by other countries. This is particularly the case for sugar, dairy, peanut, and cotton producers, whose quota protection could be dismantled. Another example of U.S. protectionism has been the striking increase in trade remedy actions, which have often involved agricultural products. In the 1979 Trade Agreements Act, Congress responded to producer pressures by changing the regulations so that import-affected industries could obtain trade relief more easily. The number of countervailing duty investigations initiated then increased from 10 in 1980 to 43 in 1985, and the number of antidumping investigations rose from 26 in 1979 to 66 in 1985. Whereas the U.S. trade remedy laws seemed to be fair and objective from the U.S. perspective, other countries viewed the procedures as being overly susceptible to politics and biased in favor of the complainant (Destler, 1986: 111–127).

It should be noted that a number of countries were taking a more active stance regarding the agricultural trade negotiations in the Uruguay Round, and that it was therefore more difficult for the United States and the EC to mask their differences. At the GATT Kennedy and Tokyo Rounds, the United States had settled for less in agriculture because of its desire to reach agreement in other areas; but this solution was not necessarily feasible at the Uruguay Round even if the United States had opted for it. The Cairns Group was an important new actor calling for major reductions in internal support and export subsidies, and eleven of its fourteen members were less-developed countries. A number of the LDCs threatened to turn down agreements in other areas, such as services and intellectual property, if no agreement was reached on agriculture, and some Latin American states backed up this threat when they led a walkout at the 1988 mid-term GATT review meeting in Montreal. In essence, the Cairns Group was insisting that the major interest principle should confer influence, not only on the GATT "Big 3," but on all members "with the most obvious stake in a given issue or negotiation" (Finlayson and Zacher, 1981: 590; see also Higgott and Cooper, 1990: 589–632). This was yet another indication that the United States (and also the European Community and Japan) could no longer shape agricultural issues in the GATT to the same extent as it had in earlier years.

SUMMARY AND CONCLUSIONS

This chapter has demonstrated the usefulness of the regime concept for assessing the principles and rules governing agricultural trade, and for comparing agriculture with other trade sectors. Theories of regime change such as hegemonic stability and surplus capacity also have been shown to contribute to our understanding of the changing role of the United States in global agricultural trading relations.

 The United States as the postwar hegemon did much to support the interdependence principles of liberalization and multilateralism in the global trade regime, but in agriculture it opted instead for the sovereignty principles of exemptionalism and special interests. The 1955 U.S. GATT waiver, in particular, was (and is) a serious threat to trade liberalization because it set a precedent that enabled other GATT members, such as the European Community and Japan, to adopt even more protectionist agricultural policies. The fact that agriculture was treated differently, however, did not mean that there was no agricultural trade regime. Despite the agricultural exceptions, there was at least an attempt to limit departures from the trade liberalization principle. Thus, GATT Article XI permits quantitative restrictions in agriculture only in cases where domestic measures such as supply management are adopted; GATT Article XVI-B states that export subsidies for agricultural and other primary products "shall not be applied in a manner which results in that contracting party having more than an equitable share of world exports"; and the FAO Principles of Surplus Disposal "seek to assure that food and other agricultural commodities which are exported on concessional terms . . . do not displace normal commercial imports" (FAO, 1980: 2).

U.S. agricultural policies in the 1950s and 1960s demonstrated that the hegemonic model does not adequately account for sectoral differentiation. Wilson and Finkle (1990: 14) have noted that "agriculture is not seen as an economic activity like the others" for a variety of economic, political, and social reasons. Although classical economists would like agricultural trade to "be made as free and unsubsidized as possible," Western states have tended to treat their agricultural sectors as special (Wilson and Finkle, 1990: 20). Some of the most important reasons for this attitude relate to the chronic problem of food surpluses (relative to effective demand), and the unpredictable fluctuations in supply and demand. Foodgrain shortages were a major issue for Western industrial states only in the early 1970s; at other times surpluses presented a persistent problem. Supplementing the hegemonic model with a surplus capacity model helps to explain the U.S. propensity toward agricultural protectionism in the 1950s and 1960s.

Surplus capacity, however, provides only a partial explanation for U.S. agricultural protectionism. The hegemonic model must also be supplemented with the factor of domestic politics, which has been particularly important in agriculture. Article I of the U.S. Constitution gives Congress the sole power "to regulate commerce with foreign nations," and no trade-specific authority is granted to the president. Yet, Congress is by nature highly attuned to special interests and "does not seem well suited" to make the decisions often required in an open international trading system (Pastor, 1983: 158–164; see also Destler, 1986: 12–15). Although Congress has delegated authority to the executive to negotiate trade agreements from the time of the 1934 Reciprocal Trade Agreements Act, the executive must continue to be responsive to congressional concerns. The congressional actions culminating in the 1955 U.S. GATT waiver were a prime example of agricultural protectionism resulting from Congress's authority over trade policy. Thus, domestic considerations caused the United States to adopt agricultural trade policies in the 1950s–1960s contrary to those predicted by the hegemonic model.

Although the United States was ambivalent about agricultural trade liberalization, it did perform one postwar function that is often attributed to a hegemon. It contributed to stability and food security in the agricultural trade regime through its food aid, its duopoly with Canada, and its policies regarding East-West issues. U.S. contributions to stability and food security could be partly explained by both the "collective goods" and the "security" versions of the hegemonic stability thesis. However, stability and security were also to some degree unintended results of U.S. policies that were adopted primarily for domestic reasons. U.S. policies that promoted stability were also pursued through extra-GATT channels such as the Canada-U.S. duopoly, which did not contribute to the interdependence principle of multilateralism.

As its trade hegemony declined from the mid-1960s, the United States began to favor the interdependence principle of agricultural trade liberalization over the sovereignty principle of exemptionalism. This provides further evidence that the effects of hegemony on trading policies must be examined on a sectoral basis. Concerned about the costs of its agricultural policies and the protectionist policies of others, the United States pressured for the inclusion of agriculture in the GATT Kennedy and Tokyo Rounds. The United States was also reacting to its growing balance-of-payments deficit by attempting to benefit from its natural comparative advantage in agriculture. Thus, a declining hegemon may become more protectionist in some economic sectors where it is less competitive while opting for greater liberalization in sectors where it has natural competitive advantages.

Although the United States was more willing to incorporate agriculture in the GATT framework, its capacity to do so became more limited. Indeed, the Kennedy and Tokyo Rounds were concluded only after the United States largely accepted the EC's position that its Common Agricultural Policy was not negotiable. The future of the CAP clearly depended more on the balance of domestic pressures for and against change than on outside pressures from the United States. The EC, of course, was not solely responsible for the failure to achieve a breakthrough in agriculture. Even as the United States suggested that agricultural trade barriers be reduced in conjunction with those for industrial products, it continued to insist upon its own special prerogatives in agriculture. A prime example was the 1955 GATT waiver, which the United States has never relinquished.

In the 1970s, global foodgrain shortages were of considerable benefit to U.S. farmers, and U.S. pressures for EC concessions were therefore limited for much of the decade. Nevertheless, the return to foodgrain surpluses and the loss of U.S. market share pushed the United States to adopt a much more aggressive stance in the 1980s. The establishment of the Export Enhancement Program in 1985 was a major factor contributing to the export subsidy war between the United States and the European Community. The EEP helped bring the European Community to the bargaining table, but it also contributed to an agricultural bargaining process based more on the sovereignty principles of reciprocity and special interests—dominated by the United States and the European Community—than on the interdependence principle of multilateralism.

At the Uruguay Round, U.S. proposals for agricultural reform were more broad ranging than ever before, and U.S. threats to link the agricultural talks with the outcome of the entire round were more serious. Although the United States now seemed to be fully committed to agricultural trade liberalization, the extreme tactics it employed contributed to instability. The decline of U.S. hegemony combined with the EC's domestic preoccupations ensured that the European Community would not yield to pressures and that a stalemate would develop. Hegemonic stability theorists often refer to the hegemon as contributing to both international economic liberalization and stability, but this chapter demonstrates that as the U.S. commitment to liberalization in agriculture increased, its contribution to stability declined.

While the EC's intransigence was a major factor accounting for the prolongation of the Uruguay Round, the uncompromising nature of U.S. demands in agriculture was also a factor. In addition, other actors such as the Cairns Group adopted strong positions, and some less-developed countries would have linked the agricultural talks with the outcome of the entire round even if the United States had not done so. Cowhey and Long (1983: 186) have maintained that "it is a combination of falling hegemony and surplus capacity that produces a transformation" in a regime, and the agricultural trade regime has been confronted with both of these conditions in the 1980s and 1990s. As a result, the United States and the Cairns Group were linking agricultural trade more closely with other trade issues than ever before, and the implications of either success or failure were exceedingly high. There are great dangers in this "all or nothing" approach because agriculture is different in some major respects, and free market economists have often underestimated the importance of social, political, and ideological factors in this sector.

Before concluding, some comments are in order about the usefulness of applying the regime concept to agricultural trade issues. Sovereignty principles have been far more important than interdependence principles in agricultural trade, and the international rules governing agriculture have been applied only weakly. Nevertheless, it is useful to view agricultural trade as a specific regime nested within the more diffuse international trade regime. In the early years of the GATT there were efforts to specify the conditions under which provisions of the General Agreement did not apply to agriculture, and thus to preserve the overall principle of trade liberalization in theory if not always in practice. The GATT Uruguay Round has demonstrated an increased commitment to linking the outcome of the agricultural talks with the results of the overall negotiations, making it clear that there is now a closer relationship between trade in agricultural and nonagricultural areas. The regime concept is useful for assessing the degree to which general trade principles and rules are accepted in the agricultural area, for comparing the relative importance attached to the various principles in agriculture versus other sectors, and for determining the extent to which verbal adherence to principles diverges from adherence in practice. Theories of regime change are also helpful in interpreting the historical development of agricultural trade issues.

International relations scholars have often discussed food and agriculture in studies on interdependence. Indeed, Rosenau (1976: 40–43) identified four "central features" of interdependence issues, and in each case he cited examples in the food and agricultural areas. Because "the growth of interdependence increases the capacity of all relevant actors to injure each other,"[9] regimes are necessary for managing conflict in highly interdependent areas such as food and agriculture. When states refuse to recognize their interdependence by emphasizing sovereignty principles—such as exemptionalism, special interests, and reciprocity—serious conflicts, such as the U.S.-EC agricultural export subsidy war, become more likely. Subsequent chapters in this volume provide detailed analyses of the tension between domestic interests and international interests in the current Uruguay Round of trade negotiations. The discussions in this chapter and those that follow offer strong evidence that a greater recognition of the international effects of domestic agricultural policies is essential if current differences in the Uruguay Round are to be resolved.

NOTES

1. The "nesting" terminology was first used by Aggarwal (1981).

2. For a discussion of the trade regime principles see Finlayson and Zacher (1981: 561-602). The Finlayson-Zacher article referred to these as "norms"; Zacher described them as "principles" in a later article. See Zacher (1987: 176, fn.8).

3. Finlayson and Zacher (1981: 578–581) have focused on a safeguard principle designed to exist temporarily; my exemptionalism principle explicitly includes exceptions that exist for a much longer period.

4. For percentage shares of the ten leading food exporters, see GATT, *International Trade* (various years).

5 A concessional sale "involves price or credit terms that contain substantial . . . government subsidies." See Knutson, Penn, and Boehm (1983: 144).

6 In 1963, the United States exported 1.8 million metric tons of grain to the Soviet Union, but the circumstances at the time were unusual. For a detailed discussion of the role of political-security issues, see Cohn (1990).

7. The founding members of the Cairns Group were Argentina, Australia, Brazil, Canada, Chile, Colombia, Fiji, Hungary, Indonesia, Malaysia, New Zealand, the Philippines, Thailand, and Uruguay. This group's role in the Uruguay Round is discussed in more detail in Chapter 6.

8. At the GATT contracting parties meeting on December 12–13, 1990, the United States accepted the fact that Canada would not alter its import restrictions on ice cream and yogurt until after the conclusion of the Uruguay Round.

9. Oran Young, quoted in Haas (1982: 210–211).

Robert L. Paarlberg 3

Why Agriculture Blocked the Uruguay Round: Evolving Strategies in a Two-Level Game

This chapter takes up two central questions: First, how did a negotiation over agriculture come to be the key component in a larger multilateral negotiation in the GATT? And second, how did that agricultural policy negotiation then come to be deadlocked in such a way as to jeopardize all the other components of the GATT's larger trade reform effort?

The answer, in brief, is that agriculture became a key component of the GATT negotiations because U.S. trade officials chose to make it so. A deadlock then ensued over agriculture because European Community officials and Japanese officials did not fully share the U.S. goal, and because U.S. domestic farm lobbies have shown themselves to be more clever than U.S. officials in manipulating the complex "two-level game" dynamic of the negotiation.

These conclusions allow us to make a larger point about the GATT itself. The post-1947 success of the GATT in opening up international industrial trade reflected mostly the interest of the industrial sector itself in liberal reform. When customs tariffs and nontariff barriers on industrial trade are brought down through a GATT negotiation, the result is mostly a reduction in mutually offsetting trade barriers, and thus an overall production and trade expansion within the industrial sectors of the nations undertaking the reform. The same does not hold for agriculture, for which industrial countries rely more on parallel internal price supports than on mutually offsetting border measures to protect the sector. If the agricultural policies of industrial countries were liberalized, the result would be a shrinkage of production and exports in most industrial countries.[1] When an economic sector has no such overall interest in liberal reform, as is the case with industrial country farming sectors, convening a multilateral GATT negotiation will not suffice to produce a liberal policy change. Instead, it can get in the way of such change.

AGRICULTURE IN THE URUGUAY ROUND

Since September 1986, delegates from 108 different countries have been negotiating in the GATT to reach agreement on new rules for international trade in a variety of product areas, including manufactured goods, services, tropical products, intellectual property, and temperate zone agricultural commodities. If successful, these negotiations could help expand the world economy by as much as $5 trillion in the 1990s.[2] As of December 1990, a certain amount of progress had been registered. A protocol had been agreed to on market access, establishing a schedule for new tariff reductions for the next five years. A draft text had been prepared on intellectual property. Progress had also been made on government procurement, tropical products, customs valuation, investment, dispute settlement, and even to some extent on the more difficult areas of services and textiles.

But in the area of agriculture, absolutely nothing had been agreed. The climactic December 1990 ministerial meeting in Brussels—the session that was to have brought the Uruguay Round to a successful conclusion—finally broke up and fell apart (it adjourned without any result), because nothing could be agreed to in the area of agriculture. The negotiators were not even able to agree upon a common "framework" for the agricultural part of the negotiation, nor even a common methodology for measuring impediments or distortions to agricultural trade. The negotiations were to have been concluded on Friday, December 7, 1990, but on the night of December 6, when it became clear that the EC was not prepared to change its position on agriculture, the agricultural negotiations collapsed. Delegates from agriculture exporting countries, including the United States, then—as threatened—pulled out of all the other negotiations, and the ministerial meeting as a whole adjourned in failure (*Wall Street Journal*, December 10, 1990: 2).

Why did the Uruguay Round, after four and a half years of effort, allow itself to be blocked by agriculture? Agriculture was only one of the fifteen separate negotiating groups in the round. Agricultural trade is only about 10 percent of total world trade. And farming represents less than 4 percent of the gross domestic product (GDP) in almost all major industrial countries (and less than 2 percent of GDP in the United States) (Commission of the European Communities, 1987; USDA, 1989b; Australian Bureau of Agricultural and Resource Economics, 1988a). How could a dispute over this relatively small agricultural sector be allowed to get in the way of a possible $5 trillion expansion in world product? The explanation can be traced to a plan, formulated by top-level U.S. agriculture and trade officials before the round began, to try to use the GATT talks abroad to solve what was mostly a domestic agricultural policy reform problem.

U.S. HOPES FOR AGRICULTURAL POLICY REFORMS

When the Uruguay Round began in 1986, U.S. agricultural policy officials were facing a difficult domestic farm policy crisis. U.S. farm commodity prices had collapsed, mostly because of tight U.S. monetary policies, high dollar exchange rates, and the still continuing effects of a world recession. As a result, the U.S. government found itself spending almost $26 billion a year to support the income of U.S. farmers, under the mandatory terms of a variety of previously legislated domestic farm "commodity programs."[3] These programs automatically offset the impact of a market price decline through such things as cash payments and direct government price supports.

These domestic commodity programs are justifiably criticized, not only for the burden they place on taxpayers (most of whom are less wealthy than the farmers receiving support), but also for the distortions they tend to impose on the production of farm commodities, and by extension on international agricultural trade. The United States is not alone in embracing such domestic farm support policies. The European Community and Japan support farm prices even more than does the United States.[4] In combination, these policies generate high-cost surplus farm production, which then can be sustained only through tight restrictions on imports, or which must be dumped onto world markets through the use of export subsidies. These import restrictions and export subsidies, in turn, tend to generate endless international trade frictions. A surprising number of U.S.-EC and U.S.-Japan trade policy disputes are concerned with trade in agricultural commodities.[5]

U.S. agricultural policy officials, especially the more "market-oriented" Reagan administration appointees, made repeated attempts, particularly in 1981 and 1985, to "reform" these domestic agricultural support policies by reducing the level at which prices and income receive guaranteed public support. Their efforts, however, had been firmly opposed by domestic farm lobbies through the influence they exerted within the agricultural committees of the U.S. Congress. A 1985 Reagan administration effort to return U.S. agriculture to the discipline of the free market had been pronounced "dead on arrival" by both the Republican and the Democratic members of these agricultural committees (Rapp, 1988: 41).

Accordingly, when official preparations began for the new "Uruguay Round" of GATT negotiations, these recently defeated Reagan administration officials sensed an opportunity to pursue their domestic objective of farm policy reform at home through an international negotiation abroad. Consequently, they took an early lead in insisting that negotiations on domestic agricultural policy reform should become a key component of the larger Uruguay Round.

Among the top U.S. officials who most enthusiastically embraced this "internationalization" of the domestic farm policy reform problem were Reagan's recently named U.S. trade representative (USTR), Clayton Yeutter, and his undersecretary of agriculture for international affairs and commodity programs, Daniel G. Amstutz. Yeutter, who held a doctorate in agricultural economics and had previously served in the U.S. Department of Agriculture

(USDA), was deeply committed to agricultural policy reform. Amstutz, who became his chief point of contact in the USDA, had come to government service from a senior position at Cargill, and was likewise a "free trader" looking for ways to dismantle government farm-support policies.

At the September 1986 ministerial conference in Punta del Este that launched the round, Yeutter insisted that agricultural policy, defined to include domestic farm price supports, be included as a priority reform objective in the Uruguay Round. Accordingly, the Punta del Este ministerial declaration was written to give prominence to agriculture, including the internal "structural surpluses" that were distorting agricultural trade (see *Ministerial Declaration on the Uruguay Round*, 1986). Amstutz then explained why he and Yeutter were planning to attack the reform problem in the GATT: "The bottom line is that we must reject the 'go it alone' approach and move toward a global solution. The new round of trade negotiations is a major opportunity for making that move. . . . The international bargaining table is where the solution lies."[6]

Yeutter and Amstutz hoped a bargain could be struck in the GATT because they knew that some of their agricultural policy counterparts in Western Europe and Japan were also looking for ways to reduce domestic farm support levels. Studies that had recently been done for the USDA, the Organization of Economic Cooperation and Development (OECD), and the World Bank had all shown that European and Japanese consumers and taxpayers were in some ways even more heavily burdened by domestic farm policies than were consumers and taxpayers in the United States. Table 3.1 shows the domestic cost to consumers and taxpayers of agricultural policy in the United States, in the European Community, and in Japan, estimated by the U.S. Department of Agriculture for the year 1986/1987, roughly at the time the Uruguay Round began. Table 3.1 indicates that the primary effects of agricultural support policies everywhere are to support the farmers of a nation at the expense of the consumers and taxpayers of that same nation. In fact, as these figures show, the costs to consumers and taxpayers exceed the benefits to farmers. A net economic cost is paid in each of these industrial regions, mostly because of welfare transferred to Eastern bloc and developing countries, in the form of expenditures on export subsidies.

From studying data such as these, and from conversations with like-minded reformers in the European Community and Japan, U.S. officials such as Yeutter and Amstutz conceived of a grand international strategy for solving everyone's domestic agricultural policy reform problems at the same time: do it through a GATT negotiation. By 1987, Yeutter had convinced President Reagan to endorse the effort. As Reagan subsequently explained, "No nation can unilaterally abandon current policies without being devastated by the policies of other countries. The only hope is for a major international agreement that commits everyone to the same actions and timetable" (Rapp, 1988: 150).

Table 3.1
Annual Benefits of Agricultural Support to Producers and
Costs to Consumers and Taxpayers, 1986/1987 (billion $)

	Producer Benefit	Consumer Costs	Taxpayer Costs	Net Economic Costs
United States	26.3	6.0	30.0	9.2
European Community	33.3	32.6	15.6	14.9
Japan	22.6	27.7	5.7	8.6

Source: USDA (1989a).

THE PRESUMED ADVANTAGES OF
INTERNATIONALIZING THE REFORM

The advantages of internationalizing the reform effort were expected to be twofold. First, as Reagan's words suggested, an internationally coordinated reform would be somewhat less painful to each of the agricultural sectors in question. A share of each nation's farm price supports—up to a 40 percent share for the United States, but a much smaller share for the European Community and Japan—are now simply going to offset the impact of other nations' supports.[7] The conclusion could be drawn that reducing support guarantees for U.S. farmers would be less painful if support level guarantees were also being reduced for European farmers. Sharing the pain of farm policy reform would actually mean reducing the pain to farmers. Whereas a unilateral elimination of U.S. farm subsidies would cost U.S. farmers roughly $26 billion, a multilateral liberalization (along with all other farmers in the OECD world) would cost measurably less—roughly $17 billion according to USDA estimates (USDA, 1989b: fig. 12).

A second presumed advantage of "internationalizing" the reform effort—a procedural advantage—was no less important. Unilateral domestic farm policy reform efforts have the disadvantage of being undertaken in political channels dominated by farmers. In the United States, domestic agricultural legislation is renewed every four to five years, mostly according to the preferences of the agricultural committees of the U.S. Congress, which are populated by farm state and farm district members. This legislation is then implemented by the U.S. Department of Agriculture, whose budget is controlled by those same agriculture committees. As discussed in Chapter 5, EC price support decisions, under the Common Agricultural Policy, are normally made each year by the Council of Agricultural Ministers, in response to proposals made by DG-VI, the Directorate General for Agriculture inside the EC Commission.

These routine channels are the target of intense, coordinated, and highly effective farm lobby demands. The only way for reformers to defeat these demands, presumably, would be to take the policy process out of these channels. This, from the vantage point of Yeutter and Amstutz, is what moving agriculture into the Uruguay Round was intended to accomplish.

Once agriculture moved into the GATT process, they presumed, reform-minded trade officials who shared their goal of lowering supports would gain the initiative. It would be the U.S. trade representative (or, in the EC, the external affairs commissioner) who would have at least nominal command over the process of developing negotiating positions and conducting the negotiation. And, once the negotiation was concluded, it would not be the agricultural committees of the Congress, or the Council of Agricultural Ministers in the EC, that would have the final say on ratification. In the United States, it would be the entire Congress, led by the trade committees (Senate Finance, House Ways and Means) that would ratify. And they would have to say "yes" or "no" to the whole agreement, in a deadline-driven, limited debate, no-amendment-up-or-down vote, according to the "fast track" procedures created in recent U.S. trade legislation. In the European Community, formal approval after a GATT negotiation would come not from the Council of Agricultural Ministers, but instead from the Council of Foreign Ministers, via a subcommittee of that council; the 113 Committee (named after an article in the Rome treaty that covers external trade), a committee dominated by member country trade ministers (Moyer and Josling, 1990: 175; Chapter 5, this volume).

Moreover, the procedural bias toward domestic political approval of an agreement on agriculture would presumably be overwhelming at this point because rejecting the agricultural reform package would mean rejecting the rest of the Uruguay Round as well, including the results of all the parallel negotiations on services, intellectual property, dispute settlement, investment, and all the rest.

Thus, the plan of these U.S. reformers was to use an international negotiation, conducted with like-minded officials abroad, as a device both to weaken and then to finesse the domestic farm lobby opponents of reform at home. In the more technical language of Putnam (1988: 427–460), who examined such intersections between international and domestic policy, they were hoping to expand their "win-set" by creating a "two-level game." They were entering a cooperative international game with reform-minded officials in the European Community and Japan in order to strengthen their hand against the powerful farm lobbies that were opposing reform in the more competitive policy game at home. Putnam has made large claims for the potential value of this "two-level game" approach. He has argued, for example, that it was used to great effect by President Jimmy Carter and Chancellor Helmut Schmidt in 1978, when each used the terms of an international agreement, reached at an economic summit conference, to defeat their respective policy opponents at home (in the United States, opponents to the decontrol of domestic crude oil prices; in Germany, opponents to the reflation of the economy). Putnam was careful, however, not to promise automatic success for a strategy of "internationalizing" domestic reform dilemmas. In fact, by classifying this situation as a "game," he at least implied that the opponents of policy reform at home may have some winning options of their own to pursue. Such, indeed, has been the story for agriculture—so far, at least—in the Uruguay Round.

DOMESTIC FARM LOBBY RESPONSE

Almost from the moment that U.S. officials chose to describe agricultural reform as the make-or-break element in the larger GATT negotiations, U.S. domestic farm lobby groups began their own maneuvers to protect themselves from this internationalization of the subsidy reduction effort. They found they had several great advantages on their side.

U.S. farm lobbies were assisted by the immediate reluctance of European and Japanese government officials to join U.S. officials in an enthusiastic embrace of the reform objective. U.S. domestic farm lobbies had less reason to feel threatened by the administration's "two-level game" strategy, because U.S. officials never really found enough like-minded counterparts in the European Community and Japan with whom they could play this game. Most of the international support for this U.S. reform strategy came from a much less important direction, from the so-called Cairns Group of nonsubsidizing and developing country exporters. This collection of fourteen countries, led by Australia, was enthusiastically committed to U.S., EC, and Japanese policy reform (Miller, 1989; Chapter 6, this volume). But as non-subsidizing exporters, these countries were not really proposing to undertake any difficult reforms of their own—a factor that, together with their relatively small size as producers of the commodities in question, undercut the impact of their arguments.

Agricultural and trade policy officials in the EC and Japan provided some mild support for the U.S. strategy when the Uruguay Round first got under way, but with many doubts and qualifications, especially concerning the wisdom of trying to eliminate surpluses by moving toward free trade (the EC preferred explicit market-sharing agreements). This mild support weakened badly as the round went on. In the European Community, support for a GATT-brokered reform of the CAP declined sharply following an EC economic summit meeting in February 1988, which produced a combination of decisions that temporarily relieved the EC's internal budget crisis. The European Community resolved its short-term financial problems in 1988; first, by agreeing upon a mild reform of the cereals price support system (a so-called "stabilizer" agreement), and second, by adjusting its revenue collection system to tap more directly into the wealth of its member countries with high gross national product (GNP), such as Germany (Moyer and Josling, 1990: 94–96). The result was a 25 percent increase in the EC's revenue base, momentary relief from its budget crisis, and a momentary loss of interest in further agricultural policy reform, through the GATT or otherwise. By the time serious budget pressures re-emerged in the European Community, late in 1990, the Uruguay Round was almost at its scheduled completion date.

In Japan, as well, support for a GATT agreement on agricultural policy reform was not sustained. By 1988–1989, a rash of political scandals had weakened Japan's political leaders so badly as to result in a shocking upper house electoral defeat for the ruling Liberal Democratic Party. So when the LDP put together its policy platform for the 1990 election, it threw in an explicit pledge not to undertake any further agricultural policy reform. (It promised that "not one single grain" of foreign rice would be permitted to enter the Japanese market.) The result was a considerable evaporation of Japanese support for U.S. agricultural objectives in the Uruguay Round (Paarlberg, 1990b; Chapter 4, this volume).

U.S. farm lobbies were also assisted, however, by what can now be understood, in retrospect, as an excessively ambitious official U.S. negotiating strategy in the round. The first official U.S. negotiating proposal on agriculture, tabled in Geneva in July 1987, was an ideologically rigid, far-fetched proposal to eliminate in ten years all agricultural subsidies that distort production or trade. This proposal was labeled the "zero option," and was for a time highly touted by some administration supporters as a bold and fitting parallel, in the world of agriculture, to the administration's equally radical—and ultimately successful—zero option arms control proposal to eliminate all intermediate-range nuclear forces in Europe.

Unfortunately, the other parties in this agricultural negotiation were not quite willing to play the role of Gorbachev. Neither EC nor Japanese officials could imagine taking a step so radical in agricultural policy. Nor, for that matter, could they imagine the U.S. Congress going along with a step so radical. It was at this point that the U.S. domestic farm lobby saw its first big tactical opportunity.

Knowing that the administration's zero option proposal would be rejected by the European Community and Japan, large parts of the U.S. domestic farm lobby decided, opportunistically, to endorse it. They endorsed it not because they were willing to give up all of their production and trade-distorting subsidies if the Europeans and Japanese did likewise, although that is what they said. Many of them endorsed it in hopes that it would deadlock the negotiation, which was an outcome they could live with quite comfortably.

A surprising number of U.S. farm lobbies began to argue in favor of the zero option, saying it was the only way to guarantee a "level playing field" against their subsidized foreign competition. In fact, they began saying they could accept nothing less than the zero option. They announced they would not settle for half measures. "No agreement," they began to say, would be better than a "bad agreement." Of course, "no agreement" was precisely the outcome that many of these farm lobbies were after. It would mean no need to give up their valuable domestic subsidies. In fact, it would mean they could hold on to those subsidies while claiming in public that they were "willing to give them up."

This hypocritical preference of some U.S. farm lobbies for the zero option in the GATT was manipulated to greatest effect just prior to the December 1988 midterm review conference in Montreal. During the run up to that conference, USTR Clayton Yeutter at one point signaled his readiness to move away from the zero option, and closer to the Cairns Group position, which sought an "early harvest" of more realistic partial reforms. U.S. farm groups, led by heavily protected sugar and dairy producers, noted this development with alarm and immediately lobbied the secretary of agriculture to force Yeutter to stick to the zero option in Montreal (*Food and Fiber Letter*, 1988: 3).

Soon after this Montreal conference deadlocked, the new and more pragmatic Bush administration decided to back away from the zero option, just enough to permit a papering over of international differences on agriculture, so that the negotiations could get started again. When it did so, however, U.S. farm lobby leaders came up with a variety of alternative reform-blocking strategies.

MANIPULATING THE ARMS CONTROL METAPHOR

U.S. farm lobbies secured their greatest tactical advantage from 1989 onward by embracing the administration's careless likening of the agricultural negotiation in the GATT to an arms control negotiation. This arms control metaphor was embraced by the U.S. farm lobby, because it allowed them to demand several things from the negotiation.

First, it allowed them to demand "no unilateral agricultural disarmament while the negotiations are under way." This slogan helped U.S. farm groups, in 1989, to resist some of the domestic farm subsidy cuts that might have otherwise occurred due to Gramm-Rudman budget requirements. Farm groups and farm supporters in Congress said "no" to such cuts, arguing that unilateral cuts at home would weaken the hand of U.S. negotiators in the GATT talks abroad.[8] The international talks that were intended to facilitate domestic reform, in other words, came to be used by farm supporters as a means to block reform.[9]

Second, the arms control metaphor was also seized upon as an excuse to demand more subsidies, for use of "bargaining chips" in the negotiation, presumably to be "traded away" at some future date, so as to "win" a better agreement in Geneva. Just as Reagan had used Pershing and cruise missile deployments in Europe to persuade Gorbachev to accept his zero-option Intermediate Nuclear Forces proposal, so (said the farm lobby) should the

United States now build up its agricultural subsidies so as to have something to trade away against EC subsidies.[10]

This "arm in order to disarm" tendency is unfortunate enough when it develops in some arms control negotiations. It has even less legitimacy, however, in an agricultural negotiation. Most agricultural subsidies, after all, are not at all like military arms. They are not primarily deployed against foreigners. They are deployed mostly against the welfare of consumers and taxpayers at home, rather than against trade competitors abroad. The difficult task of reducing these agricultural subsidies is closer to the problem of domestic gun control than to the problem of international arms control.

How was the U.S. farm lobby able to redefine what began as a multilateral attack on subsidies into a struggle mostly to reduce foreign farm subsidies, and to build up U.S. subsidies if necessary to accomplish that reduction? The administration's offering of the arms control metaphor was only part of the problem. A larger problem was the reaction of the U.S. Congress, which was all too eager to join the farm lobby in stressing the competitive aspect of the international negotiation. Congress found it easy to agree that agricultural reform was a "global problem," and then to view it as mostly a problem of "unfair subsidized foreign competition" for U.S. farmers. This view allowed members of Congress to "support the negotiations" and "attack farm subsidies" without angering any U.S. farmers. The subsidies they wanted the negotiation to attack were mostly subsidies in the EC and Japan.

Worse than this, even some U.S. trade officials eventually seemed to lose sight of the original negotiating plan. Instead of looking for ways to weaken the claim of farm lobbies at home, as the negotiation went on, they warmed to the task of defending those farm lobbies against "intransigent" foreigners. Carla Hills, who replaced Yeutter as U.S. trade representative in 1989, soon found herself reassuring the American Farm Bureau Federation that, despite her "absolute opposition" to trade-distorting subsidies, she favored keeping U.S. export subsidies in place for the moment because "we will not unilaterally disarm." Perhaps it is inevitable that negotiators will spend more time seeking relative gains for a politically powerful constituency at home, rather than (as was intended) joint gains for everyone's consumers and taxpayers.

But the U.S. farm lobby has gone even further in seeking and gaining tactical advantages from the Uruguay Round. Having embraced the concept of an international negotiation and having redefined that negotiation as a contest against foreigners (a contest in which U.S. farmers are "victims" of foreign agricultural policies, and hence deserving of more U.S. government support), and having consistently embraced extreme U.S. negotiating positions of the kind that make any significant international agreement unlikely, U.S. farm lobbies have then gone even further to re-ensure their advantage. They have demanded additional subsidies for themselves if and when the negotiations finally do fail (as "compensation" for the intransigence of their foreign competitors).

They first did this in 1988, when they wrote into the U.S. Trade Act that year a provision for expanded export subsidy spending in the event of a failed GATT negotiation. Of course, thcy were simultaneously, in 1988, blocking all progress in the negotiation by insisting on "no retreat" from the zero option.

Farm lobbies improved on this tactic, however, in the fall of 1990, when they wrote into the final budget reconciliation act a so-called "GATT trigger" provision. In the event of a failed Uruguay Round negotiation by June 1992, this provision would oblige the secretary of agriculture to spend an additional $1 billion on export subsidies, adopt a marketing loan subsidy for wheat and feed grains, and waive acreage reductions. If the negotiations are still a failure in June 1993, the secretary would be permitted to reverse all or part of the $13.5 billion in domestic farm budget cuts (over five years) that were finally imposed on the USDA in the 1990 budget reconciliation bill (USDA, 1990: 33–34).

With these provisions in place, the U.S. farm lobby is now in a position to start making an entirely new category of demands. Whenever there is an indication that the Uruguay Round might be failing, farm lobbies can invoke these GATT trigger provisions and ask for more subsidies. In January 1991, immediately following the failure of the Brussels ministerial, both the American Farm Bureau and the National Association of Wheat Growers called on the USDA to increase its spending on export subsidies "pending greater EC flexibility in the Uruguay Round," and Senator Robert Dole (R-KS) asked the president also to move up the "trigger date" (for an even larger outlay on subsidies) to June 1991 (*Inside U.S. Trade*, 1991: 2–3).

So, to the dismay of the reformers, the U.S. domestic farm lobby has so far had little trouble devising its own two-level game strategy—a strategy for blocking all internationally negotiated reforms, while simultaneously using the international negotiation as an excuse to boost, whenever possible, U.S. agricultural subsidies at home.

THE REFORMERS' DILEMMA: HOW TO END THE ROUND?

A puzzle arises at this point. Given the success of U.S. farm lobbies in countering the administration's two-level game strategy, and given the position those farm lobbies are now in to profit from a complete GATT deadlock, why did U.S. negotiators allow a complete deadlock to develop at the Brussels talks in December 1990? Why did they not "cut their losses" by agreeing to accept some variant of the weak policy reform proposals put forward by the European Community?

Table 3.2
Formal Negotiating Positions, December 1990

	U.S. Proposal	Hellstrom Proposal	EC Proposal
Internal support reductions	75% (1990–2000)	30% (1990–1995)	30% (1986–1996)
Border protection reductions	75% (1990–2000) No rebalancing	30% (1990–1995) No rebalancing	No separate pledge; rebalancing permitted
Export subsidy reductions	90% (1990–2000)	30% (1990–1995)	No separate pledge

Source: Based on information from *Inside U.S. Trade*, December 7, 1990.

The formal EC proposal presented in December 1990 is summarized in Table 3.2, along with the last formal U.S. proposal and a compromise proposal put forward by Swedish Agricultural Minister Matts Hellstrom, who chaired the final farm trade discussions.

The EC reform proposal was actually weaker than this comparison might suggest because it was offering support level reductions from a 1986 base year (meaning that "credit" would be given for some reductions that had already been undertaken), and because these were support level reductions to be measured not against current world prices, or even against a moving average of those prices, but instead against a fixed international "reference price" based on the 1986–1988 period, when world prices were unusually low (meaning the EC would be given an artificially high support level from which to fall by 30 percent) (*Inside U.S. Trade,* November 9, 1990). And worst of all, the EC proposal embraced the concept of "rebalancing," meaning the EC would be permitted to offset a larger than required cut for one crop (such as wheat) with a smaller than required cut, or even a support level increase, for some other crops. This presents a threat to U.S. producers and exporters of oilseeds (such as soybeans) and other non–grain feed ingredients (such as corn gluten feed), who otherwise enjoy a GATT guarantee of duty-free access to the EC market for their products (a concession the EC carelessly made in the Dillon Round of negotiations in 1962).

True, the EC hinted at some flexibility at the December 1990 Brussels conference. As the talks were collapsing, EC officials talked in the corridors about going slightly beyond their formal proposal, by offering some low percentage guarantees on market access, plus some limited guarantees on export subsidies, and by modifying their rebalancing demand to exempt soybeans (*Inside U.S. Trade*, December 10, 1990: S-3). But the United States still walked away from the talks.

The U.S. walkout appears to have been based on several calculations. First, the calculation that the "informal" EC concessions still came with too many strings attached (including, for example, an EC demand for a five-year "truce" on the GATT dispute settlement panels; the treatment of U.S. cash payments to farmers—"deficiency payments"—as the equivalent of an export subsidy; and a demand that the final agreement be linked to a new international monetary arrangement, so as to protect the EC against exchange-rate fluctuations).

Second, a more tactical calculation could have figured into the decision. Knowing that the negotiations could always be extended (assuming no congressional objections to an extension of the administration's fast track authority), U.S. officials probably saw some advantages to agreeing with the farm lobby in Brussels, asserting that "no agreement is better than a bad agreement." On November 2, 1990, twenty-nine separate U.S. farm lobby organizations had warned Secretary Yeutter, in a joint letter, that "no agreement would be better than what appears will be the EC's bottom line" (*Inside U.S. Trade*, November 5, 1990: S-12). The walkout allowed them to bond with the farm lobby in the short run, and thus gain some of the credit or credibility they would eventually need to sell a "bad" agreement to the farm lobby in the long run.[11]

The walkout, no doubt, also was intended to concentrate the minds of the Europeans on the real prospect of a total GATT failure. The imminent prospect of such a "Gattastrophe"—with an agricultural deadlock bringing down all the other ongoing Uruguay Round negotiations—would presumably result in stronger internal pressures within the European Community, especially pressure by Germany on France, to save the round by showing more flexibility on agriculture.

The wisdom of these presumed U.S. calculations has yet to be demonstrated. In late February 1991, responding to an emergency initiative by GATT Director General Arthur Dunkel, the EC did show just enough "new" flexibility on agriculture to satisfy the United States that the talks should be started again. At an informal meeting on February 19, 1991, the EC delegate simply remained silent when Dunkel read out not an agreement but a "negotiating plan" that had earlier been reviewed and accepted by the United States.[12] On the strength of this supposed breakthrough (EC officials insisted they had made no concessions), President Bush asked Congress, one week later, to extend his fast track ratification authority until June 1993.

Without an extension of the fast track, there could be little hope that foreign negotiating partners would take seriously any concessions on agriculture—or anything else—that U.S. officials might try to offer in the course of an extended round. By extending the round, however, the administration may be inadvertently extending the ability of farm lobbies to make their larger subsidy claims in the context of the round. Wheat and dairy producers busily pursued this advantage. In mid-March 1991, the House Agriculture Committee transmitted to the House Budget Committee a request for an additional $475 million in export subsidy funding for fiscal year 1991. The main reason given for this proposed doubling in export subsidy spending was the recently extended Uruguay Round. The committee letter noted that it would be "imprudent" for the United States to cut its export subsidy spending "at this critical stage in the [Uruguay Round] negotiations" (*Journal of Commerce*, March 14, 1991: 6A).

If this sort of domestic farm lobby exploitation of the round should continue, might administration officials attempt, perhaps later in the negotiation, to find some way to accept a "weak" agricultural agreement, and then simply come home? For many U.S. farm lobbies, a weak agreement would be almost as attractive as a continued deadlock. Most U.S. farm lobbies would not feel especially threatened by such an agreement because it would mean their own valuable domestic subsidies would not be taken away.

Still, the farm lobbies preferring a deadlock have now built a strong bargaining position for themselves. They have coaxed Carla Hills into repeating her long-standing assertion that a significant agreement on agriculture is the "key" to the whole round. In March 1991, Hills repeated to Congress that "if we don't get reforms in agriculture we won't get an agreement" (*Journal of Commerce*, March 15, 1991: 6A). And these lobbies have also persuaded Edward Madigan, Yeutter's successor as secretary of agriculture, to repeat their favored line that "no agreement is better than a bad agreement." Asked in his confirmation hearings if he were prepared to "walk away" from a bad agreement (for U.S. farmers) in Geneva, Madigan replied, "You bet I am" (*Journal of Commerce*, March 6, 1991: 6A).

REFORM WITHOUT A GATT AGREEMENT?

It is easy to be pessimistic about prospects for an agricultural reform breakthrough in what remains of the Uruguay Round. A more promising course might be to pursue farm policy reform outside of the GATT.

Pursuing policy reform one country at a time is difficult, but not impossible. After all, in late fall 1990, the U.S. Congress agreed to cut its farm support spending by $13.5 billion over the next five-year period. This cut was made unilaterally by the United States as a part of the annual congressional budget reconciliation process. This unilateral cut was made just one month before the final GATT conference in Brussels, and without any regard to the GATT. If the budget deal had been linked more closely to the GATT, the cut might have been labeled "unilateral disarmament," and it might have been more difficult to secure.

Now the European Community, as well, is moving unilaterally toward a significant farm policy reform package. In January 1991, EC Agriculture Commissioner Ray MacSharry announced a plan that might eventually cut cereals price support levels inside the European Community by as much as 40 percent. MacSharry and the EC Commission began devising this radical scheme late in 1990, mostly in response to internal social policy and budget pressures, without any explicit connection to the Uruguay Round. EC officials have consistently insisted there is no connection. It is almost as if they know this reform plan will be easier to sell to their suspicious agricultural ministers if it is not presented as a "concession" to U.S. farmers, or as a "compromise" with U.S. negotiators for the purpose of breaking the deadlock in Geneva.

So, there may indeed be some promise in the two-level game approach to farm policy reform, providing that the second-level game is an internal budget crisis of the kind that cannot be erroneously described as a "contest against foreigners," rather than a GATT negotiation.

NOTES

1. By one estimate, total U.S. farm output would fall by 1 percent following a liberalization of all industrial country farm policies. Farm output in the EC and Japan would fall by 7 percent and 32 percent, respectively (USDA, 1989a).

2. This is the estimate used by Heinrich Weiss, chairman of the Federation of German Industries (BDI), a strong supporter of the Uruguay Round (see *Inside U.S. Trade*, February 1, 1991: 18).

3. Annual spending for commodity programs, which had averaged $3 billion prior to 1982, had reached $25.7 billion in FY 1986.

4. See Paarlberg (1989b). For an insightful explanation of the tendency for developed countries to embrace such policies, see Anderson and Hayami (1986).

5. Of a total of seventy-eight "unfair trade practice" petitions accepted by the U.S. trade representative (under Section 301 of U.S. trade law) between 1974 and 1989, thirty (39 percent) involved trade in agricultural products. And seventeen of these petitions (57 percent of all agricultural trade dispute cases) specifically involved complaints about the agricultural trade practices of the European Community. See Vogt (1989: 12–13).

6. Letter from Daniel G. Amstutz, undersecretary for international affairs and commodity programs, U.S. Department of Agriculture (*Choices*, 1986: 38).

7. U.S. officials estimated, in 1986/87, that if EC policies had not been operating, U.S. producer income would have increased by roughly $8 billion. Likewise, if U.S. policies had not been operating, EC producer income would have increased by roughly $7 billion (USDA, 1989a).

8. Early in 1989, when the outgoing Reagan administration proposed to meet budget guidelines by cutting $2 billion worth of farm price and income support programs, the chairman of the Senate Agriculture Committee, Patrick Leahy (D-VT), rejected the proposal as a give-away of bargaining leverage in the GATT: "If that is not telegraphing unilateral disarmament I do not know what is," Leahy said (see *Inside U.S. Trade*, February 3, 1989: 18).

9. The U.S. sugar lobby has resisted compliance with an international GATT

panel finding that its import quotas are a violation of GATT rules, in part by arguing that it does not want to give away any bargaining leverage in the ongoing Uruguay Round. The sugar lobby, in other words, is using an ongoing negotiation over future GATT rules as its excuse to continue violating current GATT rules. European farm lobbies have done much the same. Copa and Cogeca, the two most powerful European farm organizations, rejected price cuts recommended by the EC Commission for 1989/90, "without reciprocal measures taken by our GATT partners" (see USDA, 1989b: 8).

10. In 1990, for example, Clayton Yeutter (who was by then the secretary of agriculture) was pressured by farm groups into accepting a new "marketing loan" subsidy program for soybeans. He gave in on the argument that this measure would provide more "bargaining leverage" for the United States in the GATT talks (see *Inside U.S. Trade*, August 17, 1990: 20).

11. One week after the collapse, the U.S. Feed Grain Council "saluted" Secretary Yeutter for his "courage and strength" in "walking away from the negotiating table in Brussels" (*Inside U.S. Trade*, December 14, 1990: 6).

12. *New York Times* (February 21, 1991: D1). By remaining silent, the EC did not agree to accept an agreement on the matters of greatest importance to the United States—domestic supports, market access, and export subsidies—but only to "conduct negotiations" on such matters (*Inside U.S. Trade*, February 22, 1991: 7).

David P. Rapkin
Aurelia George

4

Rice Liberalization and Japan's Role in the Uruguay Round: A Two-Level Game Approach

Putnam's (1988) framework for analyzing international negotiations as "two-level games" offers a systematic way to examine the intersection of states' international interests and obligations with well-entrenched domestic interests and the policies that benefit them. At the international level of the game, representatives of states negotiate with their counterparts from other states; at the domestic level, these same negotiators must bargain to obtain consent for any deal they strike, or may want to strike, from the bureaucracies, legislators, parties, and interest groups that their country's political system comprises.

Such two-level games often arise in the area of agricultural trade, in which the forces of internationalization run headlong into the policies many states employ to support and protect their agricultural producers. Partly because most societies view their agrarian sectors as repositories of national culture and tradition, farm interests tend to be disproportionately represented in policy processes and thus effective in resisting external pressures to liberalize. The systemic consequence is that the channels of world agricultural trade remain congested with more trade-distorting policies of internal support and external restriction than found in any other sector.

Nowhere do the dilemmas of the two-level game appear to be posed in starker terms than in the case of Japan's rice policies. The country's total prohibition on rice imports is but the external face of a complex web of farm and land-use policies that are interwoven with Japan's electoral system and party politics, vested bureaucratic interests, networks of quasi-governmental agricultural organizations, and, most broadly, with the fabric of rural life in Japan. Yet these interests underlying rice protection run directly counter to the economic interests of Japan's urban consumers, its world-class manufacturing industries, and its cosmopolitan interests in an open world-trading order.

It is frequently said that Japan has benefited more than any other country from the relatively open world-trading regime constructed in the post–World War II period under the auspices of the GATT. Today, Japan's manufacturers enjoy unparalleled competitive advantages across a wide range of technologically advanced, high value-added sectors. Their ability to exploit these advantages, however, is impeded by a variety of protectionist measures erected elsewhere in the industrialized world. Moreover, impending regionalization in the form of the post-1992 EC and a North American free trade zone at least holds the potential of further curbing Japan's access to the lucrative markets of these areas. Japan, therefore, would seem to have a compellingly large stake in furthering the GATT project in the ongoing Uruguay Round of negotiations.

Other countries and various analysts have inferred from this large stake that enlightened self-interest would induce Japan to assume a leadership role in bringing the Uruguay Round to a successful conclusion. More specifically, it has been anticipated that Japan would take the initiative by offering some kind of opening of its rice market in order to obtain agreement on other significant GATT provisions that would benefit its manufacturers. This expectation has been strengthened by the belief that concessions on rice within the multilateral GATT forum would be more palatable in terms of domestic politics than would be yet another bilateral concession in the face of U.S. pressure.

Yet, to date Japan has made no concessions on the rice issue. Rather, its GATT delegation passively stood by and watched as the Uruguay Round negotiations collapsed in December 1990 in Brussels when the United States and the European Community could not resolve their differences over reducing EC farm subsidies. Japan has since refrained from attempting to mediate or break the logjam by offering any sort of concessions on rice; instead, Japan has maintained its insistence on the right to prohibit rice imports on grounds of "food security." Although there are growing signs that the Japanese government will finally capitulate if and when the European Community and the United States reach an agreement, it is significant that any concessions will be reactive, granted only when a pressured Japan is virtually isolated and perceives itself to be backed into an international corner from which there is no other avenue of escape.[1] And this reactive stance, of course, does nothing to reduce the risk of the United States and the European Community failing to strike an agreement—an outcome that could spell the failure of the entire agenda of the Uruguay Round.

From the standpoint of the international level of the GATT negotiating game, this failure of Japan to act to secure its large stake in the GATT regime seems anomalous. In this chapter, we demonstrate why this outcome is anything but anomalous when the domestic politics level of the game is considered. We first review briefly the evolution of Japan's rice-centered agricultural regime and describe the changing demographic and economic circumstances that would seem to make this regime politically unsustainable. We then use the conceptual categories of Putnam's two-level game framework to analyze the domestic and international politics of rice liberalization, focusing in turn on the distribution of rice policy preferences across the Japanese polity and the composition of status quo and proliberalization coalitions; on how Japan's political institutions affect the prospects for ratifying possible GATT-induced reforms of the rice-control system; and on the reactive "food security" strategy Japan has pursued in the Uruguay Round negotiations. We conclude that the extent to which the Japanese state remains grounded in the political culture of rice hinders its ability to (1) secure Japan's broader interests in the Uruguay Round negotiations, and (2) assume leadership in the world trading system.

JAPAN'S AGRICULTURAL REGIME

The evolution of Japan's agricultural policies in the twentieth century conforms to a broader historical pattern in which countries have shifted from taxing to subsidizing and protecting agriculture as industrial growth proceeds and agricultural output declines as a share of national product (Anderson and Hayami, 1986: introduction, ch. 1–3; Chapter 8, this volume). What is distinctive about the Japanese case, however, is the rapidity with which government policies switched from protecting consumer interests to protecting producers and, more recently, the extent of protection that has been provided.

Throughout this century, various policy measures, institutions, and principles have evolved to form the "regime" governing Japanese agriculture around a single commodity, rice. The foundations of this regime were laid in the 1920s and 1930s when the government initiated policies to stabilize supply in response to consumer unrest. The government's role deepened with the passage in 1942, under wartime exigencies, of the Food Control (FC) Act, which added direct state control of domestic production and distribution to the already-existing total control of agricultural trade.

Occupation-era reforms established several integral features of the current regime. Land reform set the small and inefficient scale of farm operations: as recently as 1987, fully 67.9 percent of Japan's farming households cultivated areas of less than one hectare; rice production is even smaller in scale, with 83 percent of rice-growing farms consisting of one hectare or less (Australian Bureau of Agricultural and Resource Economics, 1988a: 72, table 5.4, 101). The Agricultural Cooperative Union Law institutionalized the central role of the cooperatives (Nokyo) in agricultural politics, firmly cementing a dense and extensive network of quasi-governmental organizations into the fabric of state-society relations. In addition to their functions relating to agricultural production and distribution,[2] Nokyo serves as a potent political organization that is capable of mobilizing farm votes for favored candidates.

The landmark event in the shift toward producer subsidization was the Agricultural Basic Law (ABL) of 1961, which elevated rural-urban income parity to the status of a superordinate regime principle. Because price supports for rice became the principal means for maintaining parity, the annual determination of rice prices thereby was thrust into a pivotal role in Japan's electoral politics.[3] With price supports providing a stimulus to production, by the mid-1960s rice surpluses appeared and deficits in the rice control account began to bump against the limits of the Ministry of Finance's fiscal tolerance.

The impact of the ABL on Japan's levels of agricultural protection was almost immediate. Hayami (1988: 6–7, table 1.2) reported that in 1955 Japan's agricultural price support levels were considerably below those of the European Community countries; by 1960, Japan had surpassed the EC average (although not all EC countries); by 1965, only four years after passage of the ABL, Japan had the highest levels in the industrialized world; in 1984, Japan's agricultural price support ratio had climbed to 102 percent, compared to the EC's 22 percent.[4]

An assortment of diversion and acreage control programs have made considerable headway in shifting resources out of agriculture in the last several decades, but overall these measures have fallen far short of overcoming the fundamental economic contradictions inherent to the regime. The root contradiction lies in the fact that the incentives offered by these and other rationalization programs have been overwhelmed by the continuing stimulus to rice production represented by price supports and the prohibition of imports. In turn, the artificial profitability of rice production results in "the transmission of inefficiency in one part of agriculture to the whole sector" (Hillman and Rothenberg, 1985: 60).

In the meantime, Japanese farmers' dual competitive disadvantages—in relation both intersectorally to manufacturing and internationally to farmers in exporting countries—continued to widen. These disadvantages are in large part natural in a Ricardian sense, but they are exacerbated severely by the minuscule scale of farm management and by the prevalence of part-time farming. The inability (or unwillingness) to correct the rural bias in Japan's electoral districting,[5] coupled with stiff resistance from the network of agricultural cooperatives, has blocked the kinds of comprehensive reforms necessary to overcome these contradictions.

The direction and velocity of demographic and economic trends, however, suggest that the agricultural regime built around rice price supports will not be sustainable in the long term: the farm population continues to both shrink and age; rice consumption, and thus also production, has declined steadily as the share of meat, dairy, and wheat products in the Japanese diet has grown; the productivity gap between the agricultural and manufacturing sectors continues to widen; popular awareness of the substantial food cost differentials between Japan and other countries has increased; and fiscal constraints have long curbed the government's willingness to tolerate escalation of the costs of the regime.

In the face of these trends, it appears that the "handwriting is on the wall," so to speak, that Japan's peculiar rice-centered agricultural regime eventually will collapse under the weight of its own contradictions. But the emergence of agricultural trade issues as the key to completion of the Uruguay Round has made it unlikely that Japan will have the luxury of reformulating its agricultural regime as and when it chooses. For example, agreement on the tariffication proposals being considered in the closing stages of the Uruguay Round negotiations likely would require a radical overhaul of Japan's agricultural regime and divestment of the various interests built up around it. Following a brief discussion of the two-level game approach, we then apply it to this intersection of Japan's domestic politics and the Uruguay Round's agricultural negotiations.

THE LOGIC OF TWO-LEVEL GAMES

In Putnam's (1988) framework, the international level (Level I) entails bargaining among different countries' negotiators in order to arrive at a tentative agreement. The domestic level (Level II) involves seeking *ratification* of this agreement by those actors—legislatures, ministries, interest groups, class forces, or the public at large—whose endorsement, or at least consent, is necessary to implement the Level I agreement. What is required for ratification, of course, varies cross-nationally and may consist of formal (e.g., parliamentary) or informal decision processes.

Although it is useful to conceive of the problem in terms of a Level I negotiation phase followed by a Level II ratification phase, in practice the two levels are interactive and thus not discrete in either a temporal or analytical sense. Level II constraints shape initial bargaining strategies and positions at Level I, and expectations concerning ratification prospects circumscribe the range of possible agreements throughout the entire Level I process.

Conversely, developments at Level I may "reverberate" across Level II politics so as to alter the preferences of the relevant domestic players. Reverberation effects, such as international pressures, can be either positive (if they increase the likelihood of ratification) or negative (provoking a "backlash" that diminishes ratification prospects). The overall two-level process may be iterative if inability to gain ratification forces negotiators to reconvene at the Level I negotiating table. In Putnam's (1988: 437) terms, "The only formal constraint on the ratification process is that since the identical agreement must be ratified by both sides, a preliminary Level I agreement cannot be amended at Level II without reopening the Level I negotiations."

Putnam's framework as described so far leads to a focus on what game theorists have termed the *win-set* of each Level II constituency, defined as "the set of all possible Level I agreements that would 'win'—that is, gain the necessary majority among the constituents—when simply voted up or down" (Putnam, 1988: 437). The nexus of the two levels lies in the extent to which the sides' win-sets overlap, if at all. Wider win-sets make overlap (and thus agreement) more likely; agreement is logically precluded if win-sets do not overlap. Also, "the relative size of the respective Level II win-sets will affect the distribution of the joint gains from the international bargain" (Putnam, 1988: 440). Negotiators who are perceived to have large Level II win-sets are likely to be pushed by their counterparts to the boundary of that win-set, that is, to the point at which their country's gains from a still-ratifiable agreement are minimized. Conversely, negotiators operating with a narrow win-set will tend to maintain a rigid bargaining stance by pleading that they will be unable to deliver ratification if further concessions are made.

This formulation leads to examination of the determinants of the size of win-sets and the ways in which win-sets are manipulated. Putnam (1988: 442–452) has suggested three sets of factors that affect win-set size: the distribution of power, preferences, and coalitions across Level II constituents; the nature of Level II political institutions; and the strategies employed by Level I negotiators. We will use these three categories to organize the balance of the chapter's analysis of rice liberalization and the Uruguay Round as a two-level game.

LEVEL II PREFERENCES AND COALITIONS: JAPAN'S RICE LIBERALIZATION DEBATE

The emergence of agricultural trade liberalization as the key to completion of the Uruguay Round has thrust the once-taboo issue of rice liberalization to front and center stage in several significant ways. First, GATT-related pressure to open Japan's rice markets stimulates public articulation of acceptable and unacceptable outcomes, that is, win-sets. Second, it brings to the fore explicit comparisons of the costs and benefits that would accrue to the various Level II constituents from alternative potential international agreements and from no agreement. This process leads to a kind of national summation of costs and benefits, which, when weighted by the constituents' relative political strengths, will be "revealed" in the country's ultimate position at the Level I negotiating table. Third—and a subject we later examine more closely—the GATT factor compels consideration of the decision processes by which (non)ratification will be determined, no small matter in a country noted for consensual decision processes that are ambiguous, not formally codified, and frequently opaque.

The next section describes the composition of the coalitions of interests formed around status quo and liberalization preferences, respectively.[6] Also discussed are the shifts that have occurred in these preferences and coalitions as Japan has deliberated over the boundaries of its national win-set, and as these deliberations have interacted with changes in the win-sets proclaimed by other players at Level I.

The Status Quo Coalition

1. *The Japanese Government.* The Japanese government has firmly maintained its official policy of opposition to any sort of opening of the rice market. Japan proposed in GATT negotiations in November 1989 that basic foodstuffs should be exempt from import liberalization requirements, and argued that countries heavily reliant on food imports need to maintain self-sufficiency in basic foods in the interests of food security. Although there are ample reasons to doubt that Japan's present closed rice regime is the optimal way to attain food security, the government interprets the concept as mandating that the rate of self-sufficiency be no less than 100 percent.[7]

Different versions of the food security doctrine have been used for several decades by the Japanese government, both in response to international criticism and to justify the costs of protection to Japanese consumers/taxpayers. After liberalizing most of the agricultural products subject to market-opening pressures from trading partners in the latter half of the 1980s, creation of the "basic foodstuffs" category enabled the Japanese government to build a food security rationale specifically for rice.

Although Japan has steadfastly maintained its rigid stance in the GATT negotiations, signs of governmental flexibility concerning its ultimate win-set began to appear in 1990 and increased in frequency in 1991. In addition to statements by several cabinet members suggesting it would be impossible to sustain the total ban on rice, first Prime Minister Toshiki Kaifu and then his successor, Kiichi Miyazawa, hinted that a partial opening might be acceptable. More recently, Miyazawa dropped the phrase "food security" and referred to tariffication as "reasonable" in his 1992 new year address to the Diet (*Nikkei Weekly*, January 25, 1992; *Japan Times Weekly International Edition*, January 20–26 and February 3–9, 1992). Also, during this period there have been repeated media reports that a consensus is about to be formed within the government and LDP in favor of rice concessions.[8]

Yet both Kaifu and Miyazawa are the latest in a long (but not uninterrupted) line of politically weak prime ministers, some of whom have been unable to deliver on commitments made to foreign leaders. Hence, it would be premature to conclude that a government decision to liberalize the rice trade is imminent on the basis of guarded support from Japan's chief executive. Indeed, as of spring 1992, a profusion of conflicting formal and informal signals is emanating from within the ranks of the Japanese government, suggesting that definition of its win-set on the rice issue is in a fluid and contested state. Should the United States and the European Community fail to reach agreement on agriculture, it is likely that the government's official position will continue to preserve the status quo rice regime.

2. MAFF's Agricultural Bureaucrats. Like their counterparts elsewhere, the agricultural bureaucrats of the Ministry of Agriculture, Forestry, and Fisheries (MAFF) are located at the point in Japanese state-society relations where the demands of agricultural constituents are brought to bear on government, so it is hardly surprising that they have been the strongest governmental advocates of continued protection. Moreover, as Reich, Endo, and Timmer (1985: 184) point out in relation to the earlier dispute with the United States over liberalization of beef and oranges, "a full liberalization could significantly reduce MAFF's direct influence on the economy. If governmental intervention were replaced by market mechanisms, that change could diminish MAFF's ability to distribute economic or political resources, something no bureaucratic agency easily decides to give up." Accordingly, MAFF initiatives for incremental agricultural reform, although ostensibly aimed at creating a more efficient, market-oriented farm sector, have never deviated from protection of rice and always preserve the ministry's core powers to regulate and subsidize.

The food security doctrine originated in the MAFF, which has also been responsible during the Uruguay Round for its more elaborate formulation and proposal as a regime principle of the GATT. MAFF's defense of agriculture, however, goes beyond the food security argument. It is also the chief expositor of what is essentially a modern version of agricultural fundamentalism, contending that agriculture has "special roles and characteristics," which relegate notions of economic rationality to a lower priority in the calculus of agricultural policymaking. MAFF argues that agriculture contributes public goods—such as protecting the environment, conserving national land, and preserving rural communities—the value of which cannot be measured solely in economic terms.

Given the outcomes of MAFF's previous confrontations with the United States over liberalization of trade in other farm commodities, agricultural bureaucrats have preferred deliberating the rice issue within GATT venues to bilateral negotiations with the United States. But the way the Uruguay Round has unfolded—with the inability to resolve agricultural trade problems blocking an overall agreement and with the prospect of Japan's international isolation looming—has begun to thin the ranks of hardline protectionists grouped around the MAFF. Since the Uruguay Round almost ground to a halt in December 1990, officials from other ministries have defected with increasing frequency from their government's unyielding position. MAFF has reacted testily to these and other indications that support for the win-set proscribing rice liberalization is eroding, and has been quick to remind other governmental players of jurisdictional boundaries and of their responsibility to stick to the government's official position. Yet there are also signs that even MAFF has begun to prepare for market opening by considering how to alter the laws banning rice imports, as well as measures to compensate rice growers (*Japan Times Weekly International Edition*, February 3–9, 1992).

3. *The Liberal Democratic Party.* The LDP has been electorally dependent on the overrepresented rural vote since its inception in 1955. Although agriculture has been a (perhaps the) core component in the LDP's coalition, its long reign of single-party governance has rested more broadly on a grand, or encompassing, coalition that also embraces a diversity of urban and industrial interests. It is not surprising, then, that although the LDP's official party line has not swerved from the protectionist status quo, more and more individual LDP members have defected from this position.

The farm sector's influence on the LDP runs much deeper than just the electoral connection. Agricultural interests are strongly and directly represented in the Policy Research Council (PRC), the party's policymaking machinery. The PRC consists of a number of divisions and research commissions, each focusing on a functional policy area. LDP legislators' tendency to specialize in one or a few policy areas within the PRC has led to the emergence of what are termed "policy tribes" (*zoku*). *Zoku* are groups of LDP Diet members who identify strongly with a particular policy area, develop technical expertise therein, and form policy and patronage networks with relevant bureaucrats and private sector interests.

The agricultural policy tribe (*norinzoku*) occupies a strong position within the PRC, with both the agricultural division and research commission attracting the largest number of members (Fukui, 1987: 22–23, tables 1 and 2). With reference to trade policy questions, Fukui (1987: 6) contrasted the "diversity and fragmentation" of the commercial and industrial tribes with the "monolithic facade" maintained by the agricultural policy network. Fukui (1987: 7) reported that there is a "very broad consensus among LDP leaders," that the agricultural tribe "is one of the most influential and effective in the party, mainly because the policy network binding it to the agricultural bureaucracy and the vast national network of agricultural cooperatives is extremely tight and stable."

Recent LDP policy on rice liberalization was formed in the wake of its July 1989 defeat in elections for the Upper House and with the Lower House election of February 1990 in prospect. Prior to those events, the LDP had pursued somewhat of an internationalist course on liberalization of farm trade in commodities other than rice. The electoral setback, however, prompted an "about face" on farm imports, with the LDP promising that it would not allow "even a single grain of rice" to enter Japan, a phrase that was widely quoted in the media as symbolizing the party's fierce resistance to rice liberalization. Although viewed by many farmers as a stopgap measure to impress voters, it was sufficient to stem the flow of farm votes away from the party. The agricultural cooperatives reverted to their customary backing of LDP candidates, and support for the conservative party rose by about 20 percentage points between the July Upper House election and early February

1990, reaching levels of 56–57 percent (*Asahi Evening News*, February 6, 1990). The LDP's promises of strict rice import barriers were subsequently seen as a key factor in the party's retention of majority control in the Lower House in the February election.

The electoral connection thus remains a critical factor in the LDP's rice policy, despite the ongoing shrinkage of the farm population. The GATT factor has pulled with increasing weight in the other direction, however, prompting an exodus of defections among the party's leadership and rank and file. Should the exodus reach proportions allowing the defectors to assemble a winning coalition, and assuming that the GATT factor does not abate due to failure to resolve the U.S.-EC stalemate, the LDP's win-set will widen to allow some form of market-opening solution for rice.

4. *The Opposition Parties.* The rice policies of the opposition parties exhibit no fundamental differences with those of the LDP. Uniform rejection by all parties of the idea of opening Japan's rice markets was expressed in the adoption of resolutions in both houses of the Diet against rice liberalization in September 1988. Cross-party agreement on agricultural protection has also been evident in deliberations in the agricultural, forestry, and fisheries committees in each house, which are regarded as "committees of friends." Members share similar views on agricultural policy matters, opposition dissent is uncommon, and unanimous resolutions are not unusual.

Hence, "despite all their other policy clashes, the ruling and opposition parties totally agree that Japan must not liberalize imports of rice" (*Asahi Evening News*, February 9, 1990). In a televised debate involving the five major party leaders prior to the February 1990 elections, the only point of agreement among all five was the need to preserve rice self-sufficiency.

The absence of any clearly articulated alternative to the governing party's agricultural policies is partly attributable to the opposition parties' desire to capture rural votes from the LDP. This electoral strategy dictates even more conservative and protectionist policies than those of the LDP. The Social Democratic Party of Japan (SDPJ) is already the major opposition party in rural areas, whereas the other opposition parties—Komeito (the Buddhist-affiliated "clean government" party), the Democratic Socialist Party (DSP), and the Japan Communist Party (JCP)—aspire to extend their primarily urban support bases into the countryside. As a result, "Japanese politics has become a competition among the parties for greater conservativeness. Serious policy debate never occurs and progressives who favor opening Japanese markets—a not inconsiderable number of people—are unable to develop any political power" (*Asahi Evening News*, January 29, 1990).

Among the opposition parties, only Komeito has significantly moderated its protectionist stance on rice. There have been stray statements hinting at receptivity to market opening by leaders of the SDPJ and DSP, but these have not been endorsed by their respective parties. The SDPJ has continued its polarizing rhetoric on the rice issue, as evidenced by party chairman Makoto Tanabe's statement to farmers and their supporters at a December 1991 antiliberalization rally organized by Zenchu (the national political secretariat of the agricultural cooperatives): "If the Diet fails to live up to farmers' expectations, it must be said that the Miyazawa regime has made the Japanese nation its enemy" (*Japan Times Weekly International Edition*, December 23–29, 1991). There is thus every reason to expect the opposition parties to attempt to exploit rural discontent in the next elections if the LDP does reverse its protectionist position on rice.

5. *Nokyo*. The nationwide agricultural cooperative organization, Nokyo, is the largest collector of institutional rents from the existing FC system. Not coincidentally, it is also the most vocal regime constituent opposing any expansion of Japan's win-set to include rice imports. The FC system provides the agricultural cooperatives with guaranteed income from the various functions they perform in Japan's highly regulated rice market. Nokyo has nearly monopolized the rice trade from farm gate to the wholesale level, acting on behalf of the government as designated collectors, warehousers, and marketers of rice (collecting fees at each step). It also operates as a cartel-like supplier of fertilizer and other inputs, as well as credit, and is formally exempted from Japan's antitrust laws.

The significance of the FC system to Nokyo therefore goes well beyond the financial benefits it provides. Nokyo is institutionally embedded in a privileged position in the FC system itself: the FC provides the rationale for the core functions Nokyo performs as a semiadministrative arm of the government and for the special protection and assistance it has received over the decades. In addition to this role in implementing agricultural policy, Nokyo's national political lobbying federation (Zenchu) is vested with a voice in the rice price determination process, as well as input in other areas of agricultural policymaking.

Nokyo's institutional embeddedness is manifest as well in its explicitly political role in Japan's rurally biased electoral system. Its extensive organizational network, with 5 million farm members (plus 2 million affiliated, that is, nonfarm, members) and 380,000 employees distributed throughout Japan, also serves as a political organization that represents agricultural interests, helps to set the policy agenda, and has proven itself effective in mobilizing the rural vote. Its support has predominantly served the political interests of the ruling LDP; however, as some of our earlier examples indicated, at times Nokyo has used its political weight to exert leverage on the LDP, particularly when elections are pending and the LDP's electoral dominance is perceived to be in jeopardy.

Nokyo's position on rice liberalization echoes the government's food security doctrine, but it takes the protectionist argument even further by calling for a clear differentiation within the GATT between agriculture and industry and for recognition of the principle that each country should have complete discretion over its agricultural policy.[9]

Many analysts (e.g., Hayami, 1988) view Nokyo as the principal obstacle to rice liberalization and, more generally, to reform of Japan's costly and inefficient agricultural regime. In a remarkably frank statement, Tokuo Matsumoto, director of Zenchu's central committee, asserted:[10]

> The source of the rice problem is the leadership of our organization. Their basic motivation is to preserve their positions, and they see that the best way to do that is to change nothing. They're not worried too much about farmers, to be honest. Nor do they have any specific view of how Japanese farming will turn out in the future. They're simply concerned with power, and holding on to it.

Nokyo's maximalist position led it to resist earlier proposals for partial opening of the rice market (e.g., a 5 percent market share for imported rice), even though such proposals would likely leave the FC system (and Nokyo's lucrative position within it) intact. The more market-oriented tariffication proposal that Japan now faces, on the other hand, would be much more likely to require dismantling of the FC system. If the eventual Level I agreement compels such a dismantling, and if Nokyo and its allies are unable to block ratification, it is safe to anticipate that ways will be found to preserve or reconstruct a privileged position for Nokyo in the successor regime.

6. *Most Farmers.* Most farmers continue to strongly support the rice import ban. As described above, key policy innovations in the evolution of Japan's agricultural regime have conduced and then reinforced the preponderance of small-scale, part-time, and inefficient farmers. By and large, it is this category of farmers, and especially rice farmers, who lie at the electoral core of the status quo coalition.

To illustrate the persistent political influence of farmers, we return to the LDP's loss of majority control in the Upper House elections of July 1989. LDP support in rural areas fell drastically after the 1988 decision to open Japan's beef and orange markets, a factor, along with the Recruit scandal and introduction of a controversial consumption tax, commonly cited as being responsible for the LDP's defeat. Indeed, the LDP lost eighteen of twenty-two seats in beef- and orange-producing districts. It is therefore highly unlikely that the LDP would emerge electorally unscathed from any decision to liberalize rice imports. It is fair to conclude that the official government position on agriculture is linked directly to the electoral calculus of the party at any given time.

7. *Consumer Organizations.* Generally speaking, the positions of consumer organizations on rice liberalization have not differed significantly from Nokyo's, with whom these organizations maintain close ties. Both sets of organizations have found common cause in the issues of food security and food safety, which they rank well above food prices in determining their attitudes toward imported food products. Imported food is regarded as suspect because, as the argument goes, Japanese consumers cannot be absolutely

certain if chemicals have been used in its production and transshipment, nor what these chemicals are.

These sorts of reservations about agricultural trade liberalization have often been made by the Japan Federation of Housewives (Shufuren), which is a prominent public ally of Nokyo on farm import issues. Another national consumer organization, the National Liaison Association of Consumer Associations (Zenshoren), led by a retired MAFF bureaucrat, publicly supports agricultural protection. One of the largest consumer organizations, the National Federation of Livelihood Cooperatives (Seikyo), has strongly opposed rice trade liberalization. This stance may reflect the ties between some of its leaders and the Japan Communist Party, which makes a concerted effort to support the consumer cooperative movement (as well as the rice status quo).

In summary, the status quo coalition opposed to rice imports began to fray at the margins in 1990, and then suffered much more fundamental erosion in the course of 1991. The MAFF and Nokyo sides of the "iron triangle" at the heart of the coalition remain intact, but the LDP side—owing to GATT-related pressures and to the more heterogeneous interests comprising its support base—appears to be in the process of reconciling itself to the inevitability of expanding Japan's win-set at the Uruguay Round to include some form of market opening.

The Market-Opening Coalition

1. *The Ministries of International Trade and Industry, Foreign Affairs, and Finance.* The Ministries of International Trade and Industry (MITI), Foreign Affairs (MFA), and Finance (MOF) reflect different constituencies, interests, and world views than those arrayed behind the rice status quo. Until recently, a taboo on open consideration of the rice issue effectively deterred these governmental actors from voicing their preferences. But once the taboo was broken, and when GATT pressures intensified, some high-level officials from these ministries began to publicly express that some form of rice liberalization is inevitable.

In MITI's case, support for rice liberalization stems from the interests it shares with many of the industrial constituents it represents. It is Japan's highly competitive manufacturers who stand to benefit from other Uruguay Round trade reforms that would increase their access to foreign markets, strengthen GATT's dispute settlement procedures, and curb the unilateralist tendencies of the United States. The once protectionist MITI has been "internationalized" in this sense, although it is likely much more an example of "free trade as the ideology of the strong" than a conversion of principle. But whether MITI's stance derives from principle or interest is secondary to the fact that it is a key spokesperson for free(r) trade in a traditionally illiberal society.

The Ministry of Foreign Affairs, which unlike MITI lacks any constituents demanding protection, is even more consistently antiprotectionist. This position reflects MFA's role as guardian of the U.S.-Japan relationship as well as Japanese relations with the rest of the world. Like other foreign ministries, its modus operandi is inevitably two-sided: it represents Japan's national interests to the rest of the world while also acting as spokesperson for the rest of the world (especially the United States) within Japanese policy circles. MFA often elicits foreign pressures when they are consistent with its purposes; it also augments external pressures with its own, arguing for the need for domestic adjustment in circumstances where Japan will be subject to international criticism.

The Ministry of Finance is neither a principal in the GATT negotiations nor a supporter of free trade principles per se; nor, until quite recently, has it been a publicly vocal dissenter in Japan's contemporary rice debate. Its interests in the rice issue instead stem from considerations of bureaucratic prerogative and fiscal restraint. Donnelly (1984: 346) summarizes the MOF position as a "proximate decisionmaker" on rice policy:

> MOF officials have regarded the food-control system as a nettlesome if not disastrous program because it threatens a number of central objectives pursued by the ministry. First, decisions about rice are often made outside the annual budgetary process and financial aspects of the control program are frequently at odds with the ministry's version of "correct" fiscal policies at a given time. Thus rice issues can be seen as encroaching on MOF's autonomy, jurisdiction, and power. Second, rice-related programs represent a violation of the norm of program "balance" operating in Japanese budgetary politics. Third, rice policies violate the ministry's sense of national priorities and fiscal responsibility: deficits in the food-control account are higher than what the ministry considers sound or fair.

In light of these concerns, MOF has long opposed the FC system, although not from a trade-policy standpoint. In January 1992, however, Finance Minister Tsutomu Hata (also a former MAFF minister) publicly joined the other proliberalization members of the Miyazawa government, warning that Japan cannot stand alone at the GATT if other countries accept the tariffication proposal (*Nikkei Weekly*, January 18, 1992).

2. *Japanese Business Federations.* Among the most internationalized sectors of the Japanese economy are the business federations. Those that aggregate and articulate the interests of large-scale export industries, led by the Federation of Economic Organizations (Keidanren), have adopted a strongly antiprotectionist position on agriculture since the early 1980s. These organizations make frequent policy recommendations to the government advocating reform of the FC system and market opening for agricultural products. Their highly visible stance at times has produced a war of words between Keidanren and Nokyo (whose head offices are close

neighbors in Tokyo), with Nokyo complaining that the farm sector was being sacrificed on the altar of trade friction created by Japan's aggressive exporters of manufactures.

Keidanren's preferences on agricultural liberalization in general and rice imports in particular do not derive simply from the interests of exporting industries. Its position has also been strongly influenced by the food processing firms that dominate the Food Industry Policy Subcommittee of its Agricultural Policy Committee. Japanese food processors have long called for cheaper imported rice because of the high cost of the locally grown input. The widening price gap between domestically grown rice and rice sold on world markets—caused by yen appreciation as well as price supports—has encouraged food processors to import processed rice products, such as rice confections, rice meals, pilafs, and grains. These soon will amount to 1 percent of Japan's total rice consumption (*Japan Economic Journal*, March 31, 1990).

3. *The Media.* The media, especially the national daily newspapers, have been the most audible and consistent voices in support of opening the rice market, acting as self-appointed spokespersons for Japanese consumers. Newspaper editorials time and again alert the public to Japan's international responsibilities in trade and question whether Japan can continue closure of its rice market. As they point out, the consequence of Japan ignoring its trade obligations is international isolation. An editorial in the *Asahi Evening News* (January 8, 1990) summed up the media position quite succinctly: "Japan in order to maintain its credibility and good faith with its GATT partners will have to accept partial liberalization of the rice market in one way or another."

Although the media have consistently supported partial market opening, some major newspapers have balked at the more thoroughly liberalizing tariffication proposal (for example, *Japan Times Weekly International Edition*, November 11–17 and November 25–December 1, 1991). We anticipate, however, that if the Uruguay Round end-game scenario pits an isolated Japan against a unified U.S.-EC position, the media will counsel acceptance.

4. *Consumers.* In the last several years, consumers' attitudes toward rice imports have shifted rapidly toward a more favorable position. According to a December 1988 public opinion survey, almost 50 percent of respondents were completely against rice imports. Added to those who wanted to see the domestic agricultural sector competitively strengthened before opening the rice market, those opposed to immediate rice imports totaled almost 70 percent. The reason cited by the majority for their opposition to rice imports was the threat posed to Japan's self-sufficiency in basic foodstuffs. Only 25 percent agreed that "Japan's rice prices were too high, so we should import more" (*Mainichi Daily News*, December 28, 1988).

In addition to the costs to taxpayers of Japan's budgetary outlays for agriculture, heavy reliance on price supports means that the Japanese as consumers have been saddled with paying most of the difference between domestic producer prices and world market prices. In consequence, in the mid-1980s Japanese households spent an average of about 26 percent of their incomes on food, compared to 13 percent in the United States, 15 percent in Great Britain and Germany, and 18 percent in France (Rothacher, 1989: 95). But rice accounts for only about 2 percent of household expenditures, thus dampening the economic motivation for imported rice. Also, as recently as December 1990, a survey revealed that more than half of all consumers, and nearly 60 percent of housewives, were unaware of domestic-international price differentials (*Japan Times*, February 26, 1990).

The high visibility of the rice debate and sharp increases in international travel have raised awareness of these price differentials which, in turn, account at least in part for subsequent shifts in public opinion. In a May 1990 poll, responses opposing liberalization fell to 42.2 percent, whereas those who approved of rice imports increased from the previous year's poll to 37.7 percent. Among those who answered that self-sufficiency should be maintained for basic foods, a common justification was that "we cannot check the safety of imported rice" (*Nihon Keizai Shinbun*, May 16, 1989).

Within the next year, a decisive reversal occurred in Japanese public opinion. In a May 1990 survey, 65 percent expressed support for some form of rice liberalization: 21 percent for total liberalization, 17 percent for liberalization in stages, and 27 percent for "minimum access." Support for continuation of the rice import ban fell to 30 percent—from almost 50 percent eighteen months earlier (*Asahi Shinbun*, June 4, 1990). Even more so than in other industrial democracies, however, consumer interests tend to be diffuse and weakly organized and articulated in comparison to the more intensely held interests mobilized by the agricultural cooperatives. Hence, consumers should be regarded as an inactive and largely unmobilized component in the proliberalization coalition. Nevertheless, this dramatic reversal of public opinion is working its way through Japan's democratic institutions and no doubt has influenced the LDP's ongoing transition to a pro–market opening preference. The LDP is mindful of the growing weight of urban interests in its support base and is aware as well of the fact that urban votes are far less reliable and more prone to rapid shift on policy grounds than the more stable votes the party has received in rural areas.

5. *Some Farmers.* Although lacking an effective voice, some farmers are strongly opposed to continuation of the FC system and Nokyo's pervasive role within it. The contradictions inherent in Japan's agricultural regime have created several cleavages among Japanese farmers: between more and less efficient farmers, between larger and small farmers, between those producing high-quality rice and those who sell lower grades to the government, and between those who evade the FC system and those who rely on it. The rice debate has brought these parallel cleavages to the surface, as in each case the

former, less numerous category of more viable farmers tends to be more favorable to rice imports than the latter. A significant number of farmers are eager to buy more land in order to achieve greater economies of scale. Many believe that they could compete in an open market and resent farmers who hold on to their small plots at all costs. Producers of high-quality rice are confident of their ability to survive liberalization because of revealed consumer preferences for their more costly product.

Some farmers—from the same minority segments of the farm sector described above—also oppose the FC system's restrictions on rice distribution and marketing. Many flout its provisions by selling rice directly to consumers and retailers (thereby bypassing the collection and distribution networks of the agricultural cooperatives) and by ignoring the government's rice acreage reduction schemes. These farmers' general dissatisfaction with the FC system is well expressed in one farmer's lament that "policies do not help farmers who take farming seriously" (*Nikkei Weekly*, June 8, 1991). This group would welcome a change to a free distribution system or a more genuinely decontrolled one, but they receive no support from Nokyo or MAFF.

To conclude this survey of Level II preferences and coalitions, it is clear that some constituents' preferences have shifted toward opening the market and that, in consequence, the once-tight winning coalition formed around the status quo rice regime has begun to splinter. Preferences, and thus also the composition of both coalitions, have derived historically from how any given constituent's political and economic interests relate to the FC system. The one exception has been consumers, whose economic interests in lower rice prices traditionally have been more than offset by cultural, environmental, and food security and safety concerns. Recent opinion surveys, however, indicate a large and rapid public shift toward the antiprotectionist coalition. The political implications of this shift, although not yet electorally registered, have not been lost on the LDP. With the ruling party apparently in the process of defecting from the status quo, it is not surprising that important elements of the government have drifted away from the official position on rice liberalization.

LEVEL II POLITICAL INSTITUTIONS:
THE RATIFICATION PROCESS

At the point at which the government might declare a change in policy that widens its win-set at Level I, the critical question concerns the strength at Level II of the market opening coalition. More specifically, has a winning coalition been formed, as tested by the ratification process as well as in the next elections (with the sequence and timing of the two tests possibly influencing their outcome)?

Ratification tests take place within an institutional context that prescribes, with more or less specificity, the decision rules to be employed. The Japanese case is located somewhere along the "less specific" side of the scale. As Putnam (1988: 449) observed: "Not all significant ratification practices are formalized; for example, the Japanese propensity for seeking the broadest possible domestic consensus before acting constricts the Japanese win-set, as contrasted with majoritarian political cultures."

Ratification of rice liberalization minimally will require approval at the cabinet, LDP, and parliamentary (Diet) levels. But whereas formal parliamentary decision rules are majoritarian, the LDP's are instead the consensual type to which Putnam refers. As mentioned earlier, the LDP's key decision points lie within the two relevant subdivisions of its Policy Research Council—the Agricultural and Forestry Division and the Research Commission on Comprehensive Agricultural Policy. Fukui (1987: 7, 19) described these as "the final arbiter on virtually all important issues of agricultural policy" in which "all decisions are made by consensus, none by the ballot." George (1990: 19) concurred: "No major decisions on agricultural policy are taken in Japan without the direct involvement of the LDP's formal agricultural policy committees . . . but more particularly the informal policy tribe or *norinzoku* that operates within these committees."

The decisions or recommendations of these agricultural-oriented subdivisions then must "be reviewed and ratified by the higher decisionmaking bodies, the PRC Deliberation Commission and the LDP General Council and, once they are so reviewed and ratified . . . become official party policy" (Fukui, 1987: 18). Within the former, the "PRC's formal decisionmaking body," Fukui (1987: 20) pointed out that "issues not settled by consensus are referred to its de facto standing committee composed of the PRC chairmen and deputy chairmen." This brief look at the LDP's policymaking machinery leads to the expectation that the party's role in the ratification process will be governed by decision practices that are less formal and transparent (for example, within the agricultural policy tribe) and that require more than a simple majority. How much more is indeterminate. Japan's consensual propensities—which include a norm that restrains majorities, especially bare majorities, from forcing solutions on a reluctant and vocal minority—cannot be neatly reduced to algorithmic decision rules.

Another issue arising in relation to the LDP's role in ratification is the status of the unanimous 1988 Diet resolution, which the party sponsored and which affirmed its support for a complete ban on rice imports. Advocates of the status quo, such as Takashi Sato, former MAFF minister and at the time chairman of the PRC's Research Commission on Comprehensive Agricultural Policy, maintained, "The LDP made an official pledge and we must honor the promise [to farmers]." Proliberalization LDP members such as Toshio Yamaguchi responded that the resolution has not been incorporated into the constitution, and claim that the government can override such a resolution in the event of an international emergency (with isolation at GATT presumably qualifying as an international emergency): "Although the government must respect the Diet resolution, an international emergency should be regarded as equally important. It is not unconstitutional" (*Japan Times*, October 10, 1990). We do not anticipate that the resolution will pose much of a formal obstacle to ratification. Rather, it is likely to be used in future inter- and intraparty electoral competition, with incumbent LDP members called to task for violating their pledge. In this sense, the resolution gives pause to LDP Diet members contemplating abandonment of the rice status quo.

As indicated previously (see note 8), the composition of the Miyazawa cabinet apparently was formed (in late 1991) so as to facilitate consensus on rice liberalization. George (1990: 19) predicted that the position of two influential LDP agricultural leaders, Tsutomu Hata and Koichi Kato, would be "critical to any final decision made by the government." Hata is now finance minister and has publicly supported rice concessions; Kato, who is chief cabinet secretary, has been more circumspect, maintaining the official status quo position while calling for a comprehensive study of the likely impact of tariffication (*Nikkei Weekly*, January 25, 1992). Thus, although we cannot speculate on what kind of decision rules operate in the Miyazawa cabinet, it seems clear that a tacit consensus for some form of liberalization already exists (but it cannot be asserted until necessary to avoid isolation at the GATT).

The nature of any agreement reached at Level I will, of course, affect the probability of ratification. The main distinction is between different versions of partial opening, on the one hand, and variants of the tariffication proposal,[11] on the other. Partial opening to afford imported rice a fixed share of the Japanese market would leave the 1942 FC Act and the associated agricultural regime more or less intact. The government could serve as purchaser of imported rice and then channel it through the extant FC system or, according to a proposal attributed to Foreign Minister Michio Watanabe, export it to developing countries. Hence, partial opening would be more easily ratified than tariffication, which has been widely interpreted to necessitate abolition of the FC Act. Recent reports, however, indicate that the Miyazawa government is exploring ways to implement tariffication without overturning the law (*Nikkei Weekly*, January 25, 1992; *Japan Times Weekly International Edition*, January 20–26, 1992). Such a step would, in effect, widen the Japanese government's win-set at Level I while maximizing the chances of ratification.

Revision or abolition of the FC Act would take place in the Diet, and thus would constitute the parliamentary ratification test. Miyazawa himself has expressed doubts about ratification prospects in the Diet, saying, "I can't make a promise that can't be fulfilled" (*Nikkei Weekly*, January 11, 1992).[12] His concerns stem from the LDP's lack of majority control in the (upper)

House of Councillors, where the opposition parties, perhaps with help from recalcitrant LDP members, are expected to block attempted changes in the FC Act. That there is a dispute over whether the government can circumvent the most formal, that is, parliamentary, step in the multilevel ratification process (by implementing tariffication without amending the FC Act) indicates the ambiguity surrounding the whole issue of ratification procedures.

Ratification has also become intertwined with the political fate of particular Japanese leaders, with the issue of electoral reform, and with the timing of elections. Toshiki Kaifu was selected by the LDP's faction leaders in 1989 to be prime minister in the wake of the Recruit scandal, the LDP's setback in the July 1989 upper house elections, and the resignations from the office within a space of several months of Noboru Takeshita and Sosuke Uno. With a weak factional support base within the party, Kaifu's chief political asset was his untainted public profile—a rare commodity in the LDP after the Recruit scandal. Party leaders perceived him to be a weak and manipulable figure who would stand in until the political effects of the scandal subsided and the LDP leaders who had been implicated in it could be resurrected. Kaifu, however, confounded the expectations of the party leadership, which continued to regard his leadership abilities with disdain, and surprisingly gained a high level of public popularity.

This turn of events led to hopes among the LDP's leadership and rank and file that the Kaifu government would push through a solution to the politically sensitive rice issue. The *Japan Times Weekly International Edition* (June 17–23, 1991) termed the rice issue "a true political hot potato," and opined, "No presidential aspirant in the LDP wants to be caught holding it. All would prefer that Kaifu make the unpopular decision to open the rice market, bear the brunt of the critical fallout, and then quit leadership upon expiration of his current term." This connection between rice liberalization and the party leadership question was complicated further by linkage to the issue of electoral reform. Kaifu had identified electoral and campaign financing reforms as the principal objective of his administration. In the face of considerable intraparty opposition to the reforms, party elder Shin Kanemaru signaled to Kaifu that he should abandon his plans to reform the LDP and concentrate instead on solving the rice issue (*Nikkei Weekly*, June 8, 1991).

The ill-fated electoral reforms included provisions to change Japan's large, multiseat electoral districts to a combination of single-seat districts and proportional representation. Of particular salience to the ratification question was the provision of the proposed reforms that would have rectified by redistricting the long-standing bias favoring rural areas. In the process, the number of Diet members representing rural constituencies would have been greatly reduced. Political commentator Takayoshi Miyagawa aptly summarized the connection between electoral reform and ratification of rice liberalization:

If the disparity in the value of a vote between rural and urban constituencies were corrected, Diet members would need only to give the farmers a fair hearing. Those Diet members who believe that the current electoral system will continue cannot argue for liberalization of the rice market, but those who are seriously considering changes in the voting system can. (*Japan Times*, October 9, 1990)

In other words, at least some elements within the LDP were awaiting fundamental revision of domestic political institutions *before* tackling ratification of rice liberalization. Implementation of the reforms, by blunting a rural backlash, would reduce the political damage sure to follow from agreement at Level I to open Japan's rice market.

The Kaifu government's demise was ostensibly triggered by his insistence on pushing forward with reform legislation against the wishes of the LDP's leadership, who responded by quashing his bid to run for another term. The new Miyazawa government picked up the banner of political reform, but then quickly dropped it when Miyazawa's involvement in the Recruit scandal resurfaced as a political issue. Thus it appears that the long-awaited reform of Japan's electoral districting system will not occur in the near term, at least not soon enough to transform the rice ratification equation before the Uruguay Round is over.

With 1992 upper house elections, or possibly general elections, looming, the interaction of electoral politics and rice ratification could follow a number of different paths. If the Miyazawa government were to attempt ratification prior to the elections, the LDP would then face being held accountable at the polls in the still overrepresented rural districts. Alternatively, if no Level I agreement is reached prior to the elections, LDP members could be pressured to repeat their 1988 pledge to ban rice liberalization, especially if the scandal-ridden LDP finds its general support eroding. These are but two among many possible outcomes of a process that is likely to continue to be implicated in the ebb and flow of Japanese politics.

To conclude this section, we turn to Putnam's discussion of the role of "state strength" and "state autonomy" in ratification processes. Putnam (1988: 449) posed the following hypothesis: "The greater the autonomy of central decision-makers from their Level II constituents, the larger their win-set and thus the greater the likelihood of achieving international agreement." He then suggested that the hypothesis is fraught with "disconcerting ambiguity" because state strength can exert a contradictory effect: "The stronger a state is in terms of autonomy from domestic pressures, the weaker its relative bargaining position internationally."

Although the Japanese state arguably may have exhibited a substantial measure of autonomy in the conduct of its industrial policies, we have demonstrated that its autonomy is much more limited in the area of agricultural trade policy. More generally, rather than considering state strength or autonomy as a factor affecting ratification, we submit that the (in)ability to engineer ratification can be more usefully conceived as constituting a test or measure of state autonomy.

LEVEL I STRATEGIES:
JAPAN AT THE URUGUAY ROUND

We now turn to consideration of Japan's negotiating posture at the Uruguay Round and how it has been circumscribed by the Level II preferences, coalitions, and political institutions discussed above. Following a brief discussion of Japan's motivations for helping to initiate the talks, we examine in turn Japan's articulation of the food security doctrine and the status it has been accorded in the GATT, the U.S. role in the agricultural negotiations, the collapse of the negotiations at Brussels in December 1990 and subsequent developments, and the limitations of Japan's reactive negotiating strategy.

The idea for a new round of GATT negotiations originally emerged from 1982 talks between President Reagan and Prime Minister Nakasone. Subsequently, Japan, along with the United States, sponsored the call for a new round at the 1985 Bonn summit. Japan enunciated its agenda for the prospective negotiations at a 1984 meeting of GATT members in Geneva: reversal of the erosion of discipline within the GATT system; improvement of the trade prospects of debt-ridden LDCs; and reform of the GATT to improve its ability to cope with the trade challenges of the 1980s and 1990s, including strengthening its dispute settlement procedures and widening LDC participation (Hufbauer and Schott, 1985: 29).

"This agenda addresses important systemic problems. But none of the issues requires Japan to make significant concessions." Moreover, "Japan has more to gain from the negotiating process than from the actual conclusion of agreements—agreements that would likely require Japan to make substantial concessions" (Hufbauer and Schott, 1985: 30, 29). The motivation for this processual emphasis becomes clearer with closer examination of the first item on Japan's agenda:

> The Japanese government's primary purpose in proposing and promoting the new GATT round is to arrest [the] progressive erosion of the GATT commitments. It believes that, as long as the GATT negotiations are proceeding, the member countries will not dare to act contrary to the provisions or the spirit of GATT (Yoshino, 1989: 126–127).

In other words, as long as negotiations were under way, Japan could hope to avoid a protectionist reaction to its deepening and highly visible export penetration of others' recession-troubled markets for manufactured goods.

The priority Japan places on dispute settlement procedures—an area that encompasses curbs on U.S. unilateralism—reflects a broader policy objective. A MITI official expressed this concern: "Rules and principles are more important to a country without strong political power, such as Japan, than to countries that have such power" (*Nikkei Weekly*, December 28, 1991–January 4, 1992).

Yet Japan could not have hoped to promulgate stronger rules and principles only in trading sectors where it stands to benefit. Given Japan's position as the world's largest food importer with scant agricultural exports, as well as its import policies for rice and other commodities, it was hardly surprising that Japan's agenda did not address agricultural trade. But at the GATT ministerial meeting launching the new round at Punta del Este, Uruguay, in October 1986, the United States with a strong push from the newly formed Cairns group of farm product exporting countries, thrust agriculture onto the round's agenda. The negotiating mandate for agricultural trade that was adopted at the Punta del Este meeting was much more ambitious and comprehensive than had been the case for prior GATT rounds. With everything "on the table," the stage thus was set for conflict over the agricultural policies of GATT's major players.

Japan's Advocacy of the Food Security Doctrine

The principal objective of the agricultural negotiating agenda was reduction of trade-distorting domestic and export subsidies, especially those of the European Community and the United States. But one significant feature of this agenda augured ill for Japan's food security position. As Gallagher (1988: 6) noted, "the text contained no preemptory reference to the taboos of 'special characteristics' or separate treatment which had surrounded agriculture at the outset of the previous round of GATT negotiations." Japan's food security argument, of course, rests squarely on such exceptionalist (i.e., culturalist) grounds, which George (1991: 16) described as "the defense of last resort" and "the most amorphous barrier of all":

> As a barrier it is virtually unassailable, not only because it presents such a diffuse target for attack but also because the act of bestowing a cultural identity on a commodity or market automatically converts any criticism of it into an attack on Japan's cultural identity, indeed the very nation itself.

Although this culturalist stance may provide Japan's rice status quo constituents with political advantage in their Level II struggle, the implicit denial of agricultural exceptionalism in the negotiating mandate meant that Japan's insistent assertion of the food security doctrine would prove a strategic disadvantage at Level I.

The ban on rice imports has never been challenged in the GATT, but it is clearly in violation of existing GATT rules. GATT rules exempt state-traded items from import liberalization, but they also require that a minimum share of consumption of such items be imported (however, they do not prescribe specific levels of minimum access). Without firm footing in either GATT legality or exceptionalism, the Japanese government has augmented its international defense of the food security position with more oblique economic and political rationales, some more tenable than others. Claims that agricultural policy is a domestic matter and that pressures for rice liberalization "infringe upon our sovereignty" (MAFF Minister Takashi Sato, *Japan Economic Journal*, October 10, 1990) merely restate a fundamental problem faced by many other Uruguay Round participants.

A more important line of argument begins with reference to Japan's status as the world's largest and fastest growing market for imported agricultural products,[13] and emphasizes Japan's recent record of market-opening measures (including unilateral tariff reductions and the 1988 concessions on beef and citrus imports) as evidence of Japan's contribution to expansion of world farm trade as well as its need to maintain self-sufficiency in rice. It is in this context, so it is argued, that the rice import ban should be weighed against others' agricultural protection policies, with U.S. and EC policies sometimes singled out for comparison. The point here is not simply that "other countries do it, too," which is true enough, but rather entails the more serious argument that Japan's rice policies are less distorting of overall agricultural trade than the subsidization policies of the major exporters. Rice is a minor export product (only 3 percent of total production is traded on world markets), so opening Japan's rice market is, therefore, an economically peripheral issue.[14]

These linked arguments lead to Japan's general contention that the agricultural proposals being considered in the Uruguay Round negotiations are skewed toward the logic and interests of exporters while neglecting "the arguments of importing countries" (MAFF Minister Masami Tanabu, *Nikkei Weekly*, December 28, 1991–January 4, 1992). In another MAFF official's more specific terms: "In farm trade, the U.S. has nothing to lose, and Japan has nothing to gain" (*Japan Economic Journal*, December 1, 1990). The contention of asymmetrical gains is essentially correct. As such, it reflects what Paarlberg (1988: 55) identified as a "deeper explanation for the relatively poor [historical] performance of GATT in agriculture."

The complaint of asymmetry is less relevant when a broader calculus is applied to the entire negotiating agenda. Insistence on symmetry of gains in all fifteen Uruguay Round negotiating areas, of course, would make overall agreement impossible. We have not seen any estimates, even approximate, of the balance of economic costs and benefits for Japan across all fifteen, but it is widely expected that Japan would net substantial gains from completion of the overall agenda (and, less consensually, would incur significant costs in the event of no agreement). Nonetheless, the certain distributional imbalance in any foreseeable Level I agricultural agreement is a legitimate Japanese concern. Accordingly, Japanese officials invoke the GATT norm of mutuality of concessions, although always refraining from indicating what concessions by others would suffice to bring about concessions on rice.

Whatever merit one might find in the food security and other arguments offered in defense of the rice ban, it is hard to avoid the conclusion that these arguments reduce to a case for exceptionality based solely on Japan's particularistic national characteristics, interests, and needs, namely, the claim that no comparable food with the same cultural and dietary importance exists in other countries.[15] This has been a difficult case to make in negotiations in which other major protagonists, especially the United States, have sought global solutions to overcome just such agricultural exceptionalism.

Yet, Japan's advocacy of the food security doctrine in the Uruguay Round has gone beyond simply pleading exceptionality to existing rules (or rules in formation) in hopes of preserving its domestic agricultural regime. Japan has employed a more aggressive strategy insofar as it has attempted to change the rules by trying to elevate the food security doctrine—and thus by implication exceptionality—to the status of *principle* in the Uruguay Round's redefinition of the international agricultural trading regime.

Most of the hundred or so negotiating countries apparently realize that accepting Japan's plea for exceptionality would undermine the GATT regime by legitimizing innumerable other potential claims for exception. In consequence, Japan has not been able to muster much support for its attempt to establish food security as an international regime principle. The high point of this bid, from Japan's standpoint, was the inclusion of language suggesting the importance to member countries of food security in the text emerging from the April 1989 "mid-term review" of the Uruguay Round's progress. Inclusion of this clause was interpreted by Japanese officials as at least allowing postponement of a rice decision, but more importantly as an indication that food security was gaining recognition as a legitimate principle within the GATT.

Encouraged by this development, and with the LDP stiffening its position after its defeat in the July 1989 upper house elections (and before the February 1990 elections), the Japanese government proposed in the November 1989 GATT meetings that the body's rules be revised to allow members to maintain border restrictions on "basic food items" in order to "sustain a sufficient level [100 percent] of domestic production" (quoted in *Japan Economic Almanac*, 1990). The proposal drew sharp criticism not only from the United States and the Cairns Group, as expected, but also from the European Community. At a five-part meeting in Florida in January 1990, MAFF Minister Michihiko Kano equated food security with self-sufficiency in rice and proposed that "Japan be allowed to subsidize its rice farmers and retain a ban on rice imports regardless of whether other countries move toward freer trade" (*Asahi Evening News*, January 5, 1990). The other four agricultural ministers (from the United States, Canada, the European Community, and Australia) rejected the insistence that food security required 100 percent self-sufficiency. Shortly thereafter, reflecting the divergence of views within the Japanese government, MITI Minister Hirakaru Matsunaga acknowledged that the food security argument was contradictory to GATT principles (*Japan Times*, January 19, 1990).

Despite these setbacks, mention of food security in the text of the G7 summit meeting in Houston in July 1990 was construed as evidence that Japan's position was winning wider acceptance. Hence, in August 1990 negotiations in Geneva, Japan again asked the GATT to adopt new farm trade rules that would allow member states, after merely notifying the GATT, to ban imports of staple foodstuffs (*Nihon Keizai Shinbun*, August 27, 1990).

When minimum access proposals surfaced as a real possibility in what had been scheduled as the Uruguay Round's concluding session in Brussels in December 1990, Japan rejected these proposals. Hardliners in the government regarded the proposals as violating the "commitment" to food security thought to have been secured in the April 1989 midterm review. A new negotiating draft put together by GATT Director General Arthur Dunkel for the resumption of the agricultural talks in February 1991 was rejected by Japan because it again proposed minimum access and made only the barest reference to food security (as a topic for examination).

Japan's failure to establish food security as a GATT regime principle is simply a manifestation of its inability to enlist a politically significant number of Uruguay Round participants to the food security cause. All members of what is termed the food security group, as might be expected, are countries with noncompetitive farm sectors and scant agricultural exports: South Korea (whose Level II problems resemble those of Japan), Egypt, Switzerland, and the Nordic countries. Unless viewed as no more than a form of stalling, Japan's advocacy of the food security doctrine in the GATT has been an abortive strategy. The Japanese government's tenacious adherence to this Level I strategy can be understood only as a function of its Level II constraints.

The Multi- and Bilateral Roles of the United States in Rice Liberalization

The issue of rice notwithstanding, we cannot overemphasize the fact that the U.S.-EC dispute over the latter's subsidization programs is the primary reason for the agricultural impasse that has blocked completion of the Uruguay Round. The United States has hoped to win Japanese concessions on rice as a way to isolate, and thus bring greater multilateral leverage to bear on, the EC position. Japan's strategic view of the U.S.-EC dispute (as an advantage that enables inaction) has precluded its playing this U.S.-scripted part.

The United States has played two overlapping roles in its efforts to force Japan out of its reactive stance. As protagonist in the Uruguay Round's agricultural negotiations, it has forcefully sought radically liberal solutions to the problems of world farm trade. The United States also has acted as protagonist in Japan's domestic rice debate and policymaking processes. George (1991: 18) described how this deeply penetrative role exceeds even the extraordinary bilateral leverage the United States has traditionally exerted on Japan:

> In many respects the United States is itself an actor in the Japanese policy process: as a surrogate opposition party presenting the only true set of alternative policies to the government's, as an interest group representing the voice of Japanese consumers, and as an alternative power base for Japanese prime ministers seeking to overcome both shortfalls in their own factional strength and domestic resistance to change.

Although not yet accomplishing the desired expansion of Japan's win-set on rice, the United States has subtly manipulated two roles to block Japan's efforts to escape its rice problem.

In its multilateral capacity, the U.S. role has changed in several significant ways from previous GATT rounds. First, with respect to the overall negotiations, U.S. willingness to promote a liberal world trading order by means of generously dispensing asymmetrical concessions had been exhausted by the time the Uruguay Round commenced. As Paarlberg (1988: 57) observed: "The United States has gone to Geneva this time with urgent demands to make across-the-board, and with even less than before to offer in return." Second, with respect to the agricultural negotiations, the U.S. government reversed its previous insistence on exempting certain of its agricultural products from GATT provisions. Indeed, the United States now proposed wholesale exorcism of illiberal farm trade practices, including those it once had been able to force the GATT to accept.

The U.S. position as *demandeur* in the Uruguay Round's agricultural negotiations derives from two mutually reinforcing motivations. First, the United States has aimed to use liberalization in the GATT to arrest or reverse the loss of world market share to the heavily subsidized EC agricultural exports. Second, the U.S. government has hoped to use liberalization to trim the mounting budgetary costs of its own agricultural support policies, including the growth of export subsidies used to combat EC subsidization. In other words, as Paarlberg has documented in Chapter 3, the market-oriented Reagan administration has attempted to use the *international* negotiation in the round to achieve a *domestic* objective of farm policy reform at home.[16] The weapon of choice for this "killing of two birds with one stone" was termed the "zero option": complete abolition of all production- and trade-distorting agricultural subsidies and nontariff barriers. It was clear from the outset that not all of the major players in the agricultural negotiations were willing to undergo such radical surgery, least of all the EC and Japan.

The rice issue was first thrust onto the agenda not by the U.S. government, but by the U.S. Rice Miller's Association (RMA), which filed an (old) Section 301 complaint against Japan's rice ban with the U.S. trade representative in September 1986. (This carefully timed complaint preceded commencement of the Uruguay Round by one month and the 1986 congressional elections by two months.) Japan, hoping to avoid direct bilateral pressure from the United States on rice, strongly preferred that the rice issue be dealt with in the GATT context. And the U.S. government preferred to avoid adding the sensitive rice issue to its already strained bilateral agenda with Japan.

To Japan's relief, then USTR Clayton Yeutter rejected the RMA petition on grounds that the rice issue should be resolved in the Uruguay Round's multilateral format rather than bilaterally. The United States thereby reduced the risks of (1) provoking a domestic backlash in Japan, and (2) diverting attention away from the long bilateral menu of industrial and high technology issues by focusing on the economically less consequential matter of rice (a minor U.S. export product).

The U.S. government has declined several subsequent opportunities to challenge directly Japan's rice policies through bilateral action. The RMA filed another rice complaint with the USTR two months before the 1988 presidential and congressional elections. The RMA's petition, which asked for a partial (10 percent) opening of Japan's rice market, invoked both the strengthened Section 301 provisions (the so-called Super 301) and the GATT rules prohibiting total import bans. Yeutter, despite considerable congressional pressure, rejected the RMA petition and once more deferred solution of the rice issue to the ongoing multilateral negotiations. When Japan was designated an "unfair trader" under Section 301 in 1989, rice was conspicuously absent from the products for which it was called to task, which included supercomputers, satellites, and wood products. The Bush administration's removal of Japan from the ignominious unfair trader list in April 1990, although motivated by broader considerations, was another decision point at which the United States avoided explicit bilateralization of the rice issue.[17]

While seeming to accede to Japan's choice of venue, the United States now was able to tackle the rice ban indirectly through the GATT, where its pressure on Japan could be sublimated in multilateral purpose and legitimacy. The observation of a European diplomat neatly captures how the U.S. strategy "multilateralizes" the rice issue: "The Americans really don't have a position on rice—they have a position on the Uruguay Round. Rice doesn't even have to be mentioned. What's wanted is a framework on which all commodities can be dealt with, and it doesn't really matter how high the tariff is at the start" (quoted in Smith, 1991: 116).

At the same time, the United States has never abandoned its bilateral role as source of direct (albeit less overt) pressure and as surrogate of sorts in Japan's internal political processes. However, it has displayed greater selectivity and sophistication in its performance of this role in the rice dispute than in other issue areas, thus far averting the backlash presumed to lie latent not so far beneath the surface of a resurgent and prideful Japanese nationalism. U.S. behavior has been consistent with Putnam's (1988: 451) expectation that negotiators will "try to reinforce one another's standing with their respective constituents," especially in its efforts to shore up the shaky Kaifu administration. The United States has also been skillful and subtle in its appeals to Japanese consumers.

This "good cop" posture has been mixed with intimidating "bad cop" tactics. For example, Under Secretary of Agriculture Richard Crowder's warning in Tokyo of "all kinds of bilateral action" (if Japan failed to make concessions on rice in the Uruguay Round) makes explicit the sense in which the threat of eventual 301 action on rice has loomed over the whole negotiating process (quoted in *Nihon Keizai Shinbun*, April 17, 1990). USTR Carla Hills has gone so far as to say that Japan will be in "large measure responsible" for failure of the Uruguay Round "if Japan finds itself unable to negotiate on agriculture, which includes rice" (*Japan Times Weekly International Edition*, November 25–December 1, 1991).

At other times the bad cop role has been cloaked in multilateral concerns, as in Secretary of Agriculture Clayton Yeutter's blunt assertion in Tokyo in 1990: "It's Japan versus the world on rice" (*Japan Times Weekly International Edition*, December 10–16, 1990). USTR Hills's admonishment played even more pointedly to Japan's fear of international isolation:

> If the second largest industrialized market in the world, a market spreading the rest of the world with manufactured goods, is insisting on maintaining the surplus of manufactured goods, but refusing to take the agricultural output of poor nations that have nothing else to sell, you can be sure that the poor nations will not stay at the bargaining table (*Nikkei Weekly*, November 23, 1991).

In sum, while the United States has refrained from bilateralizing the rice issue through formal action, it certainly has not shied away from application of bilateral pressure.

We now turn to two key junctures in the negotiations at which opportunities to manipulate the boundaries of the food security and tariffication win-sets to create overlap were passed or blocked: the Brussels talks in December 1990 and the Eagleburger memorandum of June 1991. These two events taken in sequence reveal the shortcomings of Japan's reactive strategy in the agricultural negotiations and the dilemma this strategy poses for Japan's broader role in the Uruguay Round.

Collapse in Brussels

The Uruguay Round was scheduled to be completed at Brussels in December 1990. Although agreements were not yet finalized in the other fourteen negotiations, agriculture loomed as the stumbling block to a comprehensive agreement as the talks approached. The collapse of the Brussels talks was due to the failure to resolve U.S.-EC differences. Therefore, what is at issue here is not Japan's rejection at Brussels of an otherwise consensual agreement, but rather its failure to act to try to secure an overall agreement from which it would benefit. In effect, Japan's refusal to yield any ground on rice at Brussels amounted to rejection of what was about the best agricultural deal that could emerge from the Uruguay Round.

Table 4.1 summarizes the negotiating positions of the United States, the European Community, and Japan at Brussels, as well as the eleventh-hour compromise proposal submitted by Swedish Agricultural Minister Mats Hellstrom, the chair of GATT's agricultural working committee. On the table were reductions in internal supports, import barriers, and export subsidies. Note that by this stage in the negotiations the United States had softened its zero option position. It was no longer demanding complete elimination of agricultural support and protection, although the targets it

Table 4.1
Comparison of Negotiating Positions at Brussels, December 1990

	Internal Support Reductions	Import Barrier Reductions	Export Subsidy Reductions
U.S. Proposal	75% (1990–2000)	75% (1990–2000)	90% (1990–2000)
EC Proposal	30% (1986–1996)	conditional introduction of tariffs no targets pledged rebalancing	no concessions offered
Japanese Proposal	30% (1986–1996)	no opening of rice market	phased elimination
Hellstrom Proposal	30% (1990–1995)	30% (1990–1995) 5% compulsory minimum access	30% (1990–1995)

Source: Adapted from Chapter 3 by Paarlberg and *Journal of Japanese Trade and Industry*, January 1991.

proposed for the end of the ten-year transition period were still considerably higher than its major negotiating partners were willing to entertain.

The EC position conceded little. The clock for the proposed 30 percent reduction in internal supports would be set back to 1986, thus crediting previously made reductions. Tariffication was accepted contingent on other concessions, but no specific targets or timetable were pledged. The EC proposal was qualified further by its insistence on "rebalancing," a provision by which larger-than-required cuts for one product would be allowed to offset smaller-than-required cuts for others. Significantly, the EC did not propose any reductions in export subsidies, instead offering only a ceiling to limit their growth.[18]

The Japanese proposal likewise did not yield much. The only concession presented was a 30 percent cut in internal supports for various products (including rice), which, like the EC proposal, was to be backdated to 1986. While calling for a phased elimination of export subsidies, Japan, which does not subsidize its scant agricultural exports, made no specific demands on this count. (Japan was probably holding this card in abeyance until it could be used to bargain down any concessions on rice it might be forced to make should the United States and the European Community reconcile their differences.) The official Japanese position was still to refuse to negotiate on rice imports on grounds of food security. A government source expressed Japan's reactive stance before the Brussels meeting: "We will not throw away our bargaining chips unless we are forced to" (*Japan Economic Journal*, December 1, 1990).

When the negotiations failed to close the considerable distance between the rigidly held U.S. and EC positions, and the talks were thus verging on collapse, Hellstrom introduced his minimum access proposal. As indicated in Table 4.1, the Hellstrom proposal struck a number of compromises— in terms of the levels, rates, and timetable of reductions it put forth— which would have required significant concessions from all sides. The United States was rumored to be giving serious consideration to the Hellstrom proposal, but neither endorsed nor rejected it. Whatever flexibility the EC was reported to have considered was blocked by strong French resistance to expansion of the EC win-set.[19] The United States then walked out of the Brussels talks.

What was Japan's role in this turn of events? As had occurred at earlier Uruguay Round negotiations, the U.S.-EC dispute consumed so much time and attention that the rice issue was hardly mentioned. This outcome suited well the Japanese (non)negotiating strategy. The sticking point for Japan was the compulsory 5 percent (of domestic consumption) minimum access for rice imports required by the Hellstrom proposal. The passive stance of the Japanese negotiators meant that they did not have to reject outright the compromise proposal; instead, they simply watched the negotiations collapse. Afterward, in Tokyo, MAFF Vice Minister Shigeru Motai described as "too big" the proposed cut in agricultural protection (*Japan Economic Journal*, December 15, 1990).

Agreements in the other negotiating areas apparently had been near at hand, as acknowledged shortly thereafter by a MITI official: "If we make progress in the agricultural talks, we can wrap up the other 14 packages . . . in a week" (*Japan Economic Journal*, February 16, 1991). Yet the Japanese delegation was content to let the entire Uruguay Round be thrown into jeopardy rather than make a small rice concession in hopes of breaking the U.S.-EC stalemate. This passivity must be weighed against Japan's substantial interest in the success of the overall Uruguay Round, which Foreign Minister Taro Nakayama described just after Brussels as "a keen necessity for Japan, a country that relies on the multilateral trading system" (*Japan Economic Journal*, December 15, 1990).

The divergent views within the government on the rice issue and its effect on Japan's role in the Uruguay Round were brought to the fore by the events in Brussels. MITI Minister Kabun Muto, who was soon to be replaced after running afoul of the MAFF with remarks suggesting MITI favored partial opening, summed up the pro-liberalization perspective: "Japan was unable to play an active role in the negotiations because its agricultural policy was an Achilles heel for the country" (*Japan Times Weekly International Edition*, December 24–30, 1990). His successor, Eiichi Nakao, inadvertently captured the fundamental dilemma the Japanese government had placed itself in by refusing to budge from its "not a single grain" policy: "It would cause a very serious problem for Japan if Europe and the United States reach a mutually acceptable resolution" (*Japan Times Weekly International Edition*, January 14–20, 1991). An agricultural agreement leading to a broader multilateral reform of the world trading system that is, on the one hand, a "keen necessity for Japan" would, on the other hand, be regarded as "a very serious problem."

Both within and outside Japan, the government's stonewalling at Brussels drew harsh criticism. An editorial in the *Japan Economic Journal* (December 22, 1990) used caustic language: "What was the 200-man strong Japanese delegation doing in Brussels, meanwhile? The officials were only intent on keeping dead silent, hiding themselves behind the showdown between Europeans and Americans." The Japan Economic Institute (JEI Report 48B, December 21, 1990) summarized its view thusly: "Commentators on three continents feel that Japan, at best, had earned a grade of 'incomplete' or perhaps even failed in an early test of its willingness to play a world leadership role." Moreover, the passive image projected at the GATT was quickly associated in the Japanese media and elsewhere with Japan's faltering, reactive response to the Gulf crisis (the "2G linkage"), even raising the question of whether its behavior during the Gulf crisis somehow obligated Japan to make concessions in post–Brussels GATT negotiations (see *JEI Report* 9B, March 8, 1991).

In early 1991, a troubled Japanese society collectively seemed to sense being adrift in the wake of these events. At issue was the fundamental question of the capacity of the state to exercise its sovereignty in the interests of the nation. A GATT negotiator aptly expressed this concern: "It seems Japan still cannot decide by itself. We are a player as major as the U.S. and the EC. Why don't we make our own decisions?" (*Japan Economic Journal*, February 16, 1991). These national (sclf) doubts were exacerbated by perceptions that Japan's much feared anathema, international isolation, was rearing its ugly head.

The Eagleburger Memorandum

It was in this context that consensual recognition of the necessity of some kind of concession on rice began to emerge. Tacit consensus for partial opening was spurred also by reports that the United States and the European Community would soon reconcile their differences. Foreign Minister Taro Nakayama cast the issue in terms of needing to secure a Uruguay Round agreement in order to counter the trend toward formation of regional blocs in Europe and North America, a more concrete manifestation of the isolation bugbear (*Japan Economic Journal*, January 26, 1991).

Prominent LDP members began to support publicly Japanese concessions that would conform with the Hellstrom proposal's 5 percent minimum access. At this point, the debate within Japan's policymaking circles broadened to consider the possibility of not simply waiting to make a reactive concession when finally faced with a united U.S.-EC position. Rather, as suggested by LDP Executive Council Chairman Takeo Nishioka, Japan should offer partial opening before the London summit of industrialized nations in July. In Nishioka's May 1991 terms: "If Japan has to compromise (on the rice issue) anyway, it should get the upper hand at the Uruguay Round negotiations by making that concession voluntarily and at the earliest possible date" (*Nikkei Weekly*, June 8, 1991).

This proactive suggestion was countered by the reactive logic of the rice hardliners, as spelled out by a MAFF official: "The name of the game is timing. If the decision is made too early, there is the danger that Japan may be pressured to make a further concession" (*Japan Times Weekly International Edition*, June 17–23, 1991). The *Nikkei Weekly* (June 22, 1991) editorially criticized this "unnecessarily timid stance," which was based on the "fear . . . that Japan's initiative in committing itself to rice liberalization will have no chance of breaking the impasse and could even be exploited by other countries."

Japan thus seemed poised on, but unable to cross, the brink of expanding its rice win-set. In an eight-day span in late May 1991, a succession of promarket opening statements were forthcoming from, among others, Prime Minister Kaifu, LDP boss Shin Kanemaru, Takeo Nishioka, Chief Cabinet

Secretary Misoji Sakamoto, LDP Secretary General Keizo Obuchi, and party boss and former prime minister Noboru Takeshita. Meanwhile, the U.S. government interpreted these developments as evidence that sufficient Level II support for a quota-based opening had been, or was about to be, consolidated. Specifically, it was anticipated that Prime Minister Kaifu might deliver a "gift" of rice market opening while visiting President Bush in Maine in July.

Just before Kaifu's visit, the United States chose to intervene bilaterally to thwart the move to open the rice market. Deputy Secretary of State Lawrence Eagleburger sent a memorandum to the U.S. embassy in Tokyo, the contents of which were promptly made known to the Japanese government. The memorandum reiterated the U.S. tariffication position and indicated that the United States would regard as insufficient a 3, 5, or even 10 percent partial opening of Japan's rice market (*Nikkei Weekly*, August 10, 1991).

Why did the United States, which perhaps would have accepted a minimum access solution at the eleventh hour in Brussels, harden its position at this critical juncture? According to one U.S. trade official, acceptance of a partial opening would have undermined the "full liberalization" position of the United States in the multilateral talks: "If Tokyo insists on only 'minimal access,' other nations might take the same stance" (*Nikkei Weekly*, August 10, 1991). U.S. negotiators also must have been keen to avoid prolongation of the "American pressure and desultory Japanese response" pattern that has characterized decades of Japan's incremental liberalization of its economy (see George, 1991). In this context, the once-and-for-all aspect of the tariffication scheme must have been strongly preferred over the expectation of protracted future wrangling over the pace of rice market liberalization beyond the initial minimum access.

Whatever the U.S. motivations, the implications for the Kaifu government were clear: even if it were to put its credibility on the line and assume the Level II political risks that would come with pronouncement of its willingness to accept a quota-based opening, the United States would still be less than satisfied. And Japan could expect continued Level I pressure to expand further its win-set. Some within the Japanese government argued that a unilateral partial opening should be announced anyway, thus staking out a conciliatory Japanese position to which the United States might find it propitious to acquiesce in subsequent multilateral negotiations. But the opportunity had come and gone, and Kaifu next found himself subjected to direct pressure for tariffication from U.S. President Bush in Kennebunkport, Maine (*Nikkei Weekly*, August 24, 1991).

As described earlier in the discussion of ratification, the rice question has since become entangled with intraparty leadership struggles and with the issue of electoral reform. Both the Kaifu government and its successor, under Kiichi Miyazawa, have attempted to build support for accepting tariffication while trying to finesse the contradiction between this solution and the FC Act that undergirds Japan's agricultural regime. Chastened by the Eagleburger episode, the Miyazawa government has reverted to the familiar reactive mode, as reflected in MAFF Vice Minister Yoshihiro Hamaguchi's comments regarding Japan's approach to submitting to the GATT its list of agricultural commodities to be subject to tariffication: "Japan is going to take a wait-and-see attitude before making any moves. This time, Japan has to be careful, watching how other countries react to it" (*Nikkei Weekly*, February 29, 1992). Indeed, rice tariffication was formally rejected shortly thereafter by virtue of its exclusion from Japan's list. If anything, the government hardened its food security position by adding wheat, dairy, starch, and some other farm products to the "basic foodstuffs" left off the list (*Nikkei Weekly*, March 7, 1992).

Evaluating Japan's Reactive Strategy

How well have Japan's interests been served by strict adherence to the food security strategy in the Uruguay Round negotiations? Because Japan now is subjected to pressure to accept—and is relatively isolated in its rejection of—tariffication,[20] the question is whether less radical reform alternatives could have been attained with a more flexible Level I strategy. Although it is impossible to answer these questions conclusively before the Uruguay Round is completed, we offer some tenable, albeit preliminary, evaluations.

It is important to point out that Japan's options have not been confined to a choice between maintaining the rice import ban or accepting proposals advanced by others (e.g., tariffication or the Hellstrom plan). At various points in the Level I negotiations, Japan could have seized the initiative and tendered an alternative proposal that (1) offered smaller (than tariffication) concessions, and (2) allowed self-defined reform of its rice-centered agricultural regime. There are various ways in which Japan's win-set could have been manipulated to enhance the probability of Level I agreement as well as to minimize the dislocating Level II impact.

For example, the Japanese government has been reported to have considered granting initial minimum access and committing to future tariffication, or accepting tariffication at the outset, but easing the schedule by which the tariffs subsequently would be reduced (*Canberra Times*, December 28, 1991). More generally, Japan has had wide latitude to define the terms and rate of agricultural reform in ways that might win Level I acceptance.[21]

As argued earlier, the Japanese government has been reluctant to exercise this decisional latitude because of Level II constraints. In short, it has been unable to muster the political courage to volunteer proposals that impose costs on the well-entrenched agricultural constituents who collect rents from the status quo regime. But if Japan waits until the Level I game generates intolerable levels of international pressure and isolation—the necessary condition for Level II acquiescence to reform—it then will have a diminished latitude to shape those reforms in ways compatible with the interests of the most affected Level II constituents.

Figure 4.1 demonstrates how this dilemma stems from Japan's refusal to modify its maximal win-set (*Jm*) in the Level I game.[22] We posit abolition of the FC Act and the associated agricultural regime as a benchmark for determining the decisional autonomy that Japan would be able to exercise in shaping reforms resulting from different Level I agreements. We assume that the Hellstrom proposal (*H*) and any solution located to its right would not require abolition and thus would allow Japan to retain decisional autonomy; and that the U.S. tariffication proposal (*USt*) would require abolition and thus dictate the terms and rate of Japan's agricultural reforms (i.e., a loss of decisional autonomy). The space between *H* and *USt* is indeterminate in this regard.

Japan's rejection of the Hellstrom proposal (H) at Brussels can be construed as a lost opportunity to retain some decisional autonomy by acceding to a proposal formulated by other players. *Jh* represents a hypothetical Japanese proposal that itself would constitute an *exercise* of decisional autonomy insofar as it would be based on Japan's preferred rate and terms of rice market opening (as described in this chapter). Following Brussels and until intimidated by the Eagleburger memorandum, Japan appeared to be following Nishioka's strategic advice and moving toward proposal of some form of *Jh*.

Should Japan have allowed itself to be so easily intimidated? We think not. Had Japan proposed (*Jh*), despite U.S. dissatisfaction, it could present itself at Level I as willing to compromise—indeed, willing to sacrifice particularistic domestic interests—in the broader cosmopolitan interest of maintaining the GATT trading regime (not to mention Japan's nonagricultural interests). It does not stretch the imagination to suppose that a *Jh* proposal, coupled with a Japanese effort to mediate the U.S.-EC dispute,

Figure 4.1
U.S. and Japanese Win-sets on Rice Liberalization

USm:	maximal outcome for the United States—the zero option			
USt:	modified tariffication			
H	Hellstrom minimum access proposal			
Jh:	hypothetical partial opening			
Jm:	maximal outcome for Japan—a rice status quo			

might have led to a Level I agreement on agriculture. And because agriculture is the last missing piece in the fifteen-piece GATT puzzle, Jh also could have facilitated completion of a comprehensive Uruguay Round agreement.

Our focus on the Brussels and Eagleburger episodes, although certainly critical junctures in the negotiations, should not obscure the central point we wish to emphasize: Japan has had numerous opportunities since the inception of the Uruguay Round in 1986 to step forth with one or another form of Jh. By doing so, it could have combined efforts to solve its formidable agricultural problems with constructive leadership in the world trading system.

Instead, Japan's strategy has been to stick to its maximal position (Jm in Figure 4.1), a stance that has produced several adverse consequences. First, in the context of the two-level game, insistence on Jm has resulted in Japan's current beleaguered circumstances: trying to stave off pressures for acceptance of USt. If it is unable to do so, and if there is a U.S.-EC agreement, then Japan's agricultural regime will be liberalized largely along lines dictated by others. Second, in the broader context of the nascent post–Cold War world order, insistence on Jm amounts to unwillingness to make Japan's domestic political economy consistent with the requirements of an open world economy. Furthermore, the bid to exalt the food security argument to the status of international regime principle reduces to little more than a futile attempt to make the world economy consistent with the requirements of Japan's domestic political economy.

CONCLUSION

This chapter has used Putnam's two-level game framework to analyze the intersecting domestic and international games of rice liberalization, with emphasis on factors affecting the range of potential bargains Japan would be able to strike in the GATT's multilateral negotiations. The distribution of rice policy preferences across the Japanese polity was described in some detail, as were the coalitions formed around and in opposition to the rice status quo. We then examined how Japan's political institutions bear on the prospects for domestic ratification of any GATT-required change in the status quo regime. Because of consensually oriented decision rules, ratification procedures are somewhat ambiguous. Moreover, the ratification question has become entangled with electoral politics, intra-LDP leadership struggles, and even the reform of the rurally biased electoral system.

We then turned to negotiating strategies in the Uruguay Round, focusing on Japan's articulation of the food security doctrine; on its interaction with the radically liberal strategy pursued by the United States; and on two key episodes in the negotiating process. Domestic constraints have limited the Japanese government to reactive tactics and strategy, an abortive approach that has placed Japan in an isolated position and has prevented initiatives that would allow self-definition of agricultural reform.

We conclude that the two-level game of rice liberalization and the Uruguay Round comprises an important test of Japan's capacity to exercise leadership in the world political economy, although not the only or even the major test. Bound by the peculiar form of state-society relations in agriculture, the Japanese state lacks sufficient domestic autonomy to exercise its sovereign autonomy in the international arena, thus blocking a constructive leadership role. We agree in this regard with Funabashi's (1992: 24, 26) provocative argument: "To internationalize this sacred staple would not only internationalize the mythic essence of Japan, it would also revolutionize political culture, which has been founded for the last 40 years on rice protectionism." Funabashi proceeds to liken rice liberalization to Britain's 1846 repeal of the Corn Laws, arguing that only when the "archaic, perverted system of political representation . . . is revolutionized by opening the rice market will Japan be capable of providing . . . real global political leadership."

To borrow a metaphor, Japan's supercharged economic engine is mounted in an anachronistic state jalopy that lacks the suspension, steering, and handling ability to exploit its potential performance characteristics. One can only speculate as to if, when, and how Japan will adapt its renowned "just in time" system to retrofit this engine into a redesigned and newly constructed state chassis. It does seem unlikely that this will transpire before the Uruguay Round expires.

NOTES

1. Throughout the chapter we use the term "reactive" in the sense of Calder's (1988: 519) definition: "the state fails to undertake major independent foreign economic policy initiatives when it has the power and national incentives to do so . . . and it responds to outside pressures for change, albeit erratically, unsystematically, and often incompletely."

2. The agricultural cooperatives provide the main organizational apparatus for administering the FC system, and thereby virtually monopolize the collection, storage, and marketing of rice. In 1985, Nokyo handled 95 percent of all rice produced, earning in the process at least ¥110 billion (about US$458.3 million at 1985 exchange rates) through marketing commissions, storage fees, and interest subsidies (George, 1988: 9, 11). For a detailed analysis of Nokyo's economic functions and their relation to its political activities, see George (1988); George and Saxon (1986) examine the role of Nokyo in maintaining agricultural protection.

3. See George (1988: 30–49) for a thorough discussion of the rice price deliberation process and its entanglement in Japan's domestic politics.

4. Price support ratios, also termed the nominal rate of protection, measure the difference, in percentage terms, between domestic and world market prices. Other comprehensive measures of agricultural support and protection show the same pattern; for example, in terms of producer-subsidy equivalents (PSEs, the

ratio of all income transfers to farmers resulting from policies to total agricultural income) from 1982 to 1984, Japan's 72 percent compares to 33 percent for the EC and 22 percent for the United States (Paarlberg, 1988: 62–63, table 5).

5. Farmers' electoral influence is understated by levels of support per se because Japan's electoral constituency system significantly overweights the vote of rural areas; additionally, voter turnout is significantly higher in rural districts. As Hemmi (1982: 224) and others have pointed out, the LDP's share of parliamentary seats won is invariably greater than its share of votes; in addition, declines in the LDP's share of votes are never translated into proportional losses of seats. Despite constitutional challenges and measures to trim the rural-urban discrepancies, substantial disproportionality persists. At the extreme, as of March 1990, 3.26 times as many votes were required in the least represented district than in the most represented to elect a member to Japan's House of Representatives; for the House of Councillors, the upper house based more on regional representation, the corresponding ratio was 6.26:1 (*Japan Times Weekly International Edition*, August 20–26, 1990).

6. This section is drawn largely from George (1990).

7. The case against interpreting food security to mean 100 percent self-sufficiency rests on the argument that this worthwhile goal is better attained by means other than a ban on imports, such as stockpiling reserve supplies and diversification of supply sources (see Hayami, 1988: 121–123). Winters's (1990) more general theoretical critique of the use of restrictive agricultural policies to achieve national security objectives is also very useful.

8. The Miyazawa cabinet was apparently put together in late 1991 with an eye toward establishing such a consensus. The appointment to key posts of four politicians considered influential in agricultural policy (including three former MAFF ministers) was reportedly motivated by the expectation that they would be able to persuade farmers and other antiliberalization constituents to consent to a change in policy (*Japan Times Weekly International Edition*, November 16, 1991).

9. The agricultural cooperative has occasionally asserted itself at Level I. For example, at various points during the last decade of U.S.-Japan agricultural trade negotiations, Zenchu has tried to exploit divergent interests among U.S. farmers by threatening to cut back on Nokyo purchases of U.S. feedgrain if the U.S. government exerts too much pressure for liberalization.

10. Quoted in Smith (1991: 110).

11. Under tariffication, initial tariffs would be set at levels equal to the combined protection provided by existing nontariff measures. In the case of rice, estimates of initial tariff levels range from 300 to 800 percent, with most converging around the U.S. government's estimate of 600–700 percent. Japan's private Forum for Policy Innovation provides the lowest (300 percent) estimate (*Japan Economic Journal*, August 25, 1990). The initial level of tariffs, the rate at which they would be "ratcheted" down, and their eventual level at the end of the tariffication timetable are subjects for negotiation.

12. Putnam (1988) used the phrase "involuntary defection" to describe the inability to deliver on a Level I promise because of failed ratification.

13. See Paarlberg (1990b) for a persuasive demonstration of the magnitude and rapid rate of expansion of Japan's food imports. From a bargaining standpoint, reminding one's trading partners of these facts also serves the salutary purpose of flexing the political muscle that accrues to the world's largest net food importer. Japan's well-established reputation for manipulating access to its partially opened markets so as to discriminate among exporters lends credibility to this implicit threat.

14. This argument about relative trade distortion in aggregate terms is valid; however, the costs of Japan's protectionist agricultural protection are nonetheless substantial. For estimates, see Anderson and Tyers (1988).

15. The MAFF bolsters the food security argument by stressing Japan's extreme reliance on food imports. For example, the percentage of daily per capita calorie intake that is produced domestically has declined steadily from 79 percent in 1960 to 60 percent in 1970, to 53 percent in 1980, and 48 percent in 1989. This compares with 1989 figures of 127 percent for the United States and 77 percent for Great Britain (*Look Japan*, April 1992, p. 46).

16. Note the contrast between the U.S. strategy of trying to change the international regime to reform its domestic regime and Japan's strategy of trying to change the international regime in order to avoid reform of its domestic regime.

17. This U.S. abstention from bilateral measures apparently stems from a tacit U.S.-Japan agreement, although the terms of that agreement are not entirely clear. Paarlberg (1990b: 139–140) reported, "In order to get concessions from Japan on beef, citrus, and processed products, U.S. trade negotiators had been forced to provide assurances that Japan would not be placed under comparable bilateral pressure any time soon to open up its rice market." George (1990: 10) interpreted this agreement a bit differently, suggesting that the United States "made it clear . . . that it regarded movement by Japan on rice as a quid pro quo for withdrawing the threat of 'Super 301' action." Depending on a temporal perspective—on which juncture in the sequence of events and bargaining commitments one focuses—the two interpretations are not necessarily inconsistent.

18. See Chapter 3 by Paarlberg for a discussion of other technical aspects of the EC proposal that diminished the value of what was ostensibly offered.

19. For a detailed discussion of the bargaining game within the EC, see Chapter 5 by Moyer.

20. The MAFF claims that by December 1991, twenty other countries had joined Japan's opposition to tariffication (*Nikkei Weekly*, December 28, 1991– January 4, 1992). One significant recent addition to this list is Canada (see Chapter 6 by Cooper and Higgott). It is important to point out that opposition to tariffication is not coterminous with endorsement of the food security doctrine.

21. The Tokyo-based Forum for Policy Innovation, led by agricultural economist Yujiro Hayami, has generated the most comprehensive reform proposal along such lines: an initial rice import quota of 200,000 tons (about 2 percent of consumption) would be increased to 300,000 tons over a five-year period, during which time the domestic support price would be reduced by 5 percent a year. After the five-year period, the quota would be converted to a 200 percent tariff, which then would be scaled down to 100 percent over the next ten years (*Japan Economic Journal*, August 25, 1990; *Nikkei Weekly*, August 10, 1991).

22. The reduction of the Uruguay Round's multilateral agricultural negotiations to the bilateral confrontation of U.S. and Japanese positions as shown in Figure 4.1, especially in light of the EC's critical role, is certainly an information-reducing simplification. Nonetheless, this simplification is suitable for the limited purposes at hand. What is depicted as the U.S. modified tariffication proposal has evolved, for all intents and purposes, to become the GATT position, as articulated in the various Dunkel drafts.

H. Wayne Moyer ⟩5

The European Community and the GATT Uruguay Round: Preserving the Common Agricultural Policy at All Costs

The current Uruguay Round of trade negotiations provides a crucial test of the GATT's effectiveness in reducing barriers to agricultural trade. European Community decisionmakers, defending the highly protectionist Common Agricultural Policy, accepted inclusion of agricultural trade issues into the negotiations only reluctantly. This reluctance was overcome only when rapidly escalating farm subsidy costs in the mid-1980s threatened to break the EC budget, necessitating an unpopular increase in the Community's value-added tax or an equally unpopular decrease in EC spending. Strong pressures from the United States and the Cairns Group, which insisted that any further liberalization in international trade must include agriculture, provided a reinforcing impetus.

Accepting the inclusion of agricultural trade issues into the Uruguay Round did not mean that the EC was prepared to abandon the CAP. Quite the contrary, the history of the Uruguay Round, from its very inception in 1986, is well characterized as a battle between the United States, generally supported by the Cairns Group, which has fought to end trade-distorting agricultural subsidies, and the EC, which has attempted to protect the current market-managing price support mechanisms of the CAP. This disagreement was largely responsible for the breakdown of the December 1990 negotiating conference in Brussels, scheduled to finalize a new GATT agreement by the accepted deadline of December 31, 1990. Although the negotiations were resumed in 1991, it is not yet clear whether either the United States or the European Community can compromise their basic positions enough to reach a new trade agreement for agriculture. However, the outlook appeared to brighten in early 1992. The EC has particular problems in that its negotiating positions are formulated through a multitier, compartmentalized, consensus-driven decisionmaking process that favors agricultural interests. This process involves bargaining at many levels and a complicated interplay between the EC GATT negotiating team, EC policymaking institutions, and member governments.

This chapter examines the evolution of the EC negotiating position, emphasizing the critical "final period" of negotiations, which began with the July 1, 1990, report of Art de Zeeuw, chairman of the GATT agricultural negotiations committee, and culminated with the breakdown of the negotiations at Brussels. It will explain how the evolving policy environment led to sufficient change in the EC negotiating position to restart the negotiations in 1991. And it will also explain why further movement has been difficult and why the EC has had difficulty compromising enough to reach the minimum agreement acceptable to the United States and the Cairns Group.

THE DEVELOPING EC POSITION
IN THE URUGUAY ROUND

During 1987, the major participants in the GATT negotiations submitted their initial proposals. The gap between the major protagonists was quite clear. The United States made a radical proposal for the elimination of "all policies which distort [agricultural] trade," known as the "zero option."[1] Progress toward liberalization would be measured by monitoring the changes in domestic support programs with an aggregate indicator such as the producer subsidy equivalent developed in the OECD. Credit would be given for any policies introduced since the start of multilateral negotiations that had contributed to reducing the imbalance on world markets. The U.S. proposal recognized that GATT rules would need strengthening to reflect the trading environment at the end of the transition period. On the short term, the United States was silent.

The Cairns Group took a position closely allied with that of the United States. Its proposal offered steady reductions in protection over a ten-year period, but suggested a three-stage agenda. First, in the short run, a freeze would be imposed on present subsidies that distort trade. This would be followed by a phased reduction of these subsidies, using a PSE-type measure of support to assess progress. In the longer run, a new set of GATT rules would be developed, which, in effect, would remove present exceptions for agriculture.

The EC proposal represented the polar opposite position. It emphasized the need for short-run actions and was specific in calls for measures to firm up cereal, sugar, and dairy prices. Like the U.S. proposal, the EC proposal endorsed an aggregate measure of support based on the OECD work, but modified it to take account of supply control policies and exchange rate variations. The EC position included provision for an unspecified but "substantial" decline in support levels, but did not endorse the notion of a zero target in support.[2]

The basic positions were spelled out further during 1988 as the negotiations continued in Geneva. The Cairns Group proposed a short-term program of action to include both a freeze and a two-year phased reduction in support as a "down-payment" on longer-term reform. Reductions in support of 10 percent were suggested for 1989 and 1990 (GATT, 1988). The United States introduced the concept of tariffication into the negotiations. Nontariff import measures would be converted to tariffs, to be reduced as protection was phased out. The EC, still not able to deal with long-term measures, could only spell out its ideas for short-term measures. Among its proposals was one to freeze PSEs at their 1984 level, which would have given full credit to the EC for CAP reforms and would have taken as a reference a period when the dollar was unusually strong.

The gap between the EC position, on the one hand, and the U.S./Cairns Group position, on the other, remained unbridged, and the December 1988 midterm review in Montreal did not produce agreement on the major issues dividing the protagonists. The United States still insisted on complete elimination of government distortions of trade, whereas the EC was only willing to consider freezing support followed by modest reductions in subsidies. From the EC perspective, the U.S. proposals threatened the very existence of the CAP, an unacceptable outcome to the negotiations.

A second and more successful attempt to conclude the midterm review took place in Geneva in April 1989. This meeting did not resolve the issues, but it did provide a timetable for agreement. The parties accepted a two-year freeze in support levels, market access, and national prices in nominal terms. They committed themselves to reduce protection in 1990 by an unspecified amount. They also agreed to a substantial progressive reduction of agricultural support over an agreed period of time. Reductions in support could come either through an Aggregate Measure of Support (AMS) or by commitments on specific policies.[3]

Following the timetable laid out in the midterm review, countries developed their views on the major issues facing the agricultural negotiations. Several changes appeared in the positions held during the first two years of negotiations. The United States, acknowledging that it could not achieve its goal of zero support, shifted away from reliance on the AMS to press for direct action on import access through tariffication. The Cairns Group also moved toward negotiation on individual policies, using the AMS to keep track of the reductions actually made. The EC, on the other hand, warmed to the AMS as a means of maintaining policy flexibility, and began to emphasize the desirability of rebalancing support between highly protected products, such as cereals, and those less protected, such as soybeans and corn gluten feed. The EC opposed negotiations on particular support instruments, which threatened the basic support mechanisms of the CAP.

Autumn 1989 brought a new crop of proposals for the GATT agriculture negotiations. As agreed at the midterm review, countries developed their "comprehensive" proposals. Despite three years of discussions, the differences between the United States and the European Community seemed as great as ever. The U.S. proposal, which has been described as a gentler approach to the zero option, called for complete elimination of export subsidies within five years of the agreement's entry into force and phasing out of trade-distorting subsidies within ten years. The proposal also elaborated on tariffication by proposing the elimination of import restrictions through the mechanism of expanding tariff-rate quotas. It placed heavy emphasis on changing GATT rules, and centered on policy-specific negotiations, with the use of AMS only for monitoring certain types of domestic subsidy.

The Cairns Group "comprehensive paper" was similar to the U.S. proposal in that it envisioned the long-term dismantling of agricultural protectionism. It differed from the U.S. proposal in that it did not demand phasing out export subsidies within five years. Instead, it demanded a freeze and subsequent phased elimination of export subsidies over ten years, substantial progressive reductions in trade-distorting domestic support, and the tariffication of import quotas, with binding reductions over time to low levels or zero. It rejected the concept of rebalancing.

The new EC proposal still emphasized the need for market management and preservation of the fundamental principles of the CAP, while rejecting the notion of free trade for agricultural products.[4] In a concession from its previous position, the EC offered partial tariffication of its variable levies in return for outside acceptance of its demands for rebalancing levels of support between high and low protection products. It accepted down-scaling of both export subsidies and import levies, but rejected the U.S. proposals for a commitment to complete elimination of subsidies over a ten-year period. Finally, the EC proposed that the commitment to reduce support must include all policies that affect farmers' production decisions—in particular, such policies as the U.S. deficiency payments as assessed through the Community's version of the PSE, the Support Monitoring Unit (SMU).

DECISIONMAKING IN THE EUROPEAN COMMUNITY

How can we account for the EC defense of the CAP and reluctance to take measures that would lead to the eventual elimination of trade-distorting domestic subsidies, export subsidies, and import restrictions? Holding the line in negotiations to the last possible moment can often be understood as a ploy to ensure the best possible deal in a final agreement (Runge and von Witzke, 1985). As previous chapters in this volume have shown, Putnam's notion of two-level bargaining games is particularly useful in analyzing agricultural trade negotiations (see Chapters 3 and 4). Additional insights into the EC negotiations are provided by examining EC policymaking as a modified form of these bargaining games. In the EC context, though, it is necessary to conceptualize the bargaining as a three-level game, with the three levels consisting of EC GATT negotiators (Level I), the EC bargaining process (Level II), and the bargaining process of national governments (Level III).

The EC Decisionmaking Process (Level II)

This analysis begins at Level II because the principal EC trade policy decisions are reached in the European Commission and Council of Ministers, the statutory EC decisionmaking bodies based in Brussels.[5] The European Commission/Council process, shown schematically in Figure 5.1, operates in an environmental context influenced by past policy decisions, economic trends, economic shocks, and political developments and interests.[6] The EC process interacts with national governments and the GATT negotiating team. It is also influenced by outside inputs such as press and public opinion, EC consultative and lobbying bodies, and by organized interest groups from member states. What stands out most visibly from this schematic is how cumbersome and complex EC decisionmaking is, a factor that intrinsically creates policy inertia.

The first stage of the EC policymaking process takes place in the European Commission, which performs the executive function for the EC.[7] Agricultural trade proposals are formulated in the Directorate General for Agriculture (DG-VI), then submitted to the Inter-Services working group, which coordinates the various directorates that have a stake in the policy.[8] The membership varies with the issue, but DG-VI always presides. The Inter-Services working group members report to the various cabinets of the "most interested" commissioners, which meet together on a regular basis.[9] For agriculture trade policy, external affairs and agriculture commissioners always appear among the "most interested." Next, the proposal is sent on to the heads of cabinet for the seventeen commissioners, who screen the proposal before forwarding it to the commissioners for debate. The commissioners must approve a proposal by simple majority vote before it is finalized.

DG-VI tends to dominate this phase of the policy process. This body is the largest directorate-general in the EC, largely because the CAP is currently the most active and completely integrated EC policy, consuming between 55 and 60 percent of the entire EC budget. It has most of the European Commission's expertise on agricultural policy questions—expertise that is critical when changes are considered that may affect the highly complex Common Agricultural Policy. DG-VI also is strengthened in that it administers the CAP and must implement any policy changes. It leads the agricultural trade negotiating group in the Uruguay Round. DG-VI has a vested interest in the CAP in that its power and many of its jobs depend on the elaborate regulatory mechanisms that are in place for EC agriculture. It thus tends to resist measures to deregulate agriculture, either in domestic policy or in international trade negotiations. This resistance is reinforced by

Figure 5.1
Bargaining Process for EC Agricultural Trade Policy Formation

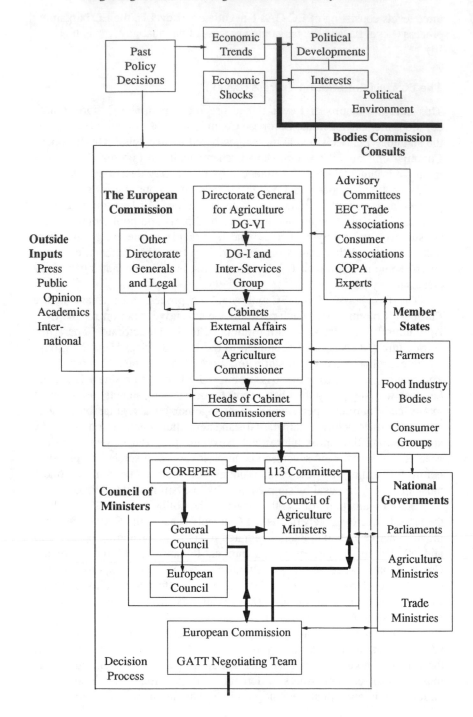

the close links between DG-VI and its farm lobby constituency, which benefits greatly from the largess of the CAP.

The External Affairs Directorate General (DG-I) comes to agricultural reform from a rather different perspective, in that it institutionally has an interest in a successful Uruguay Round. Its constituency is far broader than agriculture and includes groups from the industrial and services sector, who have much to gain from trade liberalization. DG-I derives bargaining strength in that it is responsible for coordinating EC positions for the various GATT negotiating groups and actually leads the negotiations for all the groups except agriculture. The breadth of its responsibilities also constitutes a weakness in that DG-I is spread too thin to devote much in the way of human resources to agricultural trade policy.

The external affairs commissioner and his cabinet have incentives similar to DG-VI for a successful outcome of the Uruguay Round. Moreover, greater flexibility exists at this level in that these officials do not come from the commission civil service and hence are less intrinsically committed to the status quo. Much depends on the personality of the commissioner, who appoints his own cabinet. The appointment of Frans Andriessen as foreign affairs commissioner in 1989 was seen as a favorable omen for the GATT negotiations in that Andriessen had just completed a very successful term as a reforming agriculture commissioner.

Debate among the commissioners tends to be dominated by those with dossiers directly affected by matters under consideration. Commissioners who are not directly affected tend to lay back and conserve their resources for matters more central to them. Trade policy debate has been strongly influenced by the practice of submitting proposals separately for the different GATT negotiating groups. Thus, agricultural trade proposals are considered separately from trade policy proposals in other sectors, which are prepared by different directorate-generals, although coordination occurs in DG-I and the Inter-Services working group. The net effect is that most of the commissioners have little to say when agricultural trade proposals reach the floor, as they cannot see the implications for their dossiers. This then tends to turn the commission debate to a contest between the foreign affairs commissioner and the agriculture commissioner. The foreign affairs commissioner, as we have noted, can be expected to promote the broader interests of the EC, which lie in trade liberalization. The agriculture commissioner tends to defend his constituency and can be expected to protect the CAP. The agriculture commissioner has advantages in this debate in that he commands the full resources of DG-VI to back his position, along with the implied support of the farm lobby. He also benefits in that other commissioners tend to defer to the agricultural expertise that he represents and to accept his view as worthy of special consideration, because his dossier is most strongly affected by any agreement on agriculture reached in the GATT.

After an agricultural trade proposal leaves the Commission, it goes to the "113 Committee," which consists of the senior civil servants from the national governments.[10] Each delegation will have a representative from the Ministry of Agriculture who will tend to take the initiative, thus protecting national agricultural interests. In the discussions, DG-I serves as the representative of the Commission, but DG-VI is present. The 113 Committee never votes, and discussions tend to continue until consensus is reached.

When 113 Committee approval is reached, the proposal goes to the Committee of Permanent Representatives (COREPER), which screens the proposal for the agenda of the next General Affairs Council, where it will usually be considered by foreign trade ministers.[11] The General Council also tends to decide by consensus, although the formal voting rule is by qualified majority.[12] The Council of Agricultural Ministers is not directly included in the decisionmaking process, but the General Affairs Council has tended to wait for an opinion from the Agriculture Council before making a decision. The Agriculture Council can be expected to resist any proposal that weakens the CAP. When the General Affairs Council approves a proposal, it creates a negotiating mandate for the Commission, which has the sole power to represent the European Community in trade negotiations.

National Decisionmaking Processes (Level III)

National governments have a very significant influence on EC policy decisions. As already noted, the Council of Ministers and the 113 Committee are composed of representatives from the various national governments. Thus, as a practical matter, the Commission must take national positions into account before preparing any agricultural trade policy proposal if it harbors any hope of council approval. The sectoral nature of council decisionmaking tends to ensure that national positions on agricultural trade will not be well coordinated with positions on other trade issues. This is easy to understand when one considers that the dominant voice in agricultural trade is the Agriculture Council, which consists of farm ministers from national governments. It follows that national agriculture ministries, which, of course, have mastered all the complex details of the CAP, will have the initiative in preparing position papers for cabinet consideration. The agriculture minister will thus enter cabinet discussions from a very strong position. Because the agricultural trade stance is considered separately from positions on other GATT issues, other cabinet members are disadvantaged in arguing against the agriculture minister in that they must deal directly with agricultural policy details, which neither they nor their departments normally have incentive to learn. It is not easy to talk about how agricultural trade policy must be consistent with positions on other GATT issues when the focus of the discussion is limited to agricultural trade.

Even if national cabinets can balance agricultural interests with other priorities, it is still the agriculture minister who represents the cabinet position in the EC Council of Ministers. He has strong incentives to interpret his mandate in the way most favorable to his country's domestic agricultural interests. Agricultural policy is so complicated that the only government agency likely to understand fully his actions is the national Ministry of Agriculture, which shares similar interests. Overcoming these problems will still not lead to much policy flexibility in the Agriculture Council, unless they are overcome in every member country at once. This is because the Council's practice of unanimity decisionmaking allows the most recalcitrant member government to block policy flexibility.

The EC GATT Negotiating Team (Level I)

The myriad of complicated issues included in the Uruguay Round necessitated that the negotiations be divided by sector, with bargaining in each sector going on generally in isolation from that in other sectors. National negotiators in different negotiating groups tend to be responsible to different government authorities. Loose coordination between the different groups is achieved at the national government level and at the level of the GATT through the Trade Policy Committee. Fourteen different negotiating groups were established, one of which took responsibility for agriculture trade. The net effect of this division was to discourage trade-offs between different sectors until the final stages of negotiations. The separation of agriculture ensured that agricultural interests would dominate the agricultural trade aspects of the GATT negotiations, with other interests generally denied access or lacking relevant expertise.

The Treaty of Rome, which established the EC, gives the Commission authority to negotiate for the entire EC in international trade negotiations. The Directorate-General for External Affairs has the authority to negotiate for the Commission in every sector except agricultural trade, for which the Directorate General for Agriculture exercises responsibility. This has profound implications for the Uruguay Round in that the organization with the strongest interest in maintaining the CAP is placed in the driver's seat for the actual conduct of negotiations. To be sure, DG-I chairs the EC delegation and exercises general coordinating authority, but it operates through an agent whose interests are not in trade policy reform but rather in the preservation of the CAP.

Putnam (1988: 446) noted that sometimes international negotiators, given flexibility, can arrive at an agreement that commits a nation to do things not possible to achieve domestically because of the difficulty encountered in rejecting an agreement that contains clear benefits for certain sectors in a heterogeneous society. The structure of decisionmaking for the EC GATT delegation could not be better designed to prevent such a possibility in agricultural trade negotiations. The EC nations are all members of the GATT and can observe the discussions, even if they cannot vote. The national observers with the strongest incentives to watch the agricultural trade negotiations represent, of course, the agriculture ministries. These representatives constitute the on-scene 113 Committee, which must approve any changes in EC positions or send them back to COREPER or the Council of Ministers. The practice of consensus decisionmaking in the 113 Committee, combined with the fact that the national participants come from agriculture ministries, almost guarantees EC inflexibility in day-to-day agricultural trade negotiations.

The three-level bargaining process and the complexity and compartmentalization of the EC decisionmaking process (Level II) work to reduce the EC win-set in the GATT negotiations. The practice of decisionmaking by consensus in the Council of Ministers means that any EC member nation can block changes in the EC negotiating position. So the acceptance of liberalization will occur at the pace acceptable to the most recalcitrant member. Allowing the Agricultural Council to take the initiative in agricultural trade matters strengthens the hand of agricultural interests that have an interest in blocking liberalization. The small win-set strengthens the EC in the GATT negotiations in that its credibility in resisting concessions is enhanced. But a small win-set increases the possibility of negotiating failure in that it may not overlap with the win-sets of other parties to the GATT, particularly the United States and the Cairns Group.

Asymmetries in the Political Power of Interest Groups

One can observe a multiplicity of interest groups attempting to influence EC agricultural trade policy, both at the national and Community level. Yet, without any doubt, the farm lobby exercises the most influence at all three levels of bargaining. The strength of the farm lobby can be understood by considering the incentives created by agricultural policy. To be sure, the EC has consumer groups, trade associations, and industrial groups, which all have an interest in trade liberalization. The groups favoring freer trade have diverse interests and have trouble uniting. Moreover, the impetus for action is reduced in that the benefits created by liberalization are uncertain ones that they do not already enjoy. The farm lobby does not suffer from the same problems. It has a strong interest in uniting to protect the considerable benefits accruing to farmers from the CAP. With such a large stake at risk in trade liberalization, farmers provide the financing necessary to support a vigorous defense of the status quo.

National governments have been hesitant to override their farm lobbies because of the enormous public sympathy that exists for European farmers and the asymmetrical strength of national farm lobbies compared to other lobbies.[13] Farmers have the capacity through demonstrations and elections to mobilize a high degree of political support in a number of EC countries, most notably Germany and France. The net effects are to strengthen the bargaining positions of agricultural ministries in national decisionmaking on agricultural trade issues (Level III); to strengthen the role of DG-VI, the agriculture commissioner, and the Agriculture Council in EC decisionmaking (Level II); and to impede any efforts to sacrifice agricultural interests on the part of the EC GATT negotiating team (Level I).

Effects of the Policy Environment

Some mention should be made of how past policy decisions, economic trends, economic shocks, and political developments have affected the EC posture in the Uruguay Round. In the period through 1988, the dominant economic trend was the rapidly escalating cost of the CAP, which created a budget crisis for the EC (see Figure 5.2). This tended to increase the impetus for trade liberalization and weakened the European farm lobby. An important political development, the creation of the Single European Market, seemed to reinforce this effect, in that the budget crisis prevented requisite expenditures for policy harmonization.

Subsequently, however, the Brussels agreement of February 1988, which increased EC revenues and imposed penalties for overproduction of agricultural products, along with the 1988 drought in the United States (an economic shock, which raised world food commodity prices), temporarily reduced the rate of growth of EC expenditures for agriculture and ended the

Figure 5.2
EC Outlays for Agricultural Price and Income Support, 1988–1990

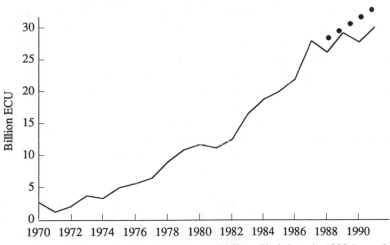

Note: ● ● ● denotes agricultural spending guidelines (limits) set in 1988 Brussels agreement.
Source: Developed from Moyer and Josling (1990: 25).

budget crisis. With budget expenditures under control, the movement to a single market could proceed without further changes in the CAP. All of this reduced the incentive for prime ministers and finance ministers to stand up to agriculture ministers, weakened the DG-I position vis-à-vis DG-VI, and strengthened the hand of the Agriculture Council vis-à-vis the General Council. Also, the enormous bargaining costs incurred in creating the Brussels stabilizers package exhausted the Commission. Hence, this body did not have the stamina to undertake the political battles necessary for a Uruguay Round proposal that would allow the CAP to be transformed.

This discussion should help clarify the question of why the EC at first showed a willingness to participate in the Uruguay Round negotiations and even made significant concessions. It also helps explain why, with the threat of a budget crisis removed, the agricultural forces prevailed, resulting in inflexibility for the EC position, which impeded the GATT negotiations from about the time of the midterm review.

THE "FINAL" PHASE OF THE URUGUAY ROUND

The de Zeeuw Proposal

With the December 31, 1990, deadline for the Uruguay Round on the horizon, the necessity increased for closing the gap between the agricultural trade position of the European Community and that of the United States and the Cairns Group. An attempt at this formidable task was made by Art de Zeeuw, chairman of the Agricultural Negotiating Group, in a July 1, 1990, proposal, after consultation with the negotiating parties. This proposal evolved from U.S., EC, and Cairns Group ideas. de Zeeuw hoped his proposal would provide the basis for a framework agreement for the final stages of the negotiations, which could lead to an agricultural trade deal and a final Uruguay Round agreement (see *Agra Europe*, July 6, 1989: E/6).

The de Zeeuw proposal called for significant reductions in domestic support using an AMS. It also called for tariffication of import restrictions, with reductions in the tariffs over time. And perhaps most important, it specified that all forms of export assistance should be substantially and progressively reduced at a faster rate than other forms of support (*Agra Europe*, July 6, 1990: E/6). The Houston summit of heads of OECD governments, meeting the following week, seemed committed to an agricultural trade deal, with the de Zeeuw report as a basis for negotiations.

Interviews held by Moyer in Brussels at this time indicated that the Commission wanted to move toward an agreement on agriculture and thought it had streamlined its decisionmaking process to allow flexibility and responsiveness.[14] The intent at that stage was for the Commission negotiating team to exercise as much leeway as possible in the negotiations, going to the Council of Ministers only when absolutely necessary, but working closely with the 113 Committee of national representatives in Geneva. The Commission planned to work directly through the General Council, without having to submit its proposals to the Agriculture Council. To put this in the terminology of the three-level bargaining game, the Commission hoped to restructure the bargaining process to allow the EC negotiators sufficient room so they could reach an agreement, which could never be approved in advance by either the EC process (Level II) or national processes (Level III). Once this agreement was reached, it was hoped that the benefits for sectors other than agriculture would be sufficient to change the bargaining balance at Levels II and III, when the choice would be a certain (although less than perfect) deal or no deal at all (see Putnam, 1988: 446).

This procedure worked, to a degree, in considering the EC's response to the de Zeeuw report, but there was a flaw, and the results should have indicated that problems lay ahead. The flaw was that the Commission response to de Zeeuw was prepared by the DG-VI representatives, who led the agricultural group negotiating team. Their critical response was then forwarded to DG-I, which took a more positive view. But DG-I was disadvantaged in that it was reacting to DG-VI rather than initiating the response. The response went directly to the General Council, but not before Agriculture Commissioner MacSharry had sharply criticized the de Zeeuw report. The General Council could not accept the de Zeeuw report as a basis for negotiations and would only go so far as to say that it could be used as a means of "intensifying negotiations" (*Agra Europe*, July 27, 1990: E/1).

The problem in the General Council was more serious than dealing with a response drafted by the section of the Commission with the greatest vested interest in the CAP. A bargaining Level III constraint on Level II also appeared in that the EC member governments were still far from agreeing that significant changes in the CAP should be made in the GATT. The most serious opposition came from Germany and France, which have managed to preserve their agricultural alliance throughout the Uruguay Round. The German government, with an agricultural sector consisting largely of small farmers who do not export very much, had little intrinsic problem with the sections of the de Zeeuw report that would reduce export subsidies.[15] However, it expressed serious reservations about domestic price cuts. The French government, on the other hand, which relied heavily on agricultural exports for a favorable balance of payments, strongly opposed reductions in export subsidies, although it could have accepted price cuts. Not surprisingly, the German government supported the French government on export subsidies, and the French government supported the German government on price supports.

The attempt to exclude the Agriculture Council from consideration of GATT proposals backfired. When this body met on July 24, the day after the EC response to the de Zeeuw report was submitted to the Trade Negotiating

Committee of the GATT, it took action to place itself in the center of the debate. The Agriculture Council appointed a high-level working group consisting of member state representatives for agriculture to shadow the agricultural trade negotiations and declared that it wanted to be updated on the current status of the talks at each subsequent meeting as long as the GATT negotiations continued. Given the public sympathy for farmers and the strength of the EC farm lobby, this action was not challenged by either the EC Commission or any national government.

The "Final" EC Negotiating Proposal

To underscore how strongly EC agricultural interests felt about preserving the CAP and how reluctant national and EC Commission leaders were to challenge the farm lobby, it is instructive to examine how the "final" EC GATT proposal developed. According to the Treaty of Rome, proposals are developed in the Commission, then submitted to the Council of Ministers. The Council is enjoined from developing its own proposals. In this case, the outline for what was to become the EC final negotiating proposal was presented informally by Agriculture Commissioner MacSharry at a meeting of the agriculture ministers of Canada, Japan, Australia, and the United States at Dromoland Castle in Ireland at the end of July, before it had been discussed either in the Commission or in the Council (*Agra Europe*, August 3, 1990: E/1). MacSharry said the EC would be willing to concede a reduction of support of 30 percent for the period 1986 to 1996 based on the SMU. About 15 percent of that amount had already been achieved, so that left only another 15 percent to be accomplished. Export subsidy reductions would be no greater than the decline in domestic support. A decrease of import barriers would have to be accompanied by rebalancing. MacSharry's action indicated that he now held the initiative rather than External Affairs Commissioner Frans Andriessen.[16]

Interestingly, MacSharry's GATT proposal received EC approval only with difficulty. When first presented to the commissioners in mid-September, it was not approved because a significant group of commissioners (Andriessen, Bangeman, and Brittan) thought MacSharry's support reductions were too small. However, the message from EC national capitals seemed supportive of MacSharry, and the full Commission approved his proposal almost intact, with the exception of allowing an 8 percent increase in soybean imports to make rebalancing more palatable to the United States.

However, when the proposal was debated in the Agricultural Council at an emergency meeting on October 8, it was rejected. The main objection was that the Commission had made no attempt to gauge the impact on farmers of the proposed cuts (*Agra Europe*, October 12, 1990: E/4). For many of the agriculture ministers, notably those from Germany and France, the cuts were acceptable only if farmers could be provided with compensatory aid to cover their losses. *Agra Europe* (October 12, 1990: P/1) noted that the Agriculture Council action exemplified the traditional unwillingness of this body to offend the farm lobby, passing the responsibility on to others—in this case the trade ministers meeting as the General Council. But the trade ministers would have none of this and refused to act until the agriculture ministers had rendered a formal opinion.

What followed was a general fiasco in which the EC proposal did not receive approval until early November, almost three weeks after the October 15 deadline to submit final GATT proposals. The Agriculture Council took the proposal up again on October 19, but still could not act, so it went to a joint Council consisting of the agriculture and trade ministers on October 26, with both MacSharry and Andriessen as Commission representatives. But agreement still could not be reached, so the proposal was put on the agenda of the European Council, meeting that weekend. However, the heads of government refused to decide the issue and it went back to the agriculture ministers. Finally, the proposal was approved in emasculated form in that the link between the decline in domestic support and reductions of export subsidies and import barriers was removed (*Agra Europe*, November 9, 1990: P/1) The main barrier to agreement was again the French-German alliance. Once again, Level II bargaining was constrained by Level III. The Germans liked the compensation provisions that had been added to the proposal, but refused to vote against the French, who had great difficulty accepting the dilution of Community preference and the reduction of export subsidies (*Agra Europe*, November 2, 1990: P/1). *Agra Europe* (November 9, 1990: P/2) commented that the EC's behavior confirmed that the EC was prepared to reduce agricultural support only as much as it was forced to do so by internal pressures—any amount of external protection reduction would clearly be secondary to internal support reduction.

The EC's difficulty in formulating its final proposal boded very badly for any further flexibility in its negotiating position, and thus made the prospects for a GATT agreement at the December 3–7 Brussels conference very dim indeed. Not surprisingly, the GATT talks collapsed on December 7, 1990, after the EC rejected the offer presented by the Swedish chairman of the agriculture negotiating group, Mats Hellstrom, for a 30 percent reduction in support, but using 1990, rather than 1986 as a base (*Agra Europe*, December 7, 1990: P/1). The EC did show some willingness to compromise by removing soybeans from rebalancing, increasing import access to 3 percent of production, reducing border tariffs by 30 percent, and agreeing to unspecified upper limits on tonnage of products eligible for export subsidies—but this clearly was not enough. Overall, the bargaining left to be done exceeded the capacity of the EC three-level bargaining structure in the narrow time frame of the Brussels conference. The decisionmaking process was overloaded and it broke down.

An Explanation for the Failure to Reach Agreement

Perhaps the most important thing that stands out in the July to December 1990 phase of the agricultural trade negotiations is that the forces supporting the CAP in unchanged form seized the initiative and dominated the decisionmaking process until the breakdown of negotiations in Brussels in December. The dominant actors were Agriculture Commissioner MacSharry, the Directorate General for Agriculture (DG-VI), and the Agriculture Council. External Affairs Commissioner Andriessen, who had overall responsibility for the negotiations, his Directorate General (DG-I), and the General Council were never able to control the EC position on agricultural trade policy. Interestingly, none of the many industrial and commercial groups in the EC with a strong interest in a successful Uruguay Round were able to influence the EC agriculture trade policy stance or to successfully trade off EC farm interests.

The explanation for this phenomenon is probably multifaceted. First, as has been indicated, the farm lobby had the greatest and most immediate interest in the Uruguay Round outcome and hence had the strongest incentive to commit resources to protect its interests. At the most fundamental level, asymmetric farm lobby pressures on member governments, particularly Germany and France, prevented any concessions that would have threatened the CAP (a Level III constraint on Levels II and I). The support of member governments for the CAP created an environment permissive for the takeover of the agricultural negotiations by DG-VI, the Agriculture Commissioner, and the Agriculture Council (a Level II constraint on Level I). DG-VI, the Agriculture Commissioner, and the Agriculture Council, in turn, had every incentive to mobilize their full resources to protect large existing benefits for their constituencies, which would be reduced by a successful agreement. DG-VI had an organizational interest in resisting deregulation in that this would have reduced its administrative power and might cost it jobs. The agricultural forces were advantaged in the EC process because they possessed a near monopoly of the expertise needed to understand the many complexities of the CAP.

The structuring of the GATT negotiations (Level I) and the EC structure of decisionmaking (Level II) did in fact shield the farm interests from outside influences. Creating a separate GATT negotiating group to handle agricultural trade issues made it difficult to bring nonagricultural interests to bear or to trade agriculture concessions for concessions in other areas. The dominant position of the Agriculture Council in the trade policy process created further difficulties in that this body is extremely receptive to the EC farm lobby and not at all receptive to industrial and services sector interests. It is even hard to bring international political pressures to bear on EC agriculture ministers, because their careers rise and fall on the basis of how they serve their domestic constituencies, not on whether the GATT succeeds or fails.

The portrayal of the Uruguay Round agricultural negotiations in the press and elsewhere as a struggle between the United States and the European Community worked to strengthen the pro-CAP forces in the EC debate, to limit flexibility, and to reduce the EC win-set. Concessions could always be construed as "caving in" to the United States, which is politically unacceptable. This is an example of negative reverberation, where developments at the GATT level of the bargaining process (Level I) had adverse consequences for bargaining in the EC and in member states (Levels II and III) (Putnam, 1988: 454). It was important not to convey the impression that the EC had been bested. A strong element of personalization crept in to the debate, with the negotiations seen as a struggle between EC Agriculture Commissioner MacSharry and U.S. Secretary of Agriculture Clayton Yeutter. Placed in this position, MacSharry, a man with admitted political ambitions in Ireland, could not afford to back down.

There were a number of economic trends and political developments in the policy environment that strengthened the pro-CAP elements in the EC. First, although EC expenditures for the CAP were increasing, they were still under budget for 1990 and considerably under the guidelines for agriculture established by the 1988 Brussels Agreement. Thus, the incentive was greatly reduced for finance ministers, prime ministers, and EC commissioners holding nonagricultural dossiers to challenge the protectors of the CAP. The recent liberation of Eastern Europe constituted an important political development, which consumed a great deal of the time of Commissioner Andriessen and DG-I, and limited the attention they could give to GATT matters. This, too, favored the farm lobby. The forthcoming December election for all of Germany constituted another important political development, one that prevented Chancellor Kohl from contemplating sacrifice of German farm interests until after the election, which occurred the day before the start of the final Brussels talks—too late for any flexibility. The conflict in the Gulf probably also benefited farm interests in that it diverted attention away from the GATT.

RESUMPTION OF THE URUGUAY ROUND IN 1991

The Changing Policy Environment

In light of the failure of the Brussels talks, the prospects for a resumption of the Uruguay Round talks seemed gloomy, indeed, particularly because President Bush's fast-track authority was due to expire on March 1, 1991. There seemed little possibility that the EC could make the concessions, particularly on export subsidies, that might get the negotiations started again. The EC's win-set seemed to show no overlap with the win-sets of the United States and the Cairns Group. Yet, this conclusion failed to contemplate the possibility of an EC budget crisis, at least in the short term—the one eventuality that had previously moved the EC to CAP reform, with dairy quotas in 1984 and stabilizers in 1988.[17]

As 1991 dawned, so did the prospect of an EC budget crisis, with evidence that agriculture spending would not only exceed budget, but exceed the 1988 expenditures guidelines as well, perhaps before the end of 1991. *Agra Europe* reported (January 11, 1991: P/1) that collapse of the cereal market meant a quadrupling of export refunds, probably adding 5–6 billion European Community units (ECU) to 1991 CAP expenditures. Dairy export expenditures were also increasing rapidly, along with beef intervention expenditures, although the full impact of this would probably be seen only in the 1992–1993 EC budget. As January progressed, the budget situation seemed to worsen. By early February, it seemed probable that spending would exceed the 1991 agriculture guideline of 32 billion ECU by more than 800 million ECU—an increase in agricultural spending of more than 25 percent from 1990, with the prospects even more ominous in 1992 (see Figure 5.3).

The Commission Response

The forthcoming budget crisis was foreseen in the Commission before the end of 1990 and the Directorate General for Agriculture had prepared a paper, dated December 5, containing both an analysis of the problem and recommendations for a solution.[18] The problem was defined as paying too high prices to the 20 to 25 percent who produce more than 80 percent of the output while failing to support the incomes of the majority of landholders for whose benefit the CAP was originally established. The paper spelled out in

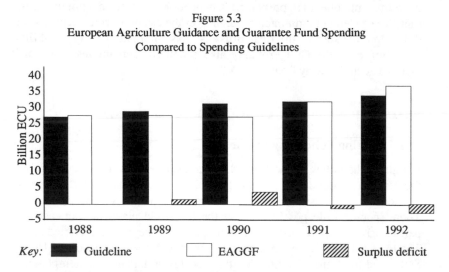

Figure 5.3
European Agriculture Guidance and Guarantee Fund Spending
Compared to Spending Guidelines

Key: ■ Guideline   □ EAGGF   ▨ Surplus deficit

Source: Developed from *Agra Europe*, February 8, 1991, P/3.

detail how the objective should be achieved. Prices should be cut to world levels with compensation to small and less prosperous landholders by direct subsidies. For cereals, oilseeds, and protein crops, an agreed level of aid would be paid in full on the first thirty hectares. It would be reduced by 25 percent for the next fifty hectares and by 35 percent on every hectare above eighty hectares.

That DG-VI should produce such a paper, which would dramatically transform the CAP, is worth some comment. As we have seen, DG-VI is a steadfast defender of the CAP and dragged its feet on GATT concessions. How could it go from defending the integrity of the CAP to transforming it? The explanation may lie in the DG-VI conception of organizational interest in the face of two different types of threat. A Uruguay Round agreement, by reducing agricultural regulations, would reduce the scope of activity for DG-VI, thus threatening its power. But an agricultural spending crisis, if it got serious enough, could threaten the very existence of both the CAP and DG-VI. Transforming the CAP could save it, while administering differential income aids would provide plenty of work for DG-VI.

Reform of the CAP, such as that contemplated by the DG-VI paper, would have significant implications for the GATT. The proposed decline in support prices would meet the demands of the United States and the Cairns Group and would allow highly significant reductions in export subsidies and import restrictions. The income supports, because they would not be production oriented, could be acceptable under GATT guidelines. Thus, a glimmer of hope appeared that the negotiations could be resumed.

Interestingly, Agriculture Commissioner MacSharry took the initiative in attempting to sell the reforms contemplated by DG-VI. At first, the Commission was divided between those who would reform the CAP, which included MacSharry, Andriessen, Christopherson, and Millan, and those who would merely modify it, led by EC President Delors, who thought the European Community should not weaken the CAP under pressure from the United States (*Agra Europe*, January 18, 1991: P/1). However, MacSharry received almost unanimous backing from the other commissioners after the DG-VI paper was discussed by the full Commission in a special January 20 seminar on CAP reform (*Agra Europe*, January 18, 1991: P/1; *Agra Europe*, January 25, 1991: P/2). The only point of contention was whether small farmers should get special benefits, with the British, Dutch, and Danish commissioners arguing that they should not.

The Response in the Agriculture Council

The response in the Agriculture Council was considerably less positive than in the Commission. MacSharry presented his CAP reform plan to the ministers on February 4, and it was received with a distinct lack of enthusiasm. Council President Rene Steichen (Luxembourg) remarked that a small majority opposed the plan (*Agra Europe*, February 8, 1991: E/1). The southern countries were prepared to sit on the fence because the plan made no difference for the products on which they relied, and the commissioner got no vocal support from any of the northern countries (*Agra Europe*, February 8, 1991: E/1). Interestingly, the strongest opposition came from the United Kingdom, the Netherlands, and Denmark—the countries that usually are most supportive of CAP reform and favored a flexible position in the GATT. These countries have relatively large, efficient farms and had little to gain from the MacSharry plan, which was designed to help the smallest and least efficient farms. Ireland also did not like the plan, because it too has a large number of farmers who would not qualify for full compensation. Germany, with its many small farms, would have been expected to support the plan, but it did not do so because the many large farms in East Germany, which need governmental aid, would have been excluded from compensation. France had divided interests: on the one hand, many small French farmers needed compensation; but on the other, no plan was acceptable if it implied the reduction of cereal exports.

Faced with the reluctance of the Agriculture Council to decide, the Commission acted within its authority to cut market support expenditures for cereals, beef, and milk to keep spending under the agricultural guidelines in 1991 (*Agra Europe*, February 22, 1991: P/1). But Commission action was stopgap at best. This left MacSharry with a dilemma. He could let things drift and ask for an increase in the agricultural guidelines. However, this would have serious political costs in that it would pit him against the budget commissioner and other commissioners whose programs would have to pay the price for an increase in agricultural spending. More ominously, national finance ministers and prime ministers, who could take the reform initiative away from the Agriculture Council, would be brought into the process.

MacSharry's other choice was to press the Agriculture Council to take action to keep expenditures under control. There were two ways that he could do this. One strategy would force reform through the 1991 price package with proposals for price cuts, quota reductions, new quotas, and increased coresponsibility levies.[19] The other, more long-term strategy would propose a price package that more or less froze supports at present levels, but insist that the Council come to grips with a thorough-going reform proposal later in the year. MacSherry seemed to move in both directions. The price package submitted to the Council for 1991 included an increase in the coresponsibility levy from 3 to 6 percent for cereals, a 2 percent cut in milk quotas, and a 5 percent reduction in the support price for sugar.[20] MacSharry also began preparing a comprehensive CAP reform proposal for debate in autumn 1991.

Placing the events of early 1991 in the context of the three-level negotiating game, it seems evident that the changing EC policy environment, particularly the prospect of a budget crisis induced by agricultural spending, altered the EC political balance (Level II) sufficiently to increase the EC GATT win-set (Level I) enough to justify reopening the GATT negotiations. Indeed, an agreement was announced at the end of February 1991 to resume the GATT talks (*Agra Europe*, February 22, 1991: P/2). The contracting parties agreed to aim to achieve "specific binding commitments" in the three main areas of the agricultural trade dispute: domestic market support, market access, and export competition (*Agra Europe*, February 22, 1991: P/2). The EC is understood to have put in written terms the modest concessions made at the December 1990 Brussels conference, including a limited commitment for market access, the removal of oilseeds from rebalancing, and a commitment to reduce subsidized exports (*Agra Europe*, February 22, 1991: P/2).

Closing the Gap Between Bargaining Positions

The negotiations were resumed in the spring of 1991 when the U.S. Congress renewed the president's fast-track negotiating authority for an additional two years. But progress in resolving the EC differences with the United States and the Cairns Group has been slow, and even in late 1992 a final agreement for the Uruguay Round is not assured.

The positions of the EC, on the one hand, and the United States and the Cairns Group, on the other, have come much closer together. At an EC-U.S. summit on November 9, 1991, President George Bush made a significant move toward the EC position by lowering U.S. demands for cuts to 35 percent for export subsidies and 30 percent in other areas to be effected in five or six years. By December, it was reported that the EC was prepared to raise its offer to cut domestic subsidies to match the 30 percent proposed by the United States although using different base years (*Financial Times*, December 23, 1991). By then the United States and EC had reduced the export subsidy dispute to the point where the EC had agreed to a mixture of quantitative and budgetary cuts that would allow 13–15 million tons of subsidized EC wheat on the international market, compared to 20 million tons exported by the EC in 1990, while the United States was demanding a maximum of 11 million tons (*Financial Times*, December 12, 1991). The EC also had made significant concessions in accepting U.S. demands for tariffication. Interestingly, the United States and the Cairns Group appear to have gone much further than the EC in modifying their negotiating positions (recall that the United States and the Cairns Group had originally demanded elimination of all market distorting subsidies). This is exactly what the three-level bargaining game analysis would lead us to expect. The small EC win-set for the GATT (Level I) dictated by the agricultural interest–dominated EC and member nation bargaining processes (Levels II and III) has in fact strengthened the EC bargaining position, although it has also made agreement difficult.

The impact of the changed EC policy climate is significant. Certainly,

DG-VI's changed conception of its interests has served as a positive factor for the success of the GATT negotiations. Another positive factor is Agriculture Commissioner MacSharry's decision to stake his political future on taking the lead in promoting CAP reform, so as to minimize the adverse effects of the inevitable on his agricultural constituency. It is also helpful that the stakes of the negotiations have become generally clear in the EC: a failure to achieve an agreement on agricultural trade will deny the Community the obvious benefits of other liberalizing elements of the Uruguay Round, most notably intellectual property and services. It may even be fair to say that the EC (Level II) constraint on a new GATT agreement largely has been removed.

Reducing the Obstacles to Agreement

Some of the obstacles at the national decisionmaking level have also been reduced. For example, Germany's position has moved significantly toward accepting compromise on agricultural trade. The linkages in the GATT of agricultural trade reform with other elements of trade liberalization with clear benefits for Germany have strengthened the hand of the groups inside Germany who would restrain agricultural spending. Moreover, the prospect that Germany, already the paymaster of Europe, might have to contribute more to bail out an unreformed CAP is a very unpleasant one indeed, particularly at a time when German financial resources are heavily committed to the reintegration of East Germany.

The most serious remaining national obstacle is France. Although the French economy would gain significantly from the nonagricultural elements of a successful Uruguay Round, French agriculture would be a clear loser. French farmers, who produce most of the EC surplus, would suffer greatly if EC agricultural export subsidies were significantly reduced or eliminated. The French government would lose as well because agricultural exports, fueled by EC subsidies, provide a very important component of national export earnings. The net benefit for France of a new GATT agreement, as opposed to no agreement at all, is probably more questionable than for any other major EC country. This severely narrows the French government's conception of an acceptable win-set in the GATT negotiations. As we have seen, neither EC GATT negotiators (Level I) nor the EC bargaining process (Level II) can easily make concessions unacceptable to the French.

The French government's conception of its balance of interests is complicated by French politics. The politically weak Mitterrand regime cannot easily withstand more massive demonstrations by farmers such as that that occurred in October 1991. Even if the government concludes that French interests are served by making concessions on agriculture, one cannot be sure that it will be able to pay the political price. Indeed, the evidence is that the French government is using the negative reverberations from the GATT negotiations to strengthen itself by saying that it will never sacrifice French farmers to the interests of the United States.

Whether the EC win-set can be broadened enough to allow a final Uruguay Round agreement may depend on how much the French position evolves. The burden of responsibility for the failure of the GATT will not be an easy one to bear, and might have a bearing on France's standing in the EC and, more generally, in the world. French policymakers must also realize that a worsening EC budget crisis induced by agricultural spending will strengthen the political forces inside the country who want to cut agricultural spending. A growing budget crisis also could slow the movement to European political and economic union, which now ranks high among France's policy priorities.

There is a chance that the French government will make the concessions that will allow the EC win-set in the GATT negotiations to be expanded enough to conclude an agreement. Should it decide to do so, the EC three-level bargaining process will be advantageous in that it will allow the necessary blame-shift. The French government will not have to make the concessions itself, but merely must allow the EC bargaining process (Level II) and the EC GATT negotiating team (Level I) to make them. It will then be able to say that it held out as long as it could, got the best deal possible, but finally acquiesced in the name of European unity.

An Opportunity for Agreement

A splendid opportunity for such concessions was provided by Arthur Dunkel, the secretary-general of the GATT, when he presented his final compromise proposal to the negotiators on December 20, 1991. This proposal appeared to split the differences between the U.S. and EC positions. It called for a 36 percent reduction in budgetary expenditures for export subsidies combined with a 24 percent reduction in the subsidized export volume. It proposed domestic support cuts of 20 percent from the average of support in the period 1986–1988, with the reductions phased in over the period 1993–1999. It recommended tariffication of all import barriers, with tariffs to be reduced by 36 percent in the 1993–1999 period and the reduction for any single product to be not less than 15 percent (*Agra Europe*, January 10, 1992: P/2). This proposal galvanized strong immediate complaints from the EC, mostly because it ignored the EC rebalancing demand and did not include the EC's proposed compensatory payments to farmers in the "green box" of nondistorting subsidies. Yet, after the initial flurry of opposition, it appeared by January 1992 that EC politicians regarded the Dunkel recommendations as a basis for agreement (*Agra Europe*, January 17, 1991: P/1). Dunkel's proposal has an intrinsic appeal in that it is balanced and may be the only alternative to no agreement. It clearly puts the agricultural interests opposed to an agricultural trade agreement on the defensive and will directly pit them against the beneficiaries of the Uruguay Round. It may provide an example of a well-formulated, well-timed, Level I bargaining proposal, providing the final impetus to definitively shift the political balance at bargaining Levels II and III, and achieve an outcome beyond the reach of domestic politics.

NOTES

1. For a discussion of the initial Uruguay Round agricultural trade proposals, see Moyer and Josling (1990: 185–187). The U.S. proposal exempted certain domestic programs considered to have only small effects on production and trade, such as domestic food programs, international food aid, and farmer income supplements not linked to production.

2. In contrast to the exporters, the Nordic countries and Japan put forward more cautious proposals. The Nordic proposal contained liberal elements, but the Japanese one carefully placed the onus on exporting countries to reduce subsidies and restore discipline in world markets. The Japanese proposal was alone in not endorsing the notion of an aggregate measure of support as an aid in negotiations.

3. The Geneva midterm accord also brought a commitment to discuss revision of the GATT rules. There seemed to be agreement that it was time to reconsider both the waivers and exceptions for quantitative barriers guaranteed by Article XI, which kept large parts of U.S. and EC agricultural policy outside the GATT, and to strengthen Article XVI, which had not been effective in preventing export subsidies for primary products. Consensus appeared to have been reached on the need to minimize the adverse trade effects of sanitary and phytosanitary regulations, but the United States and the European Community still differed on the best approach to the problem.

4. For a discussion of the EC proposal, see *Agra Europe* (December 21, 1989: P/1-P/8).

5. The European Parliament, although it is assuming increased responsibilities under the Single European Act, still has no formal responsibilities in trade negotiations. It may discuss trade policy issues in committee or in full plenary session and it may make recommendations, but it is excluded from the formal policymaking process.

6. See Moyer and Josling (1990: ch. 1) for a discussion of the underlying model of the policy process.

7. Three basic paradigms shed insight into how the process operates. Allison's (1971) Organizational Process Model helps us to understand that each of the included organizations is likely to see agricultural trade policy differently, influenced by its own organizational interests and priorities, and to take positions consistent with these interests and priorities. This model also helps us to understand that change in organizational position is inherently incremental, even in a dynamic environment, with stable parochial perceptions, satisficing and standard operating procedures exercising a strong influence. Public choice theory, which explains behavior in terms of egoistic individuals trying to maximize utility subject to constraints, helps in understanding that policy is the outcome of the way in which the preferences of egoistic institutions are combined in the political process. Allison's Bureaucratic Politics Model helps explain the bargaining outcomes, with its attention to the structure of decisionmaking, rules and procedures for bargaining, action channels controlling access to the process, and power resources of the various bargaining actors. For a more complete

discussion of how EC agricultural policy can be explained by these models, see Moyer and Josling (1990: ch. 2–4).

8. For a discussion of the function of the Inter-Service working group, see Murphy (1990: 119).

9. The Inter-Services group itself decides whether a proposal should be submitted to the full college of commissioners for their approval or be passed on directly to the 113 Committee.

10. The 113 Committee operates at two levels. When important policy issues are discussed, the national governments are represented by the chief civil servants from the ministries. When the issues are less significant, more junior officials represent their home government.

11. The COREPER has two parts: Part I consists of the deputies to the ambassadors and usually deals with agricultural trade issues; Part II consists of the ambassadors, rarely deals with CAP matters, and concentrates on more general issues. The General Affairs Council can also consist of foreign ministers, but is not usually so constituted for GATT matters.

12. The EC member states have the following votes: France, Germany, Italy, and Great Britain have ten votes each; Spain has eight votes; Belgium, Greece, the Netherlands, and Portugal have five votes each; Denmark and Ireland have three votes each; and Luxembourg has two votes. A qualified majority requires fifty-four votes, and a blocking minority requires twenty-three votes. The rule of qualified majority prevents the four large states from acting without support from at least some of the smaller states.

13. For a discussion of EC public opinion on agriculture and farmers, see Moyer and Josling (1990: 49–51).

14. Moyer conducted a series of interviews with officials in DG-I, DG-VI, and the Agriculture Council Secretariat during the period of July 11–12, 1990, to discuss the GATT negotiations.

15. Moyer conducted a series of interviews with officials in the West German Economics and Agriculture Ministries on June 28–29, 1990.

16. At the time, Andriessen was very preoccupied with responding to the emerging democratic countries of Eastern Europe.

17. For a discussion of the 1984 milk quotas decision, see Petit et al. (1987). For a discussion of the 1988 stabilizers decision, see Moyer and Josling (1990).

18. This paper was never officially released but was widely leaked by elements in the Commission supportive of reforming the CAP. For a discussion of its contents, see *Agra Europe* (February 15, 1991: P/2).

19. For a discussion of these options, see *Agra Europe* (February 8, 1991: P/3).

20. The proposed 1991 price package is detailed in *Agra Europe* (March 1, 1991: E/1–E/5).

Andrew F. Cooper
Richard Higgott

6

Australian and Canadian Approaches to the Cairns Group: Two-Level Games and the Political Economy of Adjustment

The emergence of the Cairns Group and its role in the Uruguay Round are of considerable interest for students in international relations in general and students of international political economy in particular. As has been argued elsewhere (Higgott and Cooper, 1990), the group's development has added a new dimension to the process of bargaining in the Uruguay Round of multilateral trade negotiations. Although the "pyramidal" model of decisionmaking in GATT negotiations still largely pertains (Winham, 1989: 290), neither the consensus agreement for a new round of negotiations that emanated from the 1986 Punte del Este meeting nor the progression of the round beyond the midpoint of the Geneva meeting of April 1989 can be explained simply in terms of the brute power of the major actors— the United States and the European Community. Progress in the agenda-setting and negotiating process, it may be argued, has been significantly facilitated by the activities of the Cairns Group as a constructive bridge builder and consensus seeker in the tense and often conflictual relationship, not only between the major actors, but also between the major actors and some of the secondary actors with high stakes in the agricultural negotiations.

Yet, at the same time, it must be emphasized that the activities of the Cairns Group have been constrained by the surfacing of intense tensions within this grouping of "fair trading nations." Although the group's members have common objectives with respect to their attempts to reform global agricultural trade, they have continued to have different priorities. To a certain extent, this pressure on unity resulted from the "mixed" nature of the coalition. By its heterogeneity, the Cairns Group may be regarded as a coalition unlike any other in the contemporary international political economy. Members are, in simple terms, from both sides of the north-south divide in the international order. Prominent within the group are Australia and Canada, two countries that have traditionally shared a number of common values and goals in the international system. Australia and Canada have been joined not only by New Zealand, another like-minded country, but also by a variety of "unlike" countries, namely Brazil, Hungary, Indonesia, Argentina, Chile, Colombia, Fiji, Malaysia, the Philippines, Thailand, and Uruguay.[1]

The LDCs within the Cairns Group differ considerably with regard to their comparative level of economic development and political systems. Nevertheless, their sensitivity concerning Third World, or G-77, solidarity has influenced their behavior.[2] While going along with the initiative, most were reluctant to identify themselves too closely or explicitly with a cross-cutting coalition of developed and developing countries. Their overriding concern was "special and differential" treatment for their agricultural economies. Some, such as Brazil (a member of the hard-line G-10) and Argentina, went much further in their demands, impelled as they were to come up with funds needed to cope with their enormous debt problems. Argentina showed considerably more concern for group unity than Brazil, which on several occasions failed to keep other members of the group informed of its activities in terms of agricultural policy. But Argentina also led the other Latin American countries in their "revolt" at the December 1988 Montreal midterm review meeting—a response that featured a collective threat to block progress in eleven of the other fourteen areas of negotiation in the round if there was no progress in agriculture.[3]

From the perspective of group unity, however, the tensions between Australia and Canada rather than the divisions between the developed and developing countries caused the most problems. Although Australia and Canada are quintessential middle powers, and remain like-minded in the sense that they are strong advocates of multilateralism and a rules-based approach to international economic relations, the two countries diverged considerably in the context of the Uruguay Round with respect to their approaches to the Cairns Group and agricultural trade. Whereas Australia increasingly took on the intellectual leadership and managerial responsibilities for the group, a perceptual gap grew between Canadian rhetoric and Canadian practice. Canadian policymakers persisted in talking about Canadian leadership within the group. The minister of state for the Canadian Wheat Board, for instance, claimed, "we have been taking the lead internationally in seeking a lasting solution to these problems" (Canadian House of Commons, 1987: 5357). Yet, because of Canada's apparent unwillingness to accept the burden of costs for the international campaign, the country was increasingly viewed as a backslider within the group.

In this pattern of behavior, Australia and Canada reversed their traditional roles with respect to middle-power leadership. Canada has usually been in front with respect to the thinking and practice of middle powers. One student of Canadian and Australian diplomacy has described the role of the two countries in the post-1945 era: "Canada appeared to lead the way in directions along the way which Australia has moved" (Fox, 1980: 193). This source of leadership was particularly evident in the abilities of Canadian officials during the golden age of Canadian diplomacy (late 1940s to late 1950s) to assemble coalitions and to work with other countries in the implementation of proposals. In conceptual terms, the notion of middle-power statecraft was developed in Canada—most notably by the late doyen of Canadian foreign policy studies, John Holmes—to signify an approach to diplomacy geared toward mitigating conflict and building consensus and cooperation (see, for example, Holmes, 1976).

To understand this transformation of national approaches it is necessary to adopt both an international and domestic level analysis. At the international level, the structural and situational contexts of Australian and Canadian foreign economic behavior must be examined. That is to say, Australia and Canada must be "located" in a changing international political economy. At the domestic level, the differentiated degree of state capability and the nature of state/societal relations within the two countries must be taken into account. This set of features provides both the constraints and opportunities that condition national economic performance. A useful means for exploring this dynamic is Putnam's (1988) conceptualization of two-level games. In examining the nexus between the international system and the domestic political process through this mode of analysis, the relationship between foreign economic diplomacy and domestic reform strategy may be captured.

SETTING THE CONTEXT OF INTERNATIONAL AGRICULTURAL TRADE POLITICS

A prerequisite to an inquiry into international agricultural trade politics is an acknowledgment of the change in the international political economy that has been in train over the last couple of decades. The manner of the impact of this change on Australia and Canada in the 1970s, 1980s, and early 1990s is discussed in this chapter. In caricature, the essence of this change centers on the uncertainty and increased economic conflict that has been deemed to have accompanied the erosion of the Liberal International Economic Order (LIEO).[4] In this regard, perhaps only three general points need to be made. First, the post-1970 period has witnessed a serious weakening in the principles and norms that were established at Bretton Woods and the articles of the GATT that formed the basis of the post–World War II LIEO.

Second, the chief characteristic of change in the international economic order has been the shift from hegemony to multipolarity. This is not to say that U.S. preponderance has been supplanted, nor that we have a system of advanced multilateral management of the global economy. Rather, the United States has been joined by other major—although still lesser—economic powers such as Japan and the EC, and this has complicated the power-sharing arrangements in the international political economy, the governance of which is no longer possible under the principles established in the second half of the

1940s (Odell, 1982; Block, 1977). It is, of course, possible to present empirical evidence that there has been no measurable decrease in the ratio of trade to gross national product (Webb and Krasner, 1989), and that, by logical extension, the real impact of non-tariff barriers is, in fact, limited. The point of concern for us, however, is the degree to which perceptions of a major shift from an earlier liberal ethos and of the pervasiveness of nontariff barriers are having a deleterious effect on the wider commitment to liberalism in many quarters of the global system.

Third, a major victim of these broad changes in the international economic order would appear to be the more specific principles and norms that are enshrined in the GATT and have guided the international trading system until the 1970s: multilateralism, nondiscrimination, and a legal or codified approach to regulation, rather than a negotiated approach preserving the sovereign administrative discretion of states. The codified approach represented a preferred U.S. position rather than that of its European allies in the post–World War II decades (Winham, 1986; Finlayson and Zacher, 1983). These principles and norms, however, came under increasing pressure in the 1970s and 1980s. Not only has the rise to major actor status of the EC and Japan undermined the U.S. ability to set the politico-philosophical agenda, but it would appear that there is no longer the same belief in the United States that the principles that served it well as hegemon still serve the national interest.[5] In recent years, the major debate within policymaking communities concerning the international trading system has been driven much more by the ideological-cum-philosophical questions about the relative merits of liberalism and mercantilism. Although the GATT has been successful in lowering tariffs, it has been unable to discourage the use of nontariff instruments, which have become a major reflection of "illiberality" in the trading system (Gilpin, 1987). With the emergence of the new protectionism (see, for example, Krugman, 1986; Bhagwati, 1988; Pomfret, 1988), a panoply of government-sponsored measures, described variously as strategic trade policy or industry policy, have become the norm, and the control of these measures can be brought about only by complex political processes of decisionmaking.

It is in this broad context of change that the politics of agriculture have to be understood. In the immediate post-1945 period, the United States was the dominant actor in the international agricultural trading system. By virtue of its willingness to take on the burdens of stockholder of last resort in grains, in respect to concessional transactions, the United States may be said to have performed the role of the manager of the international agricultural trading system. Indeed, the norms and rules of the post-1945 food regime reflected the liberal economic values championed (although not always practiced) by the United States—values that included comparative advantage, specialization, and the free and open exchange of goods and technology (Hopkins and Puchala, 1978). Under such conditions, U.S. policymakers argued that economic growth and economic efficiency would be maximized on a global level. As suggested, however, to make such an assertion is not to deny a history of protectionism in early post–World War II U.S. agricultural policy, which in part explains the weakness of the GATT on the issue of agriculture. After all, within the first few years of the GATT's existence, it was the United States that secured the still extant "temporary waiver" of certain quantitative export restrictions that conflicted with the interests of its own agricultural markets.[6] The issue of U.S. protectionism remained one of degree rather than substance.

The tensions found in the international relations of agricultural trade in the 1980s and 1990s reflects—and even showcases—many of the general trends found in the international political economy (IPE). The most dynamic change in this issue-area has been the ascendant position of the European Community, and other actors in the international system. Stimulated by the food "shocks" of the early 1970s, the EC moved from being a net importer of agricultural goods to a position where its production exceeded self-sufficiency in a wide range of goods. The result was a gradual globalization of the CAP, as the surpluses generated internally have been exported outside of the EC through a generous "restitution" scheme. The impact of this challenge from below was felt in a variety of ways. In terms of declaratory statements, there continued to be fundamental differences between the weight placed by the United States on open markets and the emphasis by the EC on "sovereignty" and the "management" of international transactions. At the level of action, the EC's increasingly assertive export approach prompted countermeasures from the United States. During the Carter administration and the early years of the Reagan administration, this response centered on a concerted attempt to win recourse through a revamped subsidy code of international trade under the GATT. Dissatisfaction with the slow pace involved in changing the formal rules governing export subsidies (symbolized by the failure of the November 1982 GATT ministerial to achieve agreement), though, shifted U.S. agricultural diplomacy toward a more aggressive "tit-for-tat" approach highlighted by the introduction of the Export Enhancement Program and other retaliatory measures (see, for example, Paarlberg, 1988: 91–97). By this shift in approach from residual multilateralism toward a more explicit form of unilateralism, the United States signaled to its followers as well as the challengers in the agricultural trade issue that it placed its own interests ahead of the defense of the liberal international trading order.[7]

CONTRASTING AUSTRALIAN AND CANADIAN APPROACHES TO THE CAIRNS GROUP

The erosion of the post-1945 global agricultural system and the heightened fragmentation in the global relations of agricultural trade were extremely traumatic events for Australia and Canada. As important as the role of the United States was as leader of the post-1945 agricultural trade system, an exclusively leader-centric analysis overlooks the integral role of these two first followers—Australia and Canada—in institutionalizing and legitimizing that system.[8] Although accepting the U.S. vision in terms of norms and values, Australia and Canada were not mere free riders to a hegemon distributing "international public goods." Although free riding has indeed existed, both consciously and unconsciously, among such secondary actors as Australia and Canada, not all of their behavior can be termed as free riding. On the contrary, central to Australian and Canadian followership was a form of burden-sharing within the agricultural trading system. If these countries may be said to have been riding along, to the extent they were not (given the structural limitations of the influence) in a position to maintain an open trading system by themselves, they did so only after buying a ticket to ride.

One major focus of this activity was the stabilization of international commodity markets in which Australia and Canada were significant actors. Both countries, for example, worked hard to bring the International Grains Agreement (IGA) into effect in the late 1960s and to ensure its survival in the face of defection by other actors. A second focus of this form of followership was the routinization and/or extension of the benefits of the system to a larger circle of countries. Much of this type of activity was directed at ameliorating conditions in developing countries during crisis situations, such as the devastating Indian drought in the mid-1960s, by way of food aid and other forms of relief. A third focus was the diplomacy of constraint, whereby departures from the norms by other actors were monitored and publicized. Particular attention was paid in this regard to those actors, such as the EC, less wedded to the norms of the free market. Nevertheless, as suggested, this rules-keeping activity was not confined to what may be termed the potential "spoilers" of the system (Lake, 1983). This aspect of Australian and Canadian diplomacy was directed at the system leader as well. Initially, the main target of this criticism was the U.S. demand (and receipt) of the waiver from GATT obligations, allowing it to restrict the import of agricultural products under section 22 of the U.S. Agricultural Adjustment Act. Later on, though, the focus of the criticism shifted onto the U.S. practices of disposing surplus agricultural products through a variety of practices, which were well beyond the "qualified" means of extra-market food distribution acceptable within the agricultural trade system.

The breakdown of the rules of the game experienced in the 1980s forced a rethinking of this type of traditional behavior on the part of the first followers. Economically, Australia and Canada found themselves increasingly caught in the crossfire of the "ploughshares war" between the United States and the European Community (see, for example, Bertin, 1986; Randall, 1985; Butler, 1983). The danger of this situation for third parties was demonstrated most clearly by the Reagan administration's decision in mid-

1986 to negotiate sales of subsidized wheat to the Soviet Union. Diplomatically, the influence of both of these traditional middle powers appeared to be waning vis-à-vis the larger players with which it had important but asymmetrical relationships. This vulnerability was more apparent in the case of Australia because of "outsider" status in terms of exclusive fora such as the G-7 and the quadrilaterals. By way of contrast, Canada's position was cushioned somewhat by its comparatively high international status and its varied institutional links with the United States and the EC. Yet, even with this set of advantages, Canada found it increasingly hard to rein in the unilateral behavior of the majors and establish a reordered set of rules in the trading system. Various Canadian attempts to work out a new international grains arrangement in the late 1970s and early 1980s, for example, achieved little in the face of resistance by the United States and Europe.

Certainly this new set of circumstances provided much of the stimulus toward cooperative behavior. In the prenegotiating stage of the Uruguay Round, Australia effectively used the escalating nature of the trade situation to transform the issue of agriculture to a high-level political question. Specifically, the Australian policymakers used the U.S. decision to globalize the EEP as a catalyst for moving ahead with building a larger coalition of "nonsubsidizing" agriculture-exporting nations in the four quadrants of the world, all of which were hard hit by the U.S. actions. Moving beyond the stage of informal discussions on the subject, Australia took the crucial step of formally initiating the "creation of a group . . . with common interests . . . for the long-term" by inviting ministerial representatives of fourteen carefully selected countries to a meeting at Cairns, Queensland, in the last week of August 1986 (Buckley, 1986). Justifying this step, the Australians argued that the external environment had become so threatening that it was only through the development of a "co-ordinated approach to such impositions" that these targeted middle and smaller actors might prevent "our shared interests and concerns" from being "bypassed" (*The Weekend Australian*, August 16–17, 1986; Critchley, 1986).

In embarking on this ambitious exercise in coalitional diplomacy, Australia not only tried to build new associative ties with agricultural exporting countries in the developing world, but also tried to consolidate a new sense of mutuality of interest on agricultural issues with like-minded nations. As noted, the most important country in the latter category was Canada. Although much of Australia's and Canada's followership had been conducted in a parallel rather than tandem fashion, cooperative efforts for a "joint defense" against the unilateralist activity of the majors had intensified in the early 1980s (*Globe and Mail*, December 28, 1981; *The Australian*, April 6, 1983). It is worth noting in this context that moves in this direction were buttressed by the close relationship established between Prime Ministers Hawke and Mulroney. Hawke, for example, was an observer at Mulroney's

January 1985 economic summit in Ottawa. Hawke and Mulroney were also in telephone contact during the U.S.-USSR subsidized wheat sale episode.

To some considerable degree, Australia's efforts to bring Canada on-side were successful. Canada not only "signed on" to the group, but Canada hosted a follow-up ministerial meeting of the coalition in Ottawa in 1987. The Canadian ministerial delegate at the original Cairns meeting was a relatively junior minister, the minister of state for the Canadian Wheat Board. As the group showed it had some considerable staying-power, the task of representing Canada passed over to the minister of international trade (first Pat Carney and then John Crosbie). At the same time, Canada presented the Cairns Group position at the G-7 meeting in Venice (1987) and Toronto (1988) and the quadrilateral meetings.

Yet, as the Cairns Group developed, the differences between the Australian and Canadian roles came to the fore. Not only did Australia act as the driving force behind the formation of the group, it also served as the manager of the group. Internally, Australia focused on institution building via the establishment of a division of labor, the development of monitoring activity, and the establishment of a loose form of coordinating mechanism to help maintain the cohesion of the coalition. A crucial component here was the activity of a small group of public officials such as Geoff Millter (the Secretary of the Department of Primary Industry), Peter Field (Department of Foreign Affairs), Andy Stoeckel (Bureau of Agricultural Economics), and Alan Oxley (ambassador to the GATT). Externally, with respect to the negotiation process with the United States, the EC, and other actors, Australia was instrumental in shaping the incremental step-by-step approach of the Cairns Group. The key to this approach, in broad terms, was the adoption of confidence-building techniques that would clear the air of animosity, convince all actors of the usefulness of the negotiations, and gain a collective commitment to a "standstill and rollback." At the Bariloche meeting of the Cairns Group in February 1988, Australia called for a freeze on all farm subsidies and new import barriers to commence in 1989 as part of a "down payment" or "advance" on a longer-term agreement on agriculture. At a meeting of trade ministers in Islamabad, Pakistan, in October 1988, Australia, on behalf of the Cairns Group, called for a reduction of import barriers and agricultural price supports by 10 percent for two years. By July 1989, in what was expected to be the lead up to the final stage of the negotiations, Australia was calling for complete elimination of quantitative restrictions as part of a longer-term package.

To show its own bona fides on trade reform, Australia expressed a new willingness to accelerate its own internal adjustment process. Rejecting protectionism at home as well as abroad, the Hawke government committed itself to exposing more fully the Australian economy to the forces of the international marketplace. A significant manifestation of this shift in attitude came in Prime Minister Hawke's October 1987 speech to the contracting parties of the GATT at Geneva, in which he promised that Australia was prepared to eliminate all of its restrictive barriers as part of a radical step toward trade liberalization. Intellectual support for this internal reform drive was provided by a number of well-publicized studies and publications, including the Garnaut report, the Hughes report on Australian export performance, and the Pappas, Carter, Evans, and Koop report prepared for the Australian Manufacturing Council. All of these studies reached similar conclusions about the necessity of internal adjustment in the Australian economy and helped push the Australian public policy agenda toward a neo-liberal agenda centered on deregulation and competitiveness (Garnaut, 1989; Hughes, 1989; Pappas et al., 1989).[9]

In contrast to Australia's ambitious exercise in entrepreneurial technical leadership in the agricultural trade issue area, Canada's approach to the Cairns Group was more ambivalent. If Australia was the motor for the group, Canada was the most substantial brake. The Canadian preference was to use the Cairns Group as a tactical rather than a strategic tool. By signing onto the group, Canada hoped to embellish its wider multilateral diplomacy in regard to the GATT negotiations, as well as its bilateral negotiations via the FTA, not to mesh its own approach on agricultural policy to those of its coalition partners.

The transformation of the Cairns Group from a loose assembly of "fair-trading" nations fighting exporting subsidies to an institutionalized coalition with a broad range of interests, therefore, posed serious problems in terms of Australian-Canadian relations. As the Cairns Group moved from a gambit, taken in the midst of a crisis, into an emergent third force in agricultural trade negotiations, the differences between Australia and Canada came to the fore. What had begun as a relatively minor endeavor blossomed into a serious exercise, pushed along by a "gung-ho" Australia and pulled back by a reluctant Canada. From the Australian standpoint, Canada was increasingly viewed as a country having a position in but not sharing the approach of the group. From the Canadian standpoint, the ambitious nature of the Australian proposals and the wide definition of a freeze on farm subsidies signified an unwarranted intrusion into the sphere of domestic agricultural policy.

An open rift between Canada and Australia originally appeared in 1988 about how the freeze was to be implemented. Although the subject of a great deal of crisis-management diplomacy, the differences remained so fundamental that Canada refused to sign the submission of the Cairns Group to a GATT Agriculture Committee meeting in July 1988.[10] Canada, although willing to agree to a freeze on further trade-distorting initiatives and prepared to accept an overall reduction of 10 percent over the next two years, remained adamantly opposed to any commodity-specific measures. Moreover, far from contracting as the GATT negotiations moved on, the gap in the negotiating stances of the two countries widened. Whereas Australia was willing to put everything it had on the table, Canada remained defensive about its own agricultural structures—which it considered to be non–trade distorting—and in particular wanted due allowance under Article XI for import quotas in support of supply management programs. So intransigent was Canada's position on this issue that it preferred to jeopardize its role in the coalition rather than give ground in policy terms. Agriculture Minister and Deputy Prime Minister Donald Mazankowski, for example, defended Canada's stance on the basis of sovereignty: "What's wrong with staking out a Canadian position. . . . We should be applauded for that."[11] This sense of divergence, even to the point of rupture, between Canada and the other members of the Cairns Group was reinforced in turn by autonomous Canadian diplomatic efforts to defend the marketing board system from sweeping reform. Most notably, Canada has sought the help of Japan and Korea to exempt supply management from any agreement based on tariffication (Drohan and Fagan, 1991; Ono, 1991).

COMPARING NATIONAL APPROACHES IN TERMS OF TWO-LEVEL GAMES

To a large extent, the differences between the Australian and Canadian approaches to the Cairns Group may be usefully analyzed from a structural perspective.[12] In the international political economy, the exposure of Canadian agriculture to trade tensions is seen to be far less marked than that of Australia. The profile of Canadian farm exports is a concentrated one, with grains, oilseeds, and red meats dominating in the competitive sector, and dairy and poultry producers remaining as relatively noncompetitive and domestic-oriented sectors. If Canada were a victim of the ploughshares wars, then, it was a victim with quite specific grievances. At the same time, in relative terms, Canada is in a far stronger overall position economically than Australia. Not only does Canada have a higher GNP than Australia, but by Australian standards Canada has a well-developed base in manufacturing and service industries.[13] Although the agricultural trade issue is still important for Canada, because farm products contribute only 7 percent to Canada's total exports, it is not the pivotal issue in terms of trade diplomacy.

The Australian position was very different. Not only has Australia remained more dependent on its export of resources, but its vulnerability to the denial of market access and to the competitive subsidization of agricultural commodities is far greater, given the wide range of agricultural produce it exports (rice and sugar as well as grains, dairy produce, and meat). Indeed, for the so-called "lucky country," the 1980s were a sober period because agricultural prices fell and Australia no longer had the cushion of strong mineral and energy exports. From 1973 to 1983, Australia slipped from being the twelfth largest trading nation to being the twenty-second largest in the international economy, and its share of the world export market dropped from 2.6 percent to 1.2 percent (Krause, 1984: 281). This downturn was starkly reflected in the rise in capital debt, the fall in the currency level, and the increase in the balance-of-payment deficit on the current account. Australia has, in short, undergone a process of "marginalization" in the post–World War II global economy (Higgott, 1987a, 1987b, 1987c).

The Labor government of Bob Hawke, however, not only had an economic imperative for "doing something" about the agricultural trade situation, but it had a domestic imperative for action that related specifically to the rapidly escalating "rural crisis." Mobilized by the worsening rural terms of trade, reflecting both a rise in production costs and a deterioration in world prices, the "revolt of the bush" had become a serious political force in Australia by the mid-1980s. From one perspective, this form of rural agitation was merely an irritant to a consensus-oriented government. From another perspective, though, the farmers' actions were perceived as being potentially highly damaging to the government in electoral terms. Although the Australian Labor Party (ALP) had traditionally received a minority of the votes cast in rural Australia, Labor could not afford to ignore the countryside completely. As Minister of Primary Industry John Kerin put it in a speech in November 1985, the number of marginal seats located in the countryside was too great: "Eighteen of our federal seats have a significant rural component. Nine of our most marginal seats are included on this list. We cannot hold government without these seats" (quoted in Cribb, 1987: 88).

The priority given by the ALP to the agricultural trade issue in the 1980s and 1990s, then, may be best analyzed as a two-level game (Cooper, 1990a; Higgott, 1991). Given its long-standing commitment to multilateralism, the GATT (despite all of its problems) was and still is deemed by Australian foreign economic policymakers to offer Australia the best hope for global trade reform in general, and agricultural reform in particular. Consequently, the Uruguay Round of multilateral trade negotiations has been at the apex of Australia's foreign policy agenda since the round's commencement in 1986. This international priority was, however, part of an attempt on the part of Labor to manage—by externalizing—the domestic agricultural revolt that grew in direct proportion to the downturn in commodity prices and the global "agricultural crisis" of the mid-1980s. Success in securing international reform would not only allow a very efficient Australian rural sector to reap the financial rewards in a more open global marketplace, it would lessen the widely held view in the countryside that the ALP was not doing enough to help the farming industry in a time of crisis. An externally oriented campaign against the illiberal practices of the United States and the EC, although not a complete answer to the Labor government's political problems at home, was a useful political palliative.

Labor attempted to place the blame for the trend toward economic nationalism in general, and the downturn in world commodity prices in particular, at the door of the profligate policies of the EC, the retaliatory EEP of the United States, and (in terms of access) the closed nature of the Japanese market. The specifics of the trade-distorting measures of the major actors were identified in numerous detailed and highly publicized studies by the Department of Primary Industry and the Australian Bureau of Agricultural and Resource Economics on the trade distorting and inefficient nature of the CAP, Japanese restrictions on food imports, and the protection of the U.S. grain industries (Australian Bureau of Agricultural and Resource Economics, 1985, 1989). The studies of the CAP and of Japan were translated into French and Japanese, respectively; all of the studies were distributed widely within their targeted areas.

In addition, senior members of the government, including Bill Hayden and Gareth Evans as foreign minister and John Dawkins, Michael Duffy, and Neal Blewett as ministers of trade negotiations, and even Prime Minister Bob Hawke, engaged in energetic bouts of personal diplomacy, especially vis-à-vis the United States. The U.S. subsidy policies were argued to be hitting Australian export earnings at exactly the same time as the United States was suggesting to Australia that it should be playing a more substantial role in alliance relations in the Pacific. Australian government criticism of the predatory behavior of the United States was joined by the equally vociferous condemnation of the United States and calls for retaliation by the Australian rural sector (Higgott, 1989).

Labor's domestic strategy won it some breathing space in terms of its atavistic relationship with the Australian rural sector. While its cautiousness to Labor remained, the rural sector tempered considerably much of its hostility and opposition for opposition's sake during this period. Although other factors came into play, the role of the Cairns Group was crucial. Not to denigrate the group's role in the process of the Uruguay Round negotiations, it may be stated that its importance was as much domestic in the first instance as it was international. As the *Australian Financial Review* (August 28, 1986) noted: "The harsh truth is that the Cairns Conference has been much more about posturing to domestic primary producing voters than it is about any serious initiative to change world trade patterns." Yet, even if this were the case at the outset, events outstripped this interpretation. The activities of the group in the Uruguay Round took on a significance, at both the international and the domestic levels, beyond the anticipation of the principal protagonists in 1986.

At the international level, the Cairns Group had a demonstrative effect in terms of the ability of Australia (and indeed, other middle powers) to take the lead in terms of initiatives on specific issues. This is not to suggest, of course, that entrepreneurial and technical leadership utilized in these initiatives can substitute for the structural leadership, derived from traditional power-based negotiating abilities, usually possessed only by the major powers.[14] Rather, it is to suggest that in the absence of decisive interventions by the major actors on a variety of issues, but in this instance to support an open multilateral trading system "after hegemony," that the role of smaller players—operating as conflict-mitigating, agenda-moving, and proposal-building coalitions—takes on a new importance (Higgott and Cooper, 1990: 625–632). The activities of the Cairns Group in the Uruguay Round—notwithstanding that at the time of writing the success of the round in bringing about reform may be judged a failure—represent an important exercise in complex coalition diplomacy of a kind that will likely be increasingly important in the future.

At the domestic level, the activities of the Cairns Group were put to use increasingly, not only as a political but as an educative tool. Australia has been able to occupy the high moral ground in the GATT negotiations on agriculture because it has the least subsidized agricultural economy in the world. It is, of course, less virtuous in other sectors of the economy (although the principal instrument of protection in Australian manufacturing has been the tariff rather than the nontariff barrier), and the kudos gained for Australia in the Uruguay Round have been used by the Labor government in its intellectual assault on the less-than-wholehearted commitment to liberalization that exists in some sectors of the ALP and some sectors of the economy. Not only has Australia's commitment to liberalization of agriculture in the international domain been used to exhort domestic producers in other sectors to put their houses in order, but the prospect of structural adjustment in train within Australia has also been used at the international level to invoke change in Australia's trade partners. Japan, in particular, has been constantly urged to follow the Australian example and expose its economy to the forces of the international marketplace (*Australian Financial Review*, August 15, 1986). Thus, in this discussion of agricultural reform we can see the manner in which the level of the game keeps switching and deepening.

Canada may also be analyzed through the mode of two-level—international and domestic—games. Canada's initial desire to participate in the Cairns Group reflected, to a large extent, the Mulroney government's concern to portray Canada as a good international citizen. Politically, an emphasis on Canadian middle-power diplomacy through a coalition of middle and smaller nations was useful in tempering criticism that the government was concentrating too heavily on forging a new bilateral relationship with the United States (Whalley, 1988). Diplomatically, joining this coalition of "fair-trading" nations allowed Canada to work toward solving the agricultural trade crisis without confronting the United States head-on with regard to the EEP and other retaliatory measures.

If the Canadian government's original intention was to orchestrate an externally directed reform campaign in a fashion similar to that of Australia, it was forced increasingly over time to manage the agricultural trade issue through internalized means. This gradual shift in orientation reflected the realities of the divisions and fragmentation within the Canadian farm community along commodity and regional lines. Indeed, instead of a trend toward a more pronounced sense of unity in the farm community, as evident among the Australian farm groups, the pattern has been the reverse. In other words, a shift has taken place toward even greater internal differentiation and nestling within distinct geographic and production groupings. To a considerable extent, this differentiated behavior can be explained by reference to the fact that Australian producers en masse had been forced in the 1970s and 1980s to rationalize and to become more competitive in international markets. Canadian farmers—at least those with an inward-looking focus (concentrated largely in the east of the country)—had been somewhat more removed from this process.

At the same time, the accelerated move toward agricultural unity in Australia reflected a more dynamic form of farm leadership in that country than in Canada. To a certain extent, the Australian National Farmers Federation (NFF) could be characterized as having a populist style. It organized mass rallies and demonstrations as protest vehicles, and in Ian McLachlan it had a charismatic leader who could capture media attention and who had a loyal personal following within the farming community. Beyond this populist style, however, the NFF leadership had always placed great weight on establishing the organization's credibility with respect to technical expertise. For another thing, the need for creating a better image for farmers in urban Australia was recognized. To promote this more positive image, a sophisticated "our country" multimedia awareness campaign was launched. Finally, a better relationship between the wider Australian business community and the farming interest was promoted (an approach eased by the fact that several of the Federation's leaders had links to agribusiness). All of these aspects of the business side of the NFF were facilitated, it must be added, by the Federation's ability to build up a large "fighting fund."

Whereas the Australian NFF served as an effective peak organization, the Canadian Federation of Agriculture (CFA) increasingly proved to be an ineffective umbrella organization in the 1980s. The fact that many commodity-specific groups remained outside the CFA, defected from it, or collapsed completely reduced the organization's financial resources as well as its authority to remain the general farm voice in Canada (Coleman, 1988: 101). Moreover, the CFA did not compensate for its structural deficiencies through either the presentation of an effective leadership style or sound expertise in terms of government/business relations. By choosing to stay polarized on a wide array of issues (including transportation and marketing, as well as trade policy), the CFA ended up looking more confused and indecisive. This image problem, in turn, contributed to the organization losing still further credibility as an effective actor in the policymaking process.

In this vacuum, the forces of responsiveness and resistance to change within the agricultural sector struggled to influence the agenda on the basis of their own needs and interests. At one end of the spectrum, the more export-oriented commodity producers enthusiastically embraced the concepts of efficiency and adjustment pushed forward by the Cairns Group. This reform-oriented grouping included the Canadian Cattlemen's Association, the United Grain Growers, the Western Wheat Growers' Association, and the Prairie Hog Marketing Boards. In orientation, these groups were closer to agribusiness corporations than they were to many other elements within the farm community. Confident that they were efficient enough to compete successfully in the international arena, these groups pressed for fair and consistent rules of the game. At the other end of the spectrum, the groups representing producers in the more inward-looking, domestic-oriented, and regulated forms of agriculture remained highly wary of change, fearing their needs and interests would be sacrificed on the altar of rationality. This antireform element embraced such diverse groups as the National Farmers' Union, national and provincial marketing boards, and the Quebec Union des Producteurs Agricoles (UPA).[15]

Intensifying this split was the reinforcing or accumulative tendencies inherent in the regional/commodity divide. In other words, a dominating feature in Canadian agricultural politics is what Skogstad (1990a: 48; 1990b) has termed the "provincial-producer alliance." Supporting the reform-oriented agricultural groups have been the Western provinces, led by Alberta. Conversely, the forces of resistance have been strongly backed by the provincial governments in Ontario and Quebec. The UPA, most notably, was able to get the full support of the Bourassa government in Quebec for its campaign of resistance vis-à-vis trade liberalization of agriculture. Premier Bourassa, for example, wrote to Prime Minister Mulroney in July 1990 to urge the strengthening of supply management so as to calm the fears of Quebec's 15,000 dairy farmers.

The Mulroney government attempted to manage these domestic tensions through a defensive transactional approach. One component of this approach was the initiation of an extensive process of consultation, involving a wide number of interests, through means both informal and formal (including a Federal-Provincial Agriculture Trade Policy Committee, Committee on Multilateral Trade Negotiations, and Sectoral Advisory Group on International Trade). Another component was the implementation of side deals with both adjusters and resisters in terms of subsidies and other forms of assistance. This approach was particularly visible just prior to the announcement of the 1988 federal election. On the one hand, a number of ad hoc financial support programs were directed at the Western grain farmers. On the other hand, not only were prices in the regulated dairy sector increased, but strict limits were placed on specialty products imported from the United States, including yogurt and ice cream.

In the short run, this accommodative approach must be considered to have been quite successful. By putting off clear choices between the export-oriented and import-sensitive groups rather than addressing the controversial issues head on, the Conservatives were able to retain strong political support in both the rural areas of the West and Quebec in the 1988 election (that is, in their two strongest pillars from the 1984 victory). Inevitably, though, in the longer run this approach proved problematic from both a foreign policy and a domestic political perspective. An ambiguous policy, with an emphasis on the lowest (or least harmful) common denominator, not only gradually eroded Canada's credibility in the Cairns Group (Anderson, 1990: D1), but it also had the effect of fully internalizing foreign economic policymaking so that every diplomatic move was carefully scrutinized by adjusters and resisters as a test of the government's goodwill.

THE POLITICAL ECONOMY OF ADJUSTMENT IN AGRICULTURAL TRADE

In examining the Australian and Canadian approaches to agricultural trade through the mode of two-level game analysis, identifying and explaining the "adjustment" strategies of the two countries takes on some considerable importance. Adjustment as a concept in itself is a concept fast approaching the status of a cliché. A starting point for clarification is Ikenberry's (1986) simple two-by-two conceptual breakdown of adjustment into international and domestic on the one hand, and offensive and defensive on the other. This schema provides us, in theory, with a four-level preference schedule of adjustment strategies for states to adopt: (1) offensive international adjustment, (2) defensive international adjustment, (3) offensive domestic adjustment, and (4) defensive domestic adjustment. It becomes clear in this classification how "international regimes . . . and domestic industrial trade strategies are part of a wider whole" (Ikenberry, 1986: 53). International strategies can be pursued defensively, by seeking "special" or fallback solutions, or offensively, by creating new arrangements more suited to changing arrangements. Domestic adjustment represents more territorially centered responses. Again, this can be done either by defensive measures to preserve or reinforce existing arrangements or by offensive measures that would change existing structures or create new ones. Ikenberry's model is by no means a menu from which states can choose adjustment strategies. It is not a case—for states such as Australia or Canada—of simply exercising a preference for one or another option, given the international system provides the prior structural basis for state constraint and state choice.

But the model does provide a way of schematizing the mix of approaches that have been taken by Australia and Canada in the 1980s and early 1990s. These approaches are set out in Figure 6.1. The difference that can be seen is the more offensive approach undertaken by the Australian government, as opposed to the more defensive approach taken by Canada. Faced with

Figure 6.1
Adjustment Policies—Australian and Canadian Approaches to Agriculture Trade

		International	Domestic
Offensive	Australia	Multilateral reform and strengthen the GATT	Restructuring
Defensive	Canada	Canada-US FTA	Subsidies

heightened economic problems, Canada has a greater range of options open to it that avoid hard domestic political and economic choices.[16] For one thing, Canada's more diversified economy, larger tax base, and much smaller range of export industries in the agricultural sector can much more readily prop up producers hard hit by the ploughshares war. For another thing, Canada, through the FTA and possibly the NAFTA, has a viable (albeit extremely contentious) bilateral/regional option. Whatever the costs of this type of fallback option, with respect to sovereignty and diplomatic maneuverability, the benefits of a separate deal with the United States (where well over 70 percent of Canadian exports are directed) has some economic attraction.

Australia's options are much more limited. Domestically, Australia can no longer afford to "throw money" at its agricultural producers. Internationally, Australia trades in a highly diversified set of export markets, none of which grant Australia special status. This is not to suggest that Australia does not have potential bilateral/regional options open to it. But the operationalization of these options, except, of course, in the limited context of the closer economic relationship with New Zealand, remain questionable. A privileged role for bilateralism has not been popular since the passing of the British colonial supremacy. The prospect of a special relationship with Japan, mooted and rejected in the late 1970s, is even less probable in the 1990s. And, in contrast to Canada, the notion of a free trade agreement with the United States was reviewed and rejected in the second half of the 1980s (Snape, 1986).

The pursuit of the regional option is a far more attractive, albeit even more complex, endeavor for Australia. Aside from geographical proximity, there are important complementaries between the economies of Australia and the Asia-Pacific countries, not the least of these being the potential for Australian agricultural exports to grow substantially in that dynamic growth area. Notwithstanding Australia's role in the government and nongovernment efforts to develop an institutional framework to facilitate Asian-Pacific cooperation, though, the barriers to this integrative process remain formidable. In addition to the constraints on the development of the two-way interaction attributable to the legacies of Australian industrial protection and the "White Australia" immigration policy, there are immense political barriers to forging new links with "dozens of different cultural, economic and governmental systems" (Evans, 1988).

Set against this background, the Australian APEC (Asia-Pacific Economic Cooperation) initiative must be seen in proper perspective. APEC is also a two-level signaling process (Higgott, 1990). The APEC initiative has formed part of Labor strategy at the domestic level in a manner not dissimilar to that of the Cairns Group. It was used particularly to mitigate criticism of its inability to manage the Australian economy in a time of increasing inflation, mounting interest rates, and record current account deficits. Similarly, the APEC initiative was recruited into the campaign to control the damage that John Howard's (then leader of the Opposition) use of Asian immigration as a political issue was thought to be doing to Labor's re-election chances in 1989. APEC was a signal that Australia was "of" as well as "in" the region. It was also a signal to the Australian population of the importance of recognizing this fact.

Equally important for Labor's strategy is APEC's role as part of a wider search for options and maneuverability in Australia's international economic diplomacy. Notwithstanding its firm commitment to multilateralism as its first best option, there was growing concern in the policymaking community in the late 1980s, especially following the abortive midterm review of the Uruguay Round in November 1988, that Australia needed a fall-back strategy in the event of a collapse of the multilateral order and decline into "blocism." Thus, APEC was to be a group whose pressure could be used to supplement the activities of the Cairns Group in fostering reform in the Uruguay Round, and it was also seen as the foundation of a new form of loose Asia-Pacific grouping in the event of multilateral breakdown. In this respect, it is important to emphasize the fact that APEC was not seen by Australian policymakers as the precursor of trade restricting regionalism but rather as the precursor of greater regional understanding and cooperation and trade-inducing measures. As such, the aim of the initiative has been to secure what Harris (1989) has called "open regionalism."

CONCLUSION

Obviously, this schema of adjustment strategies does not capture all of the complexity of the approaches pursued in either Australia or Canada. It would be misleading to suggest, for example, in the Australian case, that this model showcases the fundamental differences between the international constraints in the way of innovation in terms of foreign economic policy and political and institutional constraints in terms of domestic adjustment. In this regard, it is useful to return to the two-level mode of analysis discussed in this chapter to explore the question of whether the Australian government has a freer hand in the pursuit of its foreign economic goals than in the pursuit of its domestic reform package. Notwithstanding the push by the ALP to go forward with both an international and domestic adjustment strategy, it seems clear that it has been easier for the government to harness the support of domestic groups in the pursuit of international economic reform than it has been at the domestic level, where rigidities and vested interests are more germane.

Nor should the way strategies may change over time be ignored. The question of whether domestic politics drives international relations (the second image) or international relations drive domestic politics (the second image reversed) (Gourevitch, 1986) becomes less important than the question of under what circumstances and in what ways and to what degree we must see the relationship between the domestic and international policy pressures and concerns of government as symbiotic (Putnam, 1988: 427). Scholars of both the Australian and Canadian political processes have paid too little attention to this symbiosis, tending instead to favor the privileging of one group of variables over another. It was, after all, more than a decade ago that Katzenstein (1978: 4) demonstrated the way in which "the main purpose of all strategies of foreign economic policy is to make domestic policies compatible with the international political economy."

This evolving impetus for change may be illustrated by reference to the process of adjustment in Canada. As noted, it would be misleading to suggest that the FTA resulted directly in a massive restructuring of the import-oriented agricultural sectors. As the deal was negotiated, marketing boards (the main instrument of defense) were not scrapped or even radically altered. At the same time, though, the FTA did prepare the way for further pressures to build up against the existing structures. Free trade gradually chipped away at the entrenched position of the marketing boards. The most important of these incremental changes was the provision for the gradual curtailment (over ten years) of tariffs on imports of processed agricultural products. If this modification did not alter directly the system of supply management, it undercut one of the main supporting underpinnings—that Canadian processors had a "level playing field" for their raw materials. Furthermore, if the FTA provided a "little bang" in terms of reform, a "big bang" could still be set off through the GATT negotiations. Many of the major issues, such as the future of Article XI (which permitted the imposition of import quotas on agricultural products where there were government-supported marketing boards), internal price support systems, and the definition of subsidies, were left to the Uruguay Round, where the stakes were even higher. As Schott (1988: 24) put it, both Canada and the United States "kept their powder dry in the North American talks awaiting the bigger battle in the GATT."

Still, there are a series of wider messages that can be drawn from the mode of analysis adopted in this chapter. The Australian and Canadian positions in the global economic order cannot be explained solely by the impact of international economic transition. Indeed, many of the major economic problems the two countries face are endogenous and dependent on appropriate macro- and microeconomic adjustments for their resolution. What this chapter has stressed, however, is that the nature and success of the adjustment process is in large part contingent on the wider international economic environment and the manner of Australia's and Canada's integration into it. Yet it is precisely in the process of adjustment that a state's domestic economy and politics take on the appearance of an extension of the international political economy.

The contrast in strategic options available to Australia and Canada are striking. In times of heightened economic problems, a country with the economic structure and location in the wider international system, such as Canada, has the ability to adopt defensive strategies. If unable to avoid the impact of many of the changes that take place in the international economy, nor in a position to alter these changes single-handedly, Canada has at least a certain degree of flexibility in terms of its response. Internationally, this has meant the pursuit of policies driven by externalized defensive adjustment, the principal instrument of which has been the negotiation of a bilateral deal with its closest, and largest, trading partner through the FTA. Domestic adjustment strategies have also been principally defensive, including, in the agricultural sector, extensive recourse to subsidies.

This is not to say that all Canadian policies fall into the defensive category. At the domestic level, the growth and competitiveness of outward-looking Canadian agricultural products have been encouraged, at the same time as inward-looking products have been defended. At the international level, Canadian commitment to the liberalization of trade on a selected basis has been part of an offensive strategy in the Uruguay Round—which meshes with Canada's overall reformist approach on the issues of services and intellectual property. If somewhat contradictory, this approach does at least provide Canada with a comparative range of maneuverability.

By way of contrast, offensive adjustment, at both the international and domestic levels, appears to be the only option open to Australia, given its increasing marginalization in the international division of labor. An easily implemented defensive international option is not available for Australia. Furthermore, a defensive domestic adjustment strategy by itself is incapable of dealing with the challenges that Australia is currently facing. Identifying the prerequisites of successful adjustment, however, remains a lot easier than the politics of implementing the necessary kind of strategies at both levels. The difficulties of the adjustment process remain significant, given both the structural constraints facing Australia in the international economic order on the one hand, and the political and institutional constraints on domestic economic adjustment on the other.

NOTES

1. This dysfunction in the pattern of association can be seen most clearly when the Cairns Group's activities are contrasted, for example, with middle power diplomacy in the Law of the Sea negotiations. In these negotiations, Australia, Canada, and New Zealand joined with the like-minded smaller Western European democracies of Austria, Denmark, Finland, Iceland, Ireland, the Netherlands, Norway, Sweden, and Switzerland (Sanger, 1987: 52–53, 55).

2. This sensitivity to LDC solidarity is apparent, notwithstanding the divisions between food-exporting and food-importing developing countries on agricultural trade issues (see Cooper, 1990b: 13–17).

3. For an interesting account of these events, see Oxley (1990: ch. 12).

4. Of the voluminous body of secondary literature dealing with the issue, see the discussions in the following standard works: Keohane (1984); Gilpin (1987); Gill and Law (1988); Strange (1988); Nye (1990).

5. For a discussion about the early period, see Maier (1977).

6. As Warley (1976: 347) has noted, "The importance of this development can hardly be exaggerated. At a time when other exporters (including Australia and Canada) were highly agitated about agricultural trade restrictions, the architect of the trading system and the custodian of liberalism was itself giving primacy to national interests."

7. It has been argued in a variety of quarters, scholarly as well as policy-related in the United States, that the national interest may be better served by the pursuit of unilateral rather than multilateral resolution of international economic problems. Of the scholarly literature, see Krasner (1988). See also Conybeare (1985).

8. For a more general discussion of this theme, see Cooper (1992). On the concept of "followership," more generally, see Cooper, Higgott, and Nossal (1991).

9. For a fuller discussion of these trends, see Higgott (forthcoming).

10. For background, see Tyers (forthcoming) and Warley (forthcoming).

11. These differences resurfaced most clearly in the run up to the Brussels meeting at the beginning of 1991. See Drohan (1990).

12. A model for this type of analysis is Milner (1988).

13. One indication of these structural differences has been the relative lag in the competitive debate in Canada. Whereas this debate has been at the forefront of the political agenda in Australia since the mid-1980s, competitiveness has become a significant issue in Canada only since the early 1990s. See Porter (1991).

14. For an excellent discussion of these points, see Young (1991).

15. For a fuller discussion, see Cooper (1991).

16. For general discussions of Canadian foreign policy, see Dewitt and Kirton (1983).

Raymond F. Hopkins 7

Developing Countries in the Uruguay Round: Bargaining Under Uncertainty and Inequality

At the Uruguay Round of multilateral trade negotiations, less-developed countries have constituted a weak force. This weakness has been decidedly noticeable in negotiations on the issue of agricultural liberalization. This was in sharp contrast to the vocal role played by LDCs on trade issues in the 1970s. Although they offered no collective position on agriculture or on other issues in the Uruguay Round, in the 1970s LDCs pursued a concerted demand for a new economic order, including such measures as special trade preferences and a fund to stabilize and raise prices for their major exports, including agricultural goods (Gosovic and Ruggie, 1976). Their diminished and disorganized role in the 1986–1992 period illustrates several points for the analysis of international politics: (1) the problem of pursuing interests when uncertainty makes it difficult to identify them; (2) the ineffectiveness of groups that have few concessions to offer; and (3) the difficulty in establishing "compensatory measures" in multilateral arrangements, even when all participants favor doing so.

LDC bargaining on agriculture issues in the GATT talks takes place in the more general context of all GATT questions under review. In Geneva, more than 70 LDC countries—of the 108 participating countries in the GATT—have the right to express views, but within a framework scripted by the major industrialized states. Effective bargaining in MTNs requires coalition building, so that, aside from the United States and Japan, blocs of countries became the major players negotiating on all issues. Based on the experience of negotiating under these conditions, this chapter examines the actions of developing countries in agricultural negotiations. It explores the weakness of LDC bargaining, the reasons for it, and its significance for international policymaking. One major reason for the weakness of LDCs in negotiations is their failure to build effective coalitions. Another is their difficulty in determining their "interests." Their weak role, however, was not a reflection of a lack of a stake in the outcome for the LDCs, which was considerable. The chapter concludes, therefore, by considering whether there are future prospects for LDCs to influence negotiations in agricultural trade.

BACKGROUND TO THE URUGUAY ROUND NEGOTIATIONS

The failure of the Uruguay Round to agree on new rules for trade liberalization by the December 1990 deadline can be interpreted and explained in many ways. One interpretation is that the failure revealed basic weaknesses in the international political norms governing trade. An apparent consensus, at least among industrialized states, supporting the neoclassic free trade principles in the international economy may have broken down. A second interpretation is that multilateral negotiations will soon be supplanted by regional strategies to regulate trade. In spite of continuing efforts to reach an agreement, states are now more likely to use exclusionary rather than multilateral strategies for future trade management and global economic policymaking.[1] A third interpretation is that other issues, such as the end of the Cold War and the Gulf conflict, distracted senior policymakers, thus allowing parochial interests to block agreement. A fourth interpretation is that domestic protectionist sentiments in key states, encouraged by economic slowdown in the 1980s, kept negotiators from moving to further liberalization. Whatever the reasons, LDCs have been unable to play an influential role in the GATT, at least regarding agriculture. The LDCs during the 1986–1990 negotiations were the least clear on strategy and stakes, and suffered from classic weaknesses that large, disorganized interest groups face in international bargaining (Rothstein, 1979; Olson, 1965). Furthermore, it appears unlikely that they will gain much from future policy changes, whether they occur as unilateral, bilateral, regional, or global decisions. This is because changes acceptable to countries with the strongest bargaining positions are unlikely to take into account LDC interests. Further, they are unlikely to demand LDC liberalization that might create opportunities for their interests to be restructured.

The Major Players

Negotiations on agriculture are only one of the fifteen topics under discussion in Geneva. Commodity issues were discussed by negotiating groups on tropical products, textiles, intellectual property rights, and trade in services. Each has had difficulties, so agriculture is not alone in posing a stumbling block. Other negotiating groups also were set up to work on legal aspects of GATT machinery. However, the major area of dispute was over agriculture, and the principal axis of conflict was between the two largest markets, the United States and the European Community, each with major producer and export subsidies. The GDP of each of these two in 1989 was more than $5 trillion, larger than the value of domestic production of the entire set of LDCs (World Bank, 1991: 208), including China and India, which each have larger populations than the United States and Europe combined. LDC consumers have a high propensity, however, to spend on food and agricultural items—40–60 percent of any income increase compared to 12–16 percent in OECD states. As a result, LDCs collectively represent an enormous market. In current trade alone they account for over half of the world's annual food imports (World Bank, 1991: 208–209, 222–223). In addition to the United States, Europe, and the LDCs, two other "players" are important: the Cairns group, made up of industrial and developing country agricultural exporters, and Japan. Figure 7.1 depicts these major players and their situation in the negotiations. It portrays roughly their location vis-à-vis protection or trade distortions in their policies and their relative position as net agricultural exporters or importers. With respect to agricultural trade, the size of each of these groups as an exporter and importer of products also helps clarify their positions in international bargaining on this issue. Agricultural products comprise 10–12 percent of trade for OECD countries, whereas they comprise about 20 percent of trade for developing countries. Agricultural exports are relatively less important than agricultural imports for developed countries, whereas the reverse is true for developing countries (World Bank, 1991: 234–237).

Domestic Interests and Deadlock

Let us assume, as many studies of trade gains in agriculture indicate, that collaborative liberalization offers worldwide benefits, accruing to most

Figure 7.1
Major Actors in GATT Agricultural Trade Liberalization Negotiations

Aggregate Trade Distortion

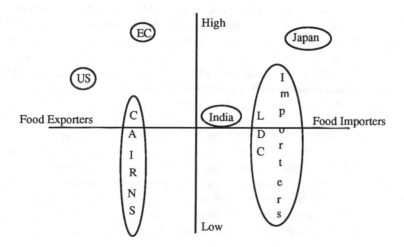

countries and to all major bargaining groups. If so, and the international actors recognize this, then failure to agree on liberalization cannot be explained by rational choice analysis, at least assuming nation-states are the unit of decision. The barriers to agreement that proved insurmountable in the first four years of GATT negotiations were not due, therefore, to the trade competition that has spawned export subsidies in the EC and United States. The bargaining set, by assumption, was one of cooperative gain. Negotiations also allow for communication. This should make side payments possible to assure that gains occur all around. The deadlock is more readily explained by distortions in rational choice arising from domestic politics and from weaknesses in the construction of the bargaining. Evidence that this is likely can be seen by looking at the estimated effects of full liberalization. Figure 7.2, derived from estimates by the U.S. Department of Agriculture (USDA, 1990c), depicts the net welfare gains and the effects on producers from liberalization. Although full liberalization is not a plausible outcome, given the politics of agricultural negotiations, it is a useful way to help assess the potential impact of liberalization moves.

Every major group had a net welfare gain, according to the USDA. These gains reflect the total effects of changes for producers, consumers, and government expenditures. The black bar in the graph shows positive gains ranging from about $1 billion for LDCs to nearly $13 billion for EC countries. There are "losers," however, within states—noticeably producers. In the five bargaining units shown in Figure 7.2, three groups (the United States, Japan, and the EC) show substantial losses for producers. Only the Cairns Group and LDC producers are gainers, and, generally, only in Cairns Group countries are producers an organized and politically potent force. Not surprisingly, countries where producers are losers have resisted GATT proposals for agricultural liberalization.

This chapter argues, as have previous chapters in this volume, that the failure to agree on agriculture reveals the effects of domestic pressures overriding aggregate national interests combined with uncertainty in the minds of negotiators. The latter reflects the role of ideas. Where understanding about consequences is low, confusion arises about what action to pursue. Ideally, the negotiations would proceed from a common orientation based on principles of economic liberalism and the prospect of material gain. Such views would anchor negotiators' outlook,[2] providing "tracks along which action can be pushed" (Goldstein and Keohane, 1990). Uncertainty, however, at least among LDCs, was also a product of ideas. It was much in evidence for LDCs in the GATT and produced substantial confusion.[3] The effect of confidence by some players and uncertainty by others was a misconstruction of common interests among negotiating blocs. In spite of an international cultural hegemony supporting liberal trade as virtuous, agriculture negotiations were resistant to this public orthodoxy. Thus, a combination of the first and fourth interpretations mentioned above

Figure 7.2
Gains and Losses in Agriculture Due to Global Liberalization

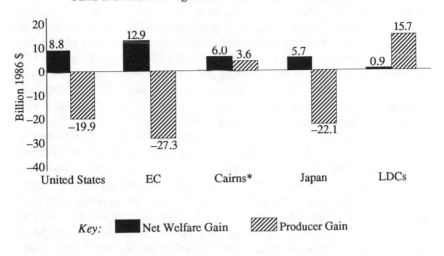

Key: ■ Net Welfare Gain ▨ Producer Gain

Source: Agricultural Trade Liberalization and Developing Countries. USDA (1990c).

*Excludes Colombia, Fiji, Hungary, and Uruguay.

was crucial to the deadlock over agriculture. Ideas arising from imbedded mercantilist institutions, such as the Common Agricultural Policy of the European Community, and uncertainties over risks and gains as well as pressure from potential domestic "losers" explain the failure of the GATT Uruguay Round in 1990 and may account for future failure.[4]

What measures of agricultural liberalization would benefit LDCs? Do they have the bargaining capacity and strategic vision to obtain agreement on such measures? The argument here is that LDCs are unsure of what interests they have and/or of how to advance or protect them in an agreement. Consequently, they are unable to exercise influence in the negotiations. Uncertainty, combined with political disorganization among the LDCs, erodes whatever bargaining power their markets and potential common interests afford them. Thus, they are in no position to influence basic issues or to prevent an "unsatisfactory" agreement. In the negotiations, therefore, at best they have been able to promise to support an agreement, both in agriculture and more generally, provided concessions were made allowing them to have "special and differential" treatment from regular GATT disciplines. Indeed, such concessions in principle were a part of the negotiating offers of the major players. Who received concessions, however, became an issue. Some newly industrializing countries (NICs) among LDCs, such as Korea, for example, were deemed undeserving of exemptions from GATT discipline or were offered compensatory benefits. Indeed, special treatment for LDCs was anticipated in the very opening of the Uruguay Round in 1986. Some analysts argue that LDCs would only harm themselves by establishing such preferential treatment. It could allow other developing countries with which they hoped to trade to cite such GATT exceptions as a basis for not lowering their own trade barriers. This would decrease South-South trade, encourage inefficiency in LDC domestic production, and create a policy tool for narrow interest groups to use in seeking government protection for inequitable privileges.

After more than 65 months of negotiation, whether differences in agriculture can be bridged among competing major groups remains questionable. But what the negotiations reveal thus far is quite interesting. As Chapters 4 and 5 have demonstrated, the gains that Japan and Europe anticipated in the collective arrangements worked out in areas other than agriculture have proven insufficient to offset strong domestic resistance to agricultural liberalization. The major lowering of trade barriers sought by developed exporting states, notably the United States and the Cairns Group, was viewed by Europe and Japan as politically impossible. One reason that industrial and service trade gains did not overcome resistance to change by agriculture sector interests is that the outcomes of the negotiations depend not only on the balance of "interests," but also on the relative power of the bargaining group and the impact of ideas about liberalization and about the distribution of benefits. Thus, multilateral trade negotiations on agriculture cannot be explained as "rational" state behavior distorted by irrational or narrow interest factions. This classic formulation of trade and agricultural theorists must be supplemented by the role of ideas and bargaining strategy.[5]

DEVELOPING COUNTRIES' PERSPECTIVES

How would liberalization affect LDCs? Although the prospect of full liberalization is practically nil, this assumption is the one most frequently modeled by economists. Such forecasting models provide information for negotiators on the direction and size of gains and losses individual countries might expect. The stakes of each negotiating party can be estimated by examining how much their protected interest groups stand to lose in transfers. Because producers, especially in more industrialized states, form smaller, more organized groups, an easy estimate of how a country would view liberalization can rest on whether their producers would gain or lose. Figure 7.2 provides some estimates on this question for five major groups. As noted earlier, the more protected a market, the more intransigent has been resistance from agricultural groups to liberalization, especially in the absence of countervailing lobbies. The studies of political dynamics in the United

States, EC, and Japan make this abundantly clear (Goldin and Knudsen 1990; Knudsen et al., 1990). Because most developing countries' producers, however, would gain—whether from liberalization by OECD countries, or, and even more so, from liberalization by all countries—it might be expected that LDCs would strongly favor liberalization. But this is not true, except for a few states (e.g., Argentina and Thailand) that joined the Australian-led Cairns Group.

Most developing countries' positions and proposals during the first five years of the round were largely in disarray. Aside from one compensatory proposal (discussed below), they drafted no special, let alone comprehensive, positions on the issues of how to liberalize agriculture. In formulating ideas and strategies, they were essentially reacting to initiatives of others.[6] In doing so, they were disadvantaged by seldom knowing the positions of the United States, the EC, or even the Cairns Group in advance. Representatives of non-LDC groups invariably were given drafts of proposals in advance; some were even reviewed and changed in private discussions. Developing countries were provided drafts only on the day of the meeting at which they were to be discussed. This left virtually no time for analyzing consequences and developing responses.

One problem important for some LDCs was a threatened rise in their import bill. Among the dozens of developing countries predicted to suffer a net loss in foreign exchange because of agricultural product price rises, however, only five countries banded together to formulate a position on this problem. They requested compensation under the GATT for food-importing countries who were very poor, if food prices rose as expected. This group, the W-74 (named after the document number of their first submission), was composed of five countries receiving food aid or concessional, highly discounted food sales. One rationale motivating them was a fear that food aid in general and concessional sales of aid in particular might be reduced or eliminated as a result of trade concessions at the GATT. In addition, they feared higher import costs. All five had significant commercial imports in addition to food aid. The W-74, organized by Jamaica under the leadership of Ransford Smith, their major and only economic official in Geneva, consisted of Egypt, Jamaica, Mexico, Morocco, and Peru. Other developing countries voiced support for their initiative, but did not cosponsor the proposal.

It might be argued that most LDC representatives at Geneva understood that their countries might gain from liberalization, and thus were glad to be pushed toward it by other negotiating parties. However, in spite of some evidence from academic models studying the effects of liberalization, most delegates interviewed were agnostic that agricultural liberalization held benefits; some even saw costs for their country outweighing benefits. Food security was a major concern and often cited as an LDC objective. Its meaning for the LDCs, of course, was quite different from that used by Japan and occasionally the Europeans. LDCs worried about inadequate domestic supplies and unreliable international markets. Wealthier states invoked food security as a nonmarket concern to legitimate protectionist national policies. Their domestic farm support programs and use of NTBs served to increase local food supplies, but the effect of such protection was to exclude farmers from reductions in agricultural protection.

The relative lack of bargaining resources of individual LDC countries, of course, played a role in the hesitant and often marginalized behavior they generally exhibited. However, another clear problem was uncertainty. As noted earlier, uncertainty encourages risk aversion. A good example of this can be seen in Table 7.1, which summarizes different predictions regarding liberalization for developing countries. The United Nations Conference on Trade and Development (UNCTAD, 1990) ran a model assuming full liberalization by OECD countries and found the net consequences for developing countries to be negative. Although some countries gained (not surprisingly, LDC members of the Cairns Group), for all LDC countries there was a net loss in foreign exchange from changes in trade and a net welfare loss. The USDA's Economic Research Service (ERS) also has done extensive modeling and has reported results under different scenarios (USDA, 1989a). The ERS results, from their Static World Policy Simulation (Swopsim) model, also show losses of $4.5 billion for LDCs, although they show a welfare gain of $2 to 3 billion if all countries liberalized. Thus, if LDCs also liberalized, then the prospective outcome would be a gain rather than a loss for them. Finally Anderson and Tyers (1990a), using somewhat different base years, project the results of liberalization. In their view, LDCs gain a net welfare in 1995 of about $11.5 billion from just the OECD countries liberalizing, and they would gain $56.3 billion in welfare if all countries liberalized (net after looking at producer, consumer, and government effects). If accepted, this last analysis supports conventional free trade wisdom that LDCs should liberalize their own markets (Krueger, Schiff and Valdes, 1988b). Anderson and Tyers's results go further, however. They disagree that effects of OECD liberalization would have a net negative effect. The difference may be explained, possibly, by noting that the other models were based on immediate effects, whereas the Anderson and Tyers model runs over several years to 1995. Further, there were differences

Table 7.1
Three Scenarios for Liberalization Effects on LDCs of Full Liberalization

	Anderson and Tyers		UNCTAD	SWOPSIM	
	OECD Only	Global	OECD Only	OECD Only	Global
Net change in welfare ($US billions)	11.5	56.3	−0.6	−4.5	2.6

in base years, commodity coverage, and elasticity estimates among the models.

The most robust result from modeling is the universal agreement that producers in LDCs would gain and consumers would lose, and the reverse would happen in most OECD countries. However, this agreement is not much solace for any particular LDC negotiator. In many cases the results for a country from one model suggest a net gain and from another a net loss. Moreover, it is clear that consumers may be a more important group to satisfy in LDCs. In fact, the power of the LDC consumer, especially in urban areas, makes it difficult politically for liberalization to proceed very far. There is a final problem for LDCs of how to improve access to industrial country markets, especially for more processed agricultural goods. In spite of the liberalization goal of the GATT, this remains a likely unattainable gain for LDC policymakers. In this context, LDC negotiators have been largely passive. They confront conflicting advice from analytical models on long-term net effects and they see short-run consequences as generally negative. They face industrialized states with little interest in opening their markets. Even if they believed in the more optimistic long-run effects of the Anderson and Tyers results, LDC action to accept liberalizing their own agriculture, especially without compensatory guarantees (ones that would run counter to market liberalization principles), is highly unlikely. They follow risk aversion when uncertainty is high.

FIVE DEVELOPING COUNTRY CASES

The Uruguay Round revealed a lack of purpose and an inability among developing countries to coalesce around common interests. As noted earlier, only a five-nation food-importing group (W-74) was able to come to agreement on a common position, but even this group saw a key member (Mexico) decide not to endorse its proposal. Why did LDCs fail to develop a coalition from which they could bargain with greater power in the GATT negotiations?

One answer to this question is that domestic pressure groups in LDCs distorted or blocked pursuit of national economic interests. Thus, the bargaining strategies chosen by LDCs were not constructed to pursue their maximum gains. On its own, however, this explanation is insufficient. It does not account for the strong pressure of export groups to gain markets through liberalization. As mentioned, some LDCs (such as Chile and Fiji) joined the Cairns Group, but many others were not in any bargaining coalition in spite of major potential gains from exports, estimated at $30 billion (*The Economist*, 1990). Thus, the additional explanation provided by levels of uncertainty faced by developing nation negotiators helps explain their role at the GATT. The centrality of additional

Table 7.2
Five Developing Country Profiles

	Nigeria	India	Egypt	Jamaica	Mexico
GDP ($ billion)	28.9	235.2	36	3.9	200.7
Share of GDP as agricultural production (%)					
1965	54.0	44.0	29.0	10.0	14.0
1988	34.0	32.0	21.0	6.0	9.0
Per capita GDP ($ hundreds)	250	340	640	1,260	2,010
Growth rates between 1965 and 1980 (%)					
GDP	6.9	3.6	6.8	4.5	6.5
agriculture	1.7	2.5	2.7	0.5	3.2
Percent of labor force in agriculture (%)	65.5	67.1	41.5	27.9	31.2
Exports					
Total ($ million)	7,390	13,313	5,849	832	20,768
Exports/GDP (%)	25.2	5.6	17.0	25.8	11.8
Agriculture ($ million)	327	2,238	728	205	2,425
Agriculture/total (%)	4.4	16.8	12.5	24.6	11.7
Largest export	cocoa	tea	cotton	sugar	coffee
Largest export/total (%)	68.5	21.1	43.2	44.0	15.1
Agriculture exports/GDP	1.1	0.9	2.1	6.4	1.4
Imports					
Total ($ million)	5,553	19,168	23,298	1,428	19,570
Imports/GDP (%)	18.9	8.1	67.9	44.3	11.1
Agriculture ($ million)	495	2,220	5,143	222	2,877
Agriculture/total (%)	8.9	11.6	22.1	15.6	14.7
Largest import	wheat[a]	palm oil	wheat	wheat	maize
Largest import/total (%)	24.3	18.4	19.8	8.7	11.9
Agriculture imports/GDP	1.7	0.9	15.0	6.9	1.6
Welfare implications of complete liberalization ($ million)					
SWOPSIM model: global liberalization					
Producer	263	7,420	313		2,298
Consumer	−543	−1,439	−1,201		−3,337
Net gain	24	1,746	−181		505
SWOPSIM model: industrialized states liberalization only					
Producer	146	4,486	511		1,111
Consumer	−220	−4,662	−801		−1,304
Net gain	−6.2	332	−529		−133
UNCTAD model					
Net	−119.1	21.2	−236.2	−29	−76.2

Sources: Country Tables (FAO, 1990); *World Development Report* (World Bank, 1991); *International Financial Statistics Yearbook* (IMF, 1990); *Agricultural Trade Liberalization and Developing Countries* (USDA, 1990c).
Note: Jamaica's figures available only from the UNCTAD model estimates; others included Jamaica in larger area groups.
[a]For Nigeria, these are 1985 data because of the embargo imposed on wheat in 1988.

considerations can be illustrated by focusing on five specific cases: Nigeria, India, Egypt, Jamaica, and Mexico (data in Table 7.2 indicate their diversity as LDCs).

Before discussing these cases, however, let us examine the suggestion that a coalition of developing nations would be an advantageous strategy to pursue. Presumably, such a coalition would offer developing countries greater bargaining leverage to achieve desired benefits. The low- and middle-income countries have a combined GDP of more than $3 trillion (World Bank, 1991). Excluding those LDC agricultural exporting countries in the Cairns Group, their combined GDP is still more than $2.4 trillion. Although this is less than the GNP of the United States or the European Community, it is still a substantial market relative to total global production, especially for agricultural trade. A coalition of developing countries, therefore, could offer market access as a concession, for example, in return for whatever guaranteed benefits they sought under the GATT framework. Another example of their potential strength at the GATT is cross-issue bargaining. LDCs could link concessions in agriculture that benefited them to their agreement on the protection of intellectual property rights, an area in which developed nations are eager for agreements. Hence, a coalition of developing countries would appear to be a rational bargaining strategy, given consideration of their total interests in the global economy.

However, this potential outcome is not realizable. Individual countries would not fare equally well under any specific outcome. Purely structural forces, based on the problem that not all developing nations could benefit from building a coalition, undercut the motivation to create one. Basically, LDC countries cannot come to an agreement on a single set of interests that might be advanced. For example, whereas Argentina sees agricultural liberalization in its interest, Jamaica gains from protectionism. Current agricultural arrangements allow Jamaica to import grain inexpensively and to sell a portion of its sugar in high-priced industrialized country markets. Another example might be the undercutting effects that access to European agricultural markets offers ACP countries under the Lomé Convention. Such existing differential treatment of certain developing countries would be eroded in a more universal agreement. Thus, special trade agreements such as Lomé have created structural interests that make it difficult for developing countries to reach common ground.

Such different structural situations among LDCs explain some, but not all, of their bargaining behavior in the current round of GATT negotiations. An exploration of five particular cases, representing some diversity of situations among the developing world, illustrates how idiosyncratic factors, such as personality and problems of uncertainty, shaped the particular actions taken by individual LDCs. These factors, coupled with the marginal opportunities to engage in the negotiations afforded many of the LDCs, also help account for the passive posture they assumed.

Jamaica

Jamaica took the leadership in the formation of the W-74 group. Its initiative may be understood as a reflection of the relative clarity of its interests. Agricultural liberalization under the GATT, causing the prices of Jamaica's food imports to rise, would leave it a clear "loser" with little offsetting gains. Moreover, Jamaica is in a unique position among developing countries. Because of its small size, its initiatives are not likely to be seen as competing with the positions of other LDCs. No one imagines it is asserting LDC leadership generally, as might be the case with a large state such as India. Rather, its motive is seen as simple: to improve specific outcomes. Its relative weakness, even among LDCs, gave Jamaica an opportunity to forge a coalition in the Uruguay Round to strengthen its relative bargaining position. Its total GDP of $3 billion is small compared to that of Mexico, which has a GDP of over $176 billion. Jamaica, then, has comparatively little to offer on its own as concessions, for example, market access.

At the same time, however, Jamaica has certain interests that it would like to see advanced in a GATT agreement concerning agriculture. Food imports are 19 percent of Jamaica's merchandise imports, whereas food is 39 percent of all household consumption (World Bank, 1991). Any move toward liberalization would result in a net welfare loss to consumers, assuming accuracy of the prediction of higher world prices for food products. Liberalization in trade would also adversely affect domestic tropical producers, whose preferential access to high-priced U.S. and European markets (the latter as an ACP country) would no longer be guaranteed. The U.S. sugar market is particularly valuable because the current sugar support and quota system protects prices inside the United States; they have been as much as four times world prices in the last decade. Thus, when Jamaica can sell sugar to the United States, it is far more profitable than sales into world markets. Although actual price changes are uncertain, Jamaican negotiators feel confident that without compensation the net welfare effects of agricultural trade liberalization would be negative.[7] With more than 10 percent of its GDP devoted to agricultural trade, Jamaica's dependence upon a favorable outcome in the agricultural negotiations is clear.

Given the relative certainty of adverse effects of trade liberalization, Jamaica has actively sought compensation as part of the Uruguay Round agreements. To do so, it has tried to increase its bargaining strength by building a coalition of nations (the W-74) with similar interests in the negotiations. The case of Jamaica illustrates the role of economic factors in shaping interests. When combined with low uncertainty, such factors help determine clear bargaining goals.

India

The case of India stands in contrast to that of Jamaica. In the past, India has acted as a leader in the international community for LDCs. In the Uruguay Round, however, India has played no active role in LDC coalitions. The most obvious reason is lack of sufficient incentive. As with Jamaica, the circumstances of India's national economic interests help explain its bargaining strategy.

India has a large economy, with a GDP of more than $200 billion, amounting to about one-quarter of all LDC gross production. It is a major producer of agricultural goods. More than 16 percent of all its exports are in the agricultural sector, and more than 60 percent of its labor force are involved in agriculture. Given these characteristics, India would appear to have a large stake in the agricultural liberalization. Indeed, most studies predict that India will have a net welfare gain if some level of trade liberalization is achieved in the agricultural sector.[8]

However, upon closer examination of India's economy, one finds that less than 2 percent of its GDP is generated by agricultural trade. In fact, India is a net food importer, although less than 1 percent of its GDP is in agricultural imports. In light of this, India has perceived itself to have a greater relative stake in the outcome of the nonagricultural negotiations in the Uruguay Round. Although Jamaica had sufficient incentives to form the W-74, India did not have a sufficient differential stake in the agricultural negotiations to incur the cost of joining any LDC coalition, even one such as the Cairns Group, which might promote its potential interest in exporting wheat. In general, India has favored low food prices in the international market, not only because it occasionally imports food, but because it also has an interest in low domestic prices. It cannot afford, however, to subsidize food to the extent that would be necessary to improve the diets of its large very poor populace to a level of minimum nutrition (e.g., enough calories to satisfy a 1.4 metabolic rate). Thus, low-priced food is sought to balance against low-income employment of domestic producers; a low-cost world market reinforces this balance. Arguably, India's interest in the lower world food prices that protectionism has fostered is offset by its interest in market access for its exports. It would therefore be indifferent to any particular outcome in agriculture; more salient would be outcomes in other spheres such as trade in services.

Egypt

Egypt has a significant stake in the outcome of the negotiations concerning agriculture. It has worked in close cooperation with other members of the W-74 to secure guarantees of food aid levels and to maintain the legitimacy of concessional agricultural sales.[9] The explanation for Egypt's participation in the W-74 is similar to that of Jamaica. It did not, however, take on the role of leader for the coalition.

Egypt relies heavily on food imports. More than 22 percent of all its imports are for agricultural products, and agricultural trade comprises more than 17 percent of its GDP. This is markedly higher than most other LDCs. Of the five cases in this analysis, for example, the next highest portion of GDP devoted to agricultural trade is Jamaica, at 13 percent; Mexico follows with only 3 percent. Not surprisingly, Egypt is expected to face the highest net welfare loss of the five cases examined here. Estimates of this loss range from about $180 million to more than $500 million annually.[10] Some of the cost of Egypt's food imports is currently reduced by food aid. Egypt has been the world's largest recipient of food aid in the last decade, receiving during 1987–1989, for example, 1.3–1.5 million metric tons of wheat.[11] Given these circumstances, one can understand the incentive for Egypt to join with Jamaica in the formation of the W-74.

Of interest is why Egypt played such a modest role in this group, despite its seeming major stake in the outcome of agricultural negotiations. Three factors appear to account for such behavior. First, domestic agriculture is heavily regulated; hence, Egypt does not favor liberalization and insists on compensation if industrialized states liberalize. Second, unlike Jamaica, Egypt has significant interests to advance in other areas of the GATT talks. Third, the Egyptian delegation is too small to provide leadership on the food import issue and cover adequately all other Egyptian interests. Moreover, unlike Jamaica's Ransford Smith, Egypt had no single negotiator willing to take personal control of the issue. Structural forces explain Egypt's membership in the W-74; questions of competing interests and a strong desire to appear in favor of liberalization as a principle for nonagricultural commodities explain its lack of initiative and leadership in the W-74 coalition.

Still, on the matter of concessions, Egypt's position is far more certain. A liberalization of agricultural trade would adversely affect consumers in Egypt through price increases (because more than five million tons of wheat are imported commercially) and call into question its food aid, which is largely in the form of "concessional sales" from the United States. The European states and the Cairns Group favor replacing such sales with grant food aid available only to the poorest states. If anything, the estimates of the effects of liberalization in Table 7.2 may understate the net welfare losses that could affect Egypt.

Mexico

Although Mexico was an original member of the W-74 group, it did not join with the other members in signing the October 1990 submission to the Negotiating Group on Agriculture. Its decision to break with the W-74 group is best viewed in light of a shift in its perception of its optimal strategy. This decision, along with its initial decision to join the W-74 coalition, reflect the uncertainty under which LDCs are negotiating in the Uruguay Round.

Of the five countries selected for analysis, Mexico has the highest per capita GDP ($2,010 in 1989). Although the value of its agricultural exports is the largest of all five countries—and hence Mexico would seem to have much to gain from global liberalization without escape or special clauses—on balance, agricultural trade is less important relative to the rest of Mexico's economy. Mexico's imports of food and agricultural products are only 1.6 percent of GDP, compared to 7 percent for Jamaica and 15 percent for Egypt.

Mexico also has a stronger bargaining position than the others in that its GDP is more than $200 billion. In the W-74, Egypt comes in next with a little over $32 billion. While the incentive is great for Egypt and Jamaica to pursue a coalition with Mexico to gain greater bargaining leverage, the incentive for maintaining a coalition with these two is relatively lower for Mexico. Moreover, Mexico's major objective is access to agricultural markets, basically those in the United States. A formula to provide access as a compensatory measure for higher priced food imports proved technically infeasible as the W-74 group refined its proposal. Food aid as compensation did not interest Mexico very much. Hence, the withdrawal of Mexico from the W-74 is understandable, given its superior interest in greater market access rather than food aid and the complex views it maintains as a country with a number of interests in the GATT negotiations.[12] However, the case of Mexico also reveals the uncertainty confronting LDCs. Mexican negotiators feel they have little control over the major decisions affecting the negotiating outcome. Further, this outcome is very unpredictable because the more powerful players show no evidence of compromising. In addition, whatever outcome might be reached among the United States, the European Community, and the Cairns Group, the actual net effect—whether an agreement leads to tiny or large reductions in trade distortions—remains unclear to countries such as Mexico, which would experience both negative and positive consequences.

Nigeria

Although not a member of the W-74, Nigeria claimed that it backed the group's proposal for larger food aid to offset higher import costs expected with trade liberalization. Seeking to determine its interest, Nigeria's trade negotiators relied heavily on studies of various negotiating areas prepared by UNCTAD, paid for by a grant from the United Nations Development Programme (UNDP). These analyses were meant to create a more level playing field for negotiations among countries. LDCs, in contrast to industrialized states, seldom had the economic staff to model consequences of various alternatives that would affect them. Thus, UNCTAD sought to give LDC negotiators information more equal to that available to those from richer states.

Nigerian support for W-74 proposals seems predictable because it has become a large importer of wheat and rice. However, Nigeria was never formally associated with the W-74 for two reasons. First, the philosophy of the Nigerian government is domestic food self-sufficiency. To this end it placed a zero quota on wheat imports in 1988, in clear violation of GATT rules. Indeed, the United States lodged a complaint against Nigeria for this action. As a result, it would have been inconsistent for Nigeria publicly to favor receiving food aid, in wheat presumably, at the same time the country was banning commercial wheat imports in an attempt to encourage local production of wheat and wheat substitutes. Second, Nigeria was once a major agricultural exporter. Oil export revenues in the 1970s, however, created a disadvantage for agriculture as a tradable good. Since that time, Nigeria has experienced a falling national income. This decline, which has fostered serious economic dislocations, has led Nigeria, once considered too wealthy for aid programs, to reappear by the mid-1980s as a country eligible for foreign assistance. It also has been working its way through a series of economic reform measures, much like Mexico. These, in turn, give it an impetus to favor liberalization in principle as it seeks gains in both agriculture and other sectors, provided it can maintain its economic liberalization policies. International pressure is a method to maintain its own adjustment program.

In analyzing the possible benefits of trade changes from the Uruguay Round, Nigeria shares the uncertainty of other LDCs. As a result Nigeria, like India, has taken cautious positions, largely on its own rather than in bargaining groups, certainly in the agricultural field. It shares with LDCs the philosophy that it wants a quid pro quo for any agreement it reaches. This would preferably be in the form of the concessions or perhaps special treatment, allowing more time or scope for domestic policy. Details such as retaining producer subsidies were not clearly worked out in Nigeria's position. Whatever concessions Nigeria might seek, however, they would not be in the area of food aid. Unlike Egypt, which charges 2–3 cents for a loaf of bread, Nigeria is disdainful of food aid and has continued its policy of national food self-sufficiency in spite of economic losses suffered by current low world prices for grain.[13]

Summary

The five country cases discussed above illustrate the variety of views among LDCs. For most, there is a high degree of uncertainty about the effects of prospective GATT agreements and about the desirability of taking positions in the bargaining itself. The grand coalitions to advance LDC economic interests that were put together in the 1970s have ebbed, if not disappeared. LDCs remain motivated to use international negotiations such as those at the GATT to improve their economic situation, but are less clear on what to seek or how to seek it. The result is risk-averse behavior for most LDCs, at least in the GATT agricultural talks.

With respect to the GATT, LDCs exemplify certain important problems in international politics. Because they could not easily identify their interests, determining appropriate strategies or forging coalitions and compromises proved elusive. Reducing uncertainty, usually aided by analytical capacity, was often beyond their reach. Senior negotiators from LDC countries were familiar with liberal economic ideals, and many professed to being true believers in free trade. Beyond this, they had seen some studies forecasting the effects of liberalization. Often, their attention focused upon trade effects and not upon total welfare gains, even though gains by agricultural producers usually were predicted to overshadow losses by consumers from more expensive imported goods (notably food). Because their central focus was on trade and not efficiency effects, their enthusiasm for agricultural liberalization was muted. Further, it was clear they were convinced that, whatever happened, it was unlikely that much liberalization would result. Large increases in agricultural import bills that some might face, therefore, were not as worrisome as they would be if they thought Europe might accept an outcome close to the U.S. or Cairns positions.

In some areas in which some LDCs could perceive clear interests to be advanced, they were able to draw up proposals, as with the food aid proposal of the W-74. These, however, suffered from a serious counterfactual problem. There seemed no way to establish the amount of compensation due a country whose import bill increased. For example, negotiators asked: "Suppose import costs increased. What portion would be caused by liberalization as opposed to increases owing to a crop shortfall in a major exporting country?" Furthermore, the choice of a base year when food prices were especially low would yield results that would not be easily accepted. Therefore, none of the other major groups took it seriously. In addition, there was a fundamental problem of compensation in the GATT. While special exemptions and treatment for LDCs could be agreed upon, the GATT has not been a funding or aid agency. Any compensation for LDCs to induce their support for a GATT agricultural accord would require another agency to arrange it.

This problem was true whether the compensation were in the form of greater food aid or in World Bank or IMF guarantees. Moving the compensation issue to another arena would require LDCs to negotiate separately on such issues. The GATT agreements, at best, might recommend that these other institutions take seriously the claims or needs of LDCs that exposed themselves to potential trade harm by agreeing to liberalization. This formula was rather a chimera as LDCs had little choice. Would they, by not agreeing, alter the prices they faced? Unlikely. Further, there was little interest in these other "appropriate" bodies to take responsibility for "compensation." The W-74 idea of market-correcting food aid flows had no organizational home.[14]

The eventual departure of Mexico from the final W-74 statement illustrates another problem in aggregating LDC interests. Although Mexico stood to lose on its import bill, the prospect that it would receive large amounts of food aid (or even any) was unlikely because it was the most wealthy of the group. It had not been a principal recipient of food aid in the 1980s, as were Egypt and Jamaica. Mexico's prime interest was in access to the U.S. market, a goal less widely shared by other LDCs. Putting market access into a compensatory proposal rather confused the issue. Market access could offer LDCs far more important economic gains, but these varied widely. Some LDCs, who already enjoyed preferential treatment in entering European markets (albeit largely for selected unprocessed goods) under the Lomé Convention, saw a universality of market access as reducing, not increasing, their economic advantage. Mexico was the major proponent of the idea of a compensatory "market share," but the idea was received as impractical. In the face of this reception, it is understandable why Mexico lost interest in the W-74 proposal as the final offers were made in October 1990. Indeed, by then, the framework for a US-Canada-Mexico free trade agreement had been accepted, further reducing Mexico's interest in the W-74 proposal.

CONCLUSION:
WEAK BARGAINING AND UNCERTAIN INTERESTS

Should LDCs have been more active in GATT agricultural talks, given their stake in the outcome? Could they have been more effective in pursuing their interests, at least to the extent these were discernable? Major studies analyzing the effects of trade liberalization all found substantial impacts on LDCs. Whether they liberalized themselves or merely faced the effects of OECD country liberalization, they did have stakes. The problem for them was the degree of confidence they could have as to the magnitude and timing of effects of liberalization. Nonetheless, the very assumptions of the GATT expected LDC negotiators to respect the "truths" of economic liberalism, thus exhibiting the same "enlightenment" as industrialized states.[15]

The short-term failure of agricultural liberalization at the Uruguay Round lies principally in the major players' inability to overcome the reluctance of certain of their domestic producer groups to lose benefits. The failure of LDCs to achieve gains from liberalization, even through the unilateral steps they could take, lies not with powerful producer opposition. Rather, it lies with a fear that the lowering of border controls would result in the loss of a major source of revenue. LDCs gain a far higher portion of their governmental budget resources from taxes on trade than industrial countries; industrial country taxpayers tend to subsidize trade rather than have it as a source of government revenue. In light of this, it is amazing that LDC trade growth has been as rapid as it has, given their high barriers to trade.

Should LDCs give more attention to seeking GATT rules that would force others to liberalize? Is this an identifiable interest around which they could organize in negotiations? Generally, the answer is yes. The experience of the fastest growing LDCs suggests that trade expansion does serve to strengthen the pace of economic development. However configured, an export-oriented, productive sector is a basic tenet of theories of comparative advantage and a rationale for trade that leads to an enhanced international division of labor in the world (World Bank, 1991). Trade growth has spurred growth in both industrial and developing countries since the 1960s, according to most analyses (Chenery and Srinivasan, 1988). If one accepts the results of the Tyers and Anderson projections for liberalization gains discussed earlier, not only would world agricultural trade grow, but LDCs would benefit somewhat from OECD country liberalization (as a group) and do even better if they were to liberalize themselves. This optimistic estimate has been a basis for ongoing macroeconomic advice to LDCs from international financial institutions. Potential benefits from trade have been proposed as a reason for LDCs to use the GATT as a political lever to liberalize their own economies (Paarlberg, 1989a). The decline in world growth rates in the last two decades has increased problems facing officials from the developing world: rapid population growth, a slowdown in productivity, growing debt and service burdens, and ecological deterioration. The difficulties of these problems dominate their attention. They make issues such as the elimination of distorting macroeconomic policies of far greater concern for most LDC countries than those raised by agriculture in the GATT. Furthermore, the GATT negotiations are part of larger global economic policymaking. As such, the roles played by various blocs in the GATT parallel patterns of weakness and strength in other international policy bargaining in the 1990s. In Geneva, the LDCs are welcomed as participants, but not expected to be decisionmakers. Their role in the world is as price and concession takers. Their capacity as producers does not yet make them able to influence global markets.

Given the marginal interest of the GATT to some LDC countries, coalition-building becomes ever harder under conditions of uncertainty. Although coalitions might make greater international gains possible, they may not materialize as long as it pays for individual countries to defect from a coalition. That is a central reason for establishing enforceable rules, that is, penalties that facilitate cooperation toward mutual gain. For LDCs, however, their position is so weak and so insufficiently clear regarding what interests they should pursue (at least as seen through their eyes) that in the agriculture negotiations they could build but one weak coalition, and even then Mexico defected from it to pursue short-run gains. The combined effects of uncertainty and inequality characterize the statements of how the LDC negotiators saw their situation. Their statements fit the literature on how belief systems can influence outcomes. They consistently saw their best strategy as caution in the face of low confidence about costs and benefits; they were risk averse under conditions of uncertainty.

It could be argued that LDCs had no choice. They could have made a fuss, however, as many LDCs did in the 1979 international talks on establishing a set of nationally coordinated grain reserves. At that juncture, LDCs walked out on a draft agreement seeking cereal price stability and food security in the world based on a high price band for cereals. After the United States and the European Community reached a compromise agreement in February 1979, the Third World states, led by India, denounced its terms and killed what was already a fragile arrangement.

In the case of the Uruguay Round, LDCs have not been interested in bargaining for lower food prices. Nor have they sought access that would be differentially helpful to developing countries. Finally, they have not sought an agreement that exempted them from all responsibilities or obligations (although some LDCs took this position). Although delegates spoke positively of looking for an agreement in which they would inevitably derive some advantages, they seldom could prescribe concretely what advantages these would be. As a group, and individually, LDC negotiators found it difficult to agree, partly because they had different interests and partly because they did not know what was in their interests.

NOTES

1. Exclusionary options include (1) unilateral strategies by a major country, e.g., the U.S. bilateral arrangements, as in the Canadian-U.S. free trade pact; (2) regional agreements, as in the expanding network of EC rules (including the relationship between the EC and the African, Caribbean, and Pacific [ACP] developing countries worked out at the Lomé Convention); and (3) arrangements negotiated by major players, as in the G-7, which become translated into working rules for policy coordination as has occurred in the area of monetary policy. See Oye (forthcoming) for an analysis of alternative political arrangements for achieving liberalization, comparing the 1930s with the 1980s.

2. The gains from freer trade do not necessarily require as universal an approach as was imbedded in the minds of policymakers at the end of World War II, when many of the principles and institutions for a liberal/capitalist world economic order were established (Ikenberry, 1992).

3. This interpretation of the role of ideas interacting with material bases for interest in shaping action is expressed by Max Weber, as cited in Goldstein and Keohane (1990).

4. On the role of ideas that drive a liberal trade perspective, see Ruggie (1982).

5. This "distortion" view to explain "illiberal" trade policy is well expressed in a recent monograph by a group of economists, some active in the GATT negotiations themselves (see Knudsen et al., 1990).

6. In Chapter 4, Rapkin and George similarly describe the Japanese state as largely reactive to the proposals and actions of others in the Uruguay Round negotiations.

7. The lack of uncertainty is also furthered by the relative sophistication of Jamaican diplomats. Many, such as Ransford Smith, Jamaica's delegate to the GATT talks, have a reasonable grounding in economic analysis. The ability to analyze and utilize information is another factor explaining why Jamaica was able to organize a group with a focused stake and interest in the outcome of the negotiations.

8. As can be seen from Figure 7.2, the welfare gains accrue to the agricultural producers, whereas the consumers suffer a net loss due to higher prices. On balance, however, the predicted net gains for India range from about $20 million (UNCTAD, 1990b) to more than $1.7 billion (USDA, 1990c).

9. This is from an interview with Maamoum Ab Del-Fatah, June 1990, Geneva. As Egypt's delegate to the GATT negotiations, he expressed a deep concern for the outcome of the negotiations on concessions for LDCs and particularly food-importing countries.

10. These results are not entirely comparable, as they result from different liberalization scenarios as outlined previously in this chapter. However, the direction of change is the same for all scenarios in this case, with the real question being that of magnitude. What is clear is that Egypt is predicted to suffer large welfare losses relative to those of other actors.

11. These levels of food aid put Egypt above Bangladesh as the largest recipient of food aid.

12. In an interview on June 19, 1990, the chief Mexican negotiator on agriculture, Counselor Alejandro de la Peña, asserted that it would be difficult for Mexico to balance its various interests in the GATT, especially when little interest was shown by the United States or EC in a formula for market access for competitive crops.

13. In an interview on June 20, 1990, Minister Udoh, Nigeria's representative to the United Nations and to the GATT in Geneva, admitted that Nigeria had a problem in losses of revenue due to food imports, which would worsen under liberalization (he had been using UNCTAD figures to organize Nigeria's position). He claimed further that food aid was a basic disincentive that should be discouraged except as a short-term bridge.

14. John Parotte, executive director of the International Wheat Council (IWC), for instance, expressed little interest or anticipation that food aid as compensation to LDCs (as discussed by the W-74 Group) would be relevant to or taken up readily by his secretariat. The IWC was asked to become the oversight body for the Food Aid Convention, a result of the sixth, or Kennedy Round, of MTNs. At that time, agriculture issues were first addressed, but not resolved, except for agreement upon food aid burden sharing. This took the form of a convention whereby food aid would be given by a number of countries—not just food exporters such as the United States and Canada, but also importers among the industrial countries in Europe and Japan. This was an appeasement to wheat exporters by increasing demand for their wheat through expanding demand in poor countries that would receive the wheat as food aid.

15. In a June 1990 interview, a delegate from one of the W-74 expressed three times the view that, whether the proposals of his country were met or not, it would accept all facets of the Uruguay Round because they appreciated the logic of "liberal" trade. Indeed, I was asked to be sure to convey this point to the U.S. delegation.

Harald von Witzke
Ulrich Hausner

8

Endogenous Agricultural and Trade Policy in Open Economies: Implications for the GATT

The economic environment of agriculture has changed significantly in the past few decades. Two of these changes have immediate implications for the topic of this chapter. In the past, agriculture in many countries produced predominantly for the domestic market and had relatively few links with the rest of the economy. Beginning in the 1960s, however, agriculture became more open, and it became more integrated into the national economies. These two developments have made agriculture increasingly sensitive to the general economic environment outside of agriculture both at home and abroad, and to agricultural and trade policies in foreign countries.

Around the globe, agriculture appears to have two characteristics in common: (1) it is subject to various kinds of government (market) intervention, and (2) there is a characteristic pattern of government involvement in the course of economic development. In less-developed countries, where agriculture is large in terms of both employment and its share in GNP, agriculture tends to be taxed, whereas in developed countries, where agriculture is only a relatively small industry, it tends to be subsidized.

This chapter analyzes the determinants of agricultural price policy intervention and discusses their implications for the reform of the international agricultural trade regime. The chapter first examines agricultural price policy formation in the course of economic development. Then it analyzes the determinants of the level of agricultural price support in developed countries. The chapter concludes with some thoughts on endogenous interactions of national agricultural policy decisions in the context of multilateral trade negotiations under the GATT, in which agricultural protectionism and agricultural policy reform have played a central role in recent years.

POLITICAL ECONOMY OF AGRICULTURAL PRICE POLICY IN ECONOMIC DEVELOPMENT

The typical pattern of government market intervention in agriculture is depicted in Figure 8.1, in which the vertical axis denotes the price and the horizontal axis denotes the GNP as an indicator of the level of economic development. The function $P_p P'_p$ depicts the producer price relative to the world price, P_w, which is identical to the horizontal axis.

Figure 8.1 suggests a rather surprising pattern of government market intervention in the course of economic development. At low levels of economic development, agriculture is taxed; that is, the producer price is below the world price. With increasing economic wealth, governments switch from taxing agriculture to subsidizing it, and the producer price exceeds the international level.

Public choice theory offers a straightforward explanation for this phenomenon.[1] In analogy to typical goods or input markets, one can think of political economic markets. Here we focus on the market for a regulated agricultural commodity price. In this market, the supply curve represents the marginal costs, and the demand curve the marginal benefits to the political decisionmaker of alternative levels of the regulated price. In Figure 8.2, the vertical axis denotes the marginal political economic costs and benefits of alternative levels of a government-regulated agricultural producer price, and the horizontal axis denotes the producer price relative to the world price.

At low levels of economic development the marginal political economic benefits of supporting the farm price above international levels are low (MB_0). The marginal political economic costs of doing so are high despite the fact that the majority of the labor force is engaged in agriculture (MC_0).

The marginal benefits of agricultural price support are low because the nonagricultural population is a relatively small group, and lives concentrated in urban areas, in close proximity to decisionmakers, with relatively good infrastructure. All of this results in comparatively low costs of organizing an interest group (see Olson, 1965). Moreover, the urban population tends to be relatively better educated than its rural counterpart; hence, it better understands the effects of agricultural policy. The prime interest of the nonagricultural population tends to be low food prices. This is because in the early stages of economic development, incomes are low and the share of income spent for food is high. Hence, low food prices have a significant impact on real wages and incomes. The agricultural population, on the other hand, represents the majority of the total population. They live dispersed in rural areas, far from decisionmaking centers, with poor infrastructure. Hence, organizing a lobby is relatively costly. Moreover, the agricultural population tends not to be very well informed. Frequently, it does not know which macroeconomic and agricultural policies are pursued by the government and what their economic implications are.

The low marginal benefits of supporting agriculture and the high marginal cost of doing so result in a political economic equilibrium in which the agricultural producer price is below the world price. In Figure 8.2, this is the intersection of MC_0 and MB_0 which results in $P_0 < P_w$.

Figure 8.1
The Agricultural Producer Price
in the Course of Economic Development

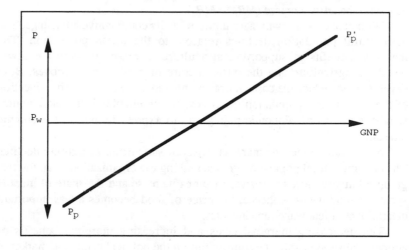

Figure 8.2
The Political Economic Equilibrium Producer Price
in the Course of Economic Development

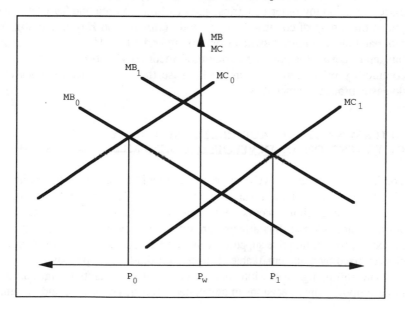

In the course of economic development, the relative political economic success of agriculture tends to grow. The marginal political economic costs of supporting agriculture decline (MC_0 to MC_1) and the marginal political economic benefits increase (MB_0 to MB_1).

With economic growth, agriculture loses its comparative advantage. The agricultural population declines relative to the urban population. The marginal benefits of supporting agriculture increase, as there are fewer people in agriculture and the infrastructure in rural areas improves. Both developments reduce the costs of organizing a lobby. Moreover, the education of the agricultural population improves, which enables it to better understand the effects of economic policy and to express its political economic interests.

At the same time, the marginal costs of supporting agriculture decline. The nonagricultural population grows, making the organization of an interest group relatively more expensive. Incomes increase and the share of income spent for food declines; hence, the price of food becomes a less important determinant of real wages and incomes.

The decreasing marginal costs and increasing marginal benefits of agricultural support shift the equilibrium on the political economic market in agriculture to the right. Countries switch from taxing agriculture to subsidizing it. In Figure 8.2, the new equilibrium is given by the intersection of MC_1 and MB_1; the resulting price is $P_1 > P_w$.

In the course of economic development, more and more countries change their agricultural policy toward subsidies. Whereas the United States and most West European countries have a long tradition of subsidizing agriculture,[2] many other countries, such as South Korea and Taiwan, have joined this group of countries only recently (Honma and Hayami, 1986). As more and more countries switch from taxing agriculture to subsidizing it, the budgetary costs of supporting agricultural incomes via distorted agricultural commodity prices tend to increase because the world price declines and domestic production increases.

DETERMINANTS OF AGRICULTURAL POLICY INTERVENTION IN DEVELOPED COUNTRIES

The level of economic development is only one in a number of determinants of agricultural policy formation. Economic development, although fluctuating over time, occurs continuously—in rolling waves rather than abrupt changes—and thus affects agricultural policy only over longer time periods. Agricultural price support levels in developed countries, however, are characterized by quite remarkable changes over shorter time periods.

The following discussion focuses on the determinants of agricultural price support policy decisions in developed countries over time and presents empirical evidence for the United States. It concentrates on the right-hand-sides of Figures 8.1 and 8.2, in which the producer price is above the world price. The theoretical framework used is a reduced form model of wheat and corn policy formation in the United States. It represents a supply-side approach to policy modeling in that it is based on the political economic calculus of the agricultural policymaker as the supplier of a minimum producer price. Although we specifically focus on the United States, analogous models can be, and have been, tested empirically for other developed countries, such as Japan or the European Community, with results comparable to those reported here (Riethmuller and Roe, 1986; von Witzke, 1986).

System of Agricultural Price Support

One central element of U.S. grain policies in the last few decades has been the loan rate, which provides a price floor to producers. In the early 1960s, producer prices were "decoupled" from the loan rate. Beginning in 1963–1964, the loan rate was supplemented by direct payments proportional to production. A target price was introduced in 1974–1975, in which the difference between the target price and the loan rate or market price (whichever is higher) is a deficiency payment.

Other measures of market intervention have been employed as well, such as "payment-in-kind" subsidies or acreage reduction programs.[3] Although it may be desirable to incorporate some of these instruments into an analysis of U.S. wheat and corn price policy decisions, this discussion focuses only on the level of producer price support in the form of a target price.

The target price does not affect consumers in the form of a higher price. Consumers pay the loan rate or the world market price, whichever is higher. In fact, during the time period analyzed here, loan rate and world market price were usually very close. Taxpayers, however, are affected by this type of agricultural producer price support, as there are budgetary expenditures involved. Total deficiency payments are the difference between the target price and the loan rate or world price, multiplied by the quantity produced at the target price. If the loan rate is above the world price, there are additional budgetary expenditures; their extent depends on storage costs, the extent of surplus production, the form of surplus disposal, and the difference between the loan rate and world price.

Theoretical Framework

A single agricultural policymaker is assumed to have preferences over consumers and producers. These preferences can be represented by a utility function, u, which is assumed to be strictly concave. The policymaker's constrained maximization problem is:

$$\max u(x_1, x_2) \tag{1}$$

such that

$$c_1(x_3) \geq x_1 \tag{2}$$

and

$$c_2(x_3) \geq x_2 \tag{3}$$

In equation (1), agricultural producer income (x_1) can be interpreted to represent the policymaker's political support from farmers, and budgetary expenditures (x_2) caused by the deficiency payment system represent the loss in political support from the rest of the electorate. The two constraints, equations (2) and (3), are assumed to be linear and continuous. Both agricultural producer income in equation (2) and budgetary expenditures in equation (3) are functions of the target price, or minimum producer price (x_3). The policymaker chooses x_3 in order to maximize utility. The optimum condition of this maximization problem is given by equation (4).[4]

$$\frac{\partial u}{\partial x_1} \cdot \frac{\partial c_1}{\partial x_3} + \frac{\partial u}{\partial x_2} \cdot \frac{\partial c_2}{\partial x_3} = 0 \tag{4}$$

Equation (4) has an obvious political economic interpretation. The policymaker sets the target price such that the marginal political economic benefits via growing political support from agricultural producers equals the marginal political economic costs via reduced support from taxpayers resulting from an increase in the target price.

As the policymaker's utility function is assumed to be strictly concave, there is a solution to this problem for x_3. Let the solution be approximated by the following statistical model:

$$x_{3t}^0 = \alpha_0 + \alpha_1 x_{1t} + \alpha_2 x_{2t} + \phi_t \tag{5}$$

where x_{3t}^0 denotes the optimum price in period t. Appendix I to this chapter presents the derivation of equation (5).

In the real world, policymakers face various contractual constraints in adjusting a government regulated price over time. Usually, decisions on the price level involve time costs, which tend to increase with increasing extent of price adjustments. Major price changes may even require special legislation. Often, policymakers are also constrained by bills that contain guidelines for price adjustments over time. U.S. farm bills represent examples of this kind of constraint.[5]

A very common and convenient way to account for such constraints is the Nerlovian partial adjustment approach (Nerlove, 1958), which implies that the actual difference in the target price between two periods is a constant fraction of the difference between the optimal price and the past price, as represented by equation (6).

$$x_{3t} - x_{3t-1} = \gamma(x_{3t}^0 - x_{3t-1}) + \theta_t \tag{6}$$

where $0 < \gamma \le 1$; and θ_t is the error term, assumed to be normally and independently distributed. Combining equations (5) and (6) yields:

$$x_{3t} = \beta_0 + \beta_3 x_{3t-1} + \beta_1 x_{1t} + \beta_2 x_{2t} + \mu_t \tag{7}$$

where $\quad \beta_0 = \gamma\alpha_0; \ \beta_3 = 1 - \gamma; \ \beta_1 = \gamma\alpha_1; \ \text{and} \ \beta_2 = \gamma\alpha_2.$

Empirical Analysis

In equation (7), the producer price for t is determined by the agricultural policymaker at some prior time. Let this be at time $t-1$. At this time, the policymaker knows neither x_{1t} nor x_{2t}. Hence, x_{1t} and x_{2t} have to be substituted by their respective expected values x_{1t*} and x_{2t*}. Economic theory suggests that economic agents form expectations based on the available information at the time of the decision, which is commonly denoted as:

$$x_{1t*} = E(x_{1t}|I_{t-1}) \tag{8}$$

$$x_{2t*} = E(x_{2t}|I_{t-1}) \tag{9}$$

Moreover,

$$x_{1t} = x_{1t*} + v_t \tag{10}$$

$$x_{2t} = x_{2t*} + w_t \tag{11}$$

Substituting equations (10) and (11) into equation (7) yields:

$$x_{3t} = \beta_0 + \beta_3 x_{3t-1} + \beta_1 x_{1t}^* + \beta_2 x_{2t}^* + \varepsilon_t \tag{12}$$

where ε_t is an error term.

The nature of the error term in equation (12) deserves some further discussion. As Nelson (1975) has noted, the error term typically results in some complications when exogenous variables have to be substituted by their anticipations. A closer look at ε_t reveals that this is the case here. As $\varepsilon_t = \mu_t + \beta_1 v_t + \beta_2 w_t$, the use of Ordinary Least Squares (OLS) would yield inconsistent estimates. In essence, this problem requires the use of suitable instrument variables for the anticipations (e.g., Wallis, 1980; McCallum, 1976).

We are now in a position to discuss the expected signs of the parameters. According to the theoretical analysis, the sign of β_0 is not determined a priori. In developed countries in which agriculture tends to be subsidized, such as in the United States, one would expect the signs of β_1 and β_2 to be negative. That is, a relatively low (high) expected agricultural income or relatively low (high) expected budgetary expenditures lead to a relatively high (low) producer support price. As $0<\gamma\leq 1$ and $\beta_3 = 1-\gamma$, β_3 can be expected to be greater than or equal to zero.

The empirical analysis is over the time period 1963–1964 to 1983–1984. The data used are from USDA (1984) publications. All monetary variables have been deflated by the consumer price index. Detailed information on the specific income situation of U.S. wheat and corn farmers is not available. As policymakers do not have such information either, a proxy can be used without a major risk of biased estimates. A number of different proxies for x_3 could be used in principle, such as overall farm income or farm income in major grain-producing states. We have elected to use the U.S. share in world wheat and corn exports. The U.S. grain sector was very export oriented during the time period analyzed here. Hence, the U.S. share in world exports is commonly perceived as a good indicator of the income situation of farmers producing wheat and/or corn.

The instruments for the anticipations x_{1t^*} and x_{2t^*} were estimated via autoregressions. The time lag was chosen for each time series based on the significance of the coefficients. The results are summarized in Appendix II to this chapter. The superscripts w and c denote wheat and corn, respectively.

The empirical test of equation (12) gives the following results:[6]

$$x_{3t}^w = 4.207 + 0.6362\,x_{3t-1}^w - 0.0808\,x_{1t^*}^w - 0.6049\,x_{2t^*}^w$$
$$\phantom{x_{3t}^w =}(2.90)\quad\ (5.21)\qquad\ \ (-2.73)\qquad (-2.59)\qquad\qquad (13)$$
$$\overline{R}^2 = 0.853;\ \rho = -0.291\ (-1.16)$$

$$x_{3t}^c = 1.023 + 0.9313\,x_{3t-1}^c - 0.0090\,x_{1t^*}^c - 0.2898\,x_{2t^*}^c$$
$$\phantom{x_{3t}^c =}(3.09)\quad\ (7.62)\qquad\ \ (-3.04)\qquad (-2.74)\qquad\qquad (14)$$
$$\overline{R}^2 = 0.801;\ \rho - 0.175\ (-0.696)$$

Based on the results of the regression analyses, the central hypotheses developed in this chapter cannot be rejected. All coefficients have the expected signs and are highly significant. The coefficients for x_{3t-1} have positive signs, and those for x_{1t^*} and x_{2t^*} have negative signs in both equations: that is, a relatively low (high) expected share in world exports (proxy for producer income) or relatively low (high) budgetary expenditures result in a comparatively high (low) producer support price, ceteris paribus. These results are similar to those obtained in time series analyses of the determinants of agricultural price support in other developed countries, such as Japan or the European Community (e.g., Riethmuller and Roe, 1986; von Witzke, 1986). They suggest that in developed countries, fluctuations in agricultural price support over time are largely determined by producer incomes and budgetary expenditures caused by price support.

ENDOGENOUS AGRICULTURAL POLICY INTERDEPENDENCE: SOME IMPLICATIONS FOR INTERNATIONAL AGRICULTURAL AND TRADE POLICY REFORM

Multilateral trade negotiations under the General Agreement on Tariffs and Trade have been quite successful in removing barriers to trade and distortions of international competition in many industries. One of the most notable exceptions has been agriculture. Until the Uruguay Round, agricultural trade and policy issues have rarely been dealt with in GATT negotiations. The endogenous nature of agricultural policy together with increasing global trade in food and agricultural commodities have created incentives for many countries, especially food-exporting developed countries that subsidize agriculture, to pursue internationally coordinated strategies aimed at leading to a more liberal world agricultural trade regime.

As discussed earlier, with economic growth, government reduces the taxation of agriculture, or increases its subsidization; some countries switch from taxing agriculture to subsidizing it. Due to this endogenous change in agricultural policy, world prices of agricultural commodities have become more and more depressed relative to what they would be under free trade.[7]

This also suggests that the effects of agricultural and trade policies of those countries that attempt to support their agricultural sectors are, to a large extent, offsetting each other (Resources for the Future, 1988). A country, in an attempt to support agriculture, can reduce the world price. This, in turn, triggers additional upward adjustments in support price levels in other countries with an analogous effect on world prices. Nowhere is agriculture likely to be much better off than before the price-support escalation. Taxpayers and/or consumers—depending on the specific form of price support—have to bear the budgetary consequences of this process. In the 1980s, budgetary expenditures in the United States and in the European Community—the two most important food and agricultural commodity-trading countries—more than doubled. As the persistent agricultural income problem in developed countries cannot be alleviated in the long run by price support, and as agricultural price support appears to result in growing budgetary expenditures, there certainly is a growing incentive for each developed country to initiate agricultural and trade policy reform.

Unilateral liberalization of agricultural and trade policy, however, is not very likely to be a feasible strategy in open economies when policy decisions are endogenous. Under these conditions, one country's agricultural and trade policy reform would be counteracted by other countries' endogenous policy adjustments. To illustrate the political economic problems of unilateral agricultural and trade policy "disarmament," assume a world of only two large countries, here referred to as the European Community and the United States.[8] Assume further that the United States discontinued agricultural price support. The resulting decline in U.S. production and exports would increase world market prices. The main driving forces of agricultural price support over time in the European Community are essentially the same as in the United States, namely, agricultural incomes and budgetary expenditures (von Witzke, 1986). Under the system of price support in the European Community and the present surplus production, increasing world prices of agricultural commodities would reduce EC budgetary expenditures. This, in turn, would lead to higher support prices there and thus increased EC exports and declining world prices. Compared to an unchanged EC agricultural policy, U.S. agriculture would have to bear higher costs of adjustment to the unilateral policy change. These higher costs of adjustment in U.S. agriculture are simply due to the fact that agricultural policymakers in the European Community would be free-riding on U.S. agricultural and trade policy liberalization.

In fact, such a policy reaction could be observed in the past under comparable circumstances. In the early to mid-1980s, the European Community was expected by many to face financial collapse or to reduce significantly the level of price support. For a number of reasons, this did not happen, however, until the second half of the 1980s. Two of the reasons are linked to macroeconomic and agricultural policy decisions in the United States. In the first half of the 1980s, the value of the U.S. dollar steadily increased against the currencies of the EC countries. This acted to reduce the difference between EC support prices and world market prices in terms of the ECU. It also reduced the export subsidies per unit and, thus, total budgetary expenditures, which, in turn, led to higher support prices in the European Community. In the same time period, budgetary expenditures of agricultural price support in the United States had reached levels that were politically no longer tolerable. As it appeared infeasible to reduce real support prices to an extent that would significantly reduce budgetary expenditures, acreage reduction programs were introduced. These programs, together with unfavorable weather conditions in the United States, reduced agricultural production and thus exports, again increasing world prices and thereby contributing to relatively higher price support in the European Community.

CONCLUSION

The theory of endogenous institutional choice stipulates that changes in the economic environment act to induce institutional change (Hayami and Ruttan, 1985). Several changes in the economic environment of world agriculture have rendered the existing international agricultural trade regime inadequate. Food has become increasingly abundant (see Ruttan and von Witzke, 1990). More and more countries have switched from taxing agriculture to subsidizing it; and the international interdependence of national farm economies has grown.

Results from time series analyses of the determinants of agricultural price support in developed countries such as the United States, Japan, and the European Community are rather consistent; suggesting fluctuations in agricultural price support over time are largely determined by producer incomes and budgetary expenditures. In the United States, a relatively low (high) expected share in world exports of corn and wheat (a proxy for producer income) or relatively low (high) budgetary expenditures for corn and wheat result, ceteris paribus, in a comparatively high (low) producer support price. Elements of inertia, as measured by the lagged producer support price, significantly constrain the effects of the other determinants on the yearly price adjustments.

Due to their high budgetary costs, policymakers can no longer provide political economic rents to farmers via distortionary agricultural and trade policies. Most developed countries have an incentive to reform their policies. However, unilateral policy changes, intended to further agricultural trade liberalization, are not likely to be politically feasible, as they would be counteracted by other countries' free riding on one country's policy reform. That is, increasing world market prices would decrease budgetary pressures and, applying the central hypothesis of this chapter, result in higher support prices in other countries. Increased exports from these countries would lead to declining world prices and thus higher costs of adjustments to the country that unilaterally discontinued its agricultural price support.

A liberal agricultural trade regime now favored by many countries represents an international public good. No country, acting on its own, can supply itself with such institutional change of the international agricultural trade regime except through cooperation with other countries (Runge, von Witzke, and Thompson, 1989). A better understanding of the forces that have shaped national agricultural and trade policies as well as the present international agricultural and trade regime will certainly facilitate the development of institutional arrangements that can lead to free(r) trade in agriculture. As previous chapters in this volume have shown, the story of agriculture in the Uruguay Round suggests that the design of a politically feasible reform of the international agricultural trade regime remains an important challenge for policymakers and for agricultural economic research.

APPENDIX 8.1:
THE THEORETICAL DERIVATION
OF THE REDUCED FORM MODEL

The policymaker's constrained maximization problem is given by

$$\max u(x_1, x_2) \tag{A1}$$

such that

$$c_1(x_3) \geq x_1 \tag{A2}$$

and

$$c_2(x_3) \geq x_2 \tag{A3}$$

where

$x_1 \equiv$ producer income
$x_2 \equiv$ budgetary expenditure
$x_3 \equiv$ target price (minimum producer price)

It is assumed that $u: R^2 \rightarrow R$ is twice differentiable and strictly concave, and that the underlying preferences are locally nonsatiated. Both constraints are assumed to be continuously differentiable and linear. Given the strict concavity of the objective function and the linear constraints, we know that if there exists an x^0 that locally maximizes $u(x)$ such that $c_j(x) \geq 0$ ($j = 1, 2$, and $x \in R^3$) then x^0 also globally maximizes $u(x)$ such that $c_j(x) \geq 0$. Furthermore, because preferences are locally nonsatiated, equations (A2) and (A3) hold with equality; that is, we have an equality-constrained maximization problem. Because the rank condition is satisfied (i.e., rank $[D\,c(x)] = 2$), we can apply Lagrange's Theorem. Define the Lagrangian L: $R^3 \times R^2 \rightarrow R$ by

$$L(x,\lambda) = u(x_1, x_2) - \lambda_1(c_1[x_3] - x_1) - \lambda_2(c_2[x_3] - x_2). \tag{A4}$$

The first-order derivative of the Lagrangian with respect to x and λ provides the First Order Necessary Conditions (FONCs) for x_0 being a local (and global) maximizer of $u(x)$ such that $c(x) = 0$:

$$D\,L(x^0, \lambda^0) = 0 \tag{A5}$$

$$x_1: \quad \partial u/\partial x_1(x^0) + \lambda_1^0 = 0 \tag{A5a}$$

$$x_2: \quad \partial u/\partial x_2(x^0) + \lambda_1^0 = 0 \tag{A5b}$$

$$x_3: \quad -\lambda_1^0(\partial c_1/\partial x_3)\,(x^0) - \lambda_2^0(\partial c_2/\partial x_3)\,(x^0) = 0 \tag{A5c}$$

$$\lambda_1: \quad -c_1(x_3^0) + x_1^0 = 0 \tag{A5d}$$

$$\lambda_2: \quad -c_2(x_3^0) + x_2^0 = 0 \tag{A5e}$$

Combining equations (A5a) and (A5b) yields the equilibrium condition for a government-controlled producer support price:

$$\frac{\partial u/\partial x_1}{\partial u/\partial x_2}(x^0) = -\frac{\partial c_2/\partial x_3}{\partial c_1/\partial x_3}(x^0) \tag{A6}$$

That is, the agricultural policymaker sets the minimum producer price x_3, such that the ratio of marginal political benefits equals minus the reverse ratio of marginal costs.

Assuming that $D^2 u(x)$ is negative for all $x \in R^2$ (which is sufficient for u to be strictly concave on R^2), that is, assuming that

$$\partial^2 u/\partial x_1^2\,(x) < 0 \tag{A7a}$$

$$\partial^2 u/\partial x_2^2\,(x) < 0 \tag{A7b}$$

$$\partial^2 u/\partial x_1^2(x)\partial^2 u/\partial_2^2(x) - (\partial^2 u/\partial x_1\partial x_2[x])^2 > 0 \tag{A7c}$$

and assuming that

$$\partial u/\partial x_1(x) > 0 \tag{A7d}$$

$$\partial u/\partial x_2(x) < 0 \tag{A7e}$$

$$\partial c_1/\partial x_3\,(x) > 0 \tag{A7f}$$

$$\partial c_2/\partial x_3\,(x) > 0 \tag{A7g}$$

$$\partial^2 c_1/\partial x_3^2(x) = \partial^2 c_2/\partial x_3^2(x) = 0 \tag{A7h}$$

$$\partial^2 u/\partial x_1\partial x_2(x) = \partial^2 u/\partial x_2\partial x_1(x) < 0 \tag{A7i}$$

for all $x \in R^3$ guarantees that the determinant of the second derivative of L with respect to x^3 and λ is strictly less than zero,

$$\det [D^2 L(x^0, \lambda^0)] < 0 \tag{A8}$$

that is, $D^2 L(x^0, \lambda^0)$ is nonsingular.

The assumptions formulated in equations (A7a) through (A7i) are consequences of basic economic considerations about (decreasing) marginal returns, the strict concavity of the objective function, the linear constraints, and Young's Theorem. Albeit somewhat restrictive, they constitute an economically plausible theoretical framework. An increase (decrease) in producer income, at the margin, increases (decreases) the policymaker's utility—that is, political support, equation (A7d)—whereas an increase (decrease) in budgetary expenditures leads to a decrease (increase) in utility, equation A7e. Equations (A7f) and (A7g) imply increasing marginal costs of "producing" income and budgetary expenditures via setting the support price. The equalities in equation (A7h) are a consequence of the linear constraints. The second-order cross partial derivatives of the objective function, equation (A7i), are assumed to be negative: given that an increase in political support (utility) based on an increase in producer income (x_1) occurred, a subsequent increase in budgetary expenditures (x_2) (via an increase in support prices set by the policymaker) decreases the policymaker's utility. We get a trade-off between increasing support from producers and decreasing support from taxpayers. The equality in equation (A7i) is guaranteed by Young's Theorem.

Because, for (x^0, λ^0), $D\,L(x^0, \lambda^0) = 0$ and $D^2L(x^0, \lambda^0)$ is nonsingular, by the Implicit Function Theorem (IFT), the FONCs described by equation (A6) determine x_3^0 (locally) as a function of x_1^0 and x_2^0. That is, there exists a neighborhood V of x_1^0 and x_2^0 in R^2, and a neighborhood U of x_3^0 in R, and a unique continuously differentiable function g: $V \to U$ such that

$$x_3^0 = g(x_1^0, x_2^0) \qquad (A9)$$

Given the constrained maximization problem in which the policymaker's control variable is the minimum producer price, x_3, and the assumptions listed above, the IFT guarantees a solution x_3^0 functionally dependent on x_1^0 and x_2^0, the producer income and the budgetary expenditure. That is, the solution to the maximization problem can be approximated by the statistical model described in equation 5.

APPENDIX 8.2: ESTIMATES OF THE INSTRUMENT VARIABLES

$$Y_t^w = 23.09 + 0.4385 Y_{t-1}^w\,;\ \overline{R}^2 = 0.151$$
$$\quad (2.79) \qquad (2.21)$$

$$B_t^w = 204{,}233 + 448.93 B_{t-1}^w\,;\ \overline{R}^2 = 0.123$$
$$\quad (1.88) \qquad (1.98)$$

$$Y_t^c = 23.66 + 0.6398 Y_{t-2}^c\,;\ \overline{R}^2 = 0.374$$
$$\quad (2.21) \qquad (3.68)$$

$$B_t^c = 949{,}233 + 318.6 B_{t-1}^c\,;\ \overline{R}^2 = 0.096$$
$$\quad (2.94) \qquad (1.46)$$

NOTES

1. The following discussion is based on Honma and Hayami (1986). See also Olson (1986).

2. This tradition dates as far back as the eighteenth century in Great Britain.

3. Whereas it may be defensible to neglect most of the other instruments employed in grains and to focus on the producer price only, it may be less so with regard to the base acreage for deficiency payments. However, producer price support and base acreage are not unrelated, as base acreage is included implicitly in the functional relationship of equation (2) (below).

4. For the derivation of the optimum condition see Appendix I. For a detailed proof, see Hausner (1992).

5. The 1985 Farm Bill, for example, permitted the loan rate to be set based on past market prices, but limited to a 5 percent annual drop (USDA, 1990b). Because the target price is connected to the loan rate via the deficiency payment rate and resulting budgetary expenditures, the target price, set annually by the U.S. Congress, can be expected to develop in a similar pattern.

6. The t-values are in parentheses. The support price is in \$/bushel, the U.S. share in world exports is in percentages, and budgetary expenditures are in \$1,000. For alternative specifications, see von Witzke (1990) and Hausner (1992).

7. Estimates of the impact of agricultural producer price support in grains indicate that world wheat prices would be significantly higher in the absence of agricultural price support. See, for example, Sarris and Freebairn (1983), Koester (1982), and Anderson and Tyers (1988b).

8. These two political entities are the two most important food and agricultural commodity trading countries in the world.

C. Ford Runge 9

Beyond the Uruguay Round: Emerging Issues in Agricultural Trade Policy

Much of the focus on agricultural trade in the 1980s and early 1990s has been on the problems and prospects for trade reform in the eighth round of global trade negotiations, the Uruguay Round. Although the round included fifteen separate negotiating areas in all, the agricultural negotiations proved central to the interests of both the rich countries of the North, where agriculture is heavily subsidized, and the poor countries of the South, where it is the principal source of export earnings and economic growth. At this writing, and after six years of negotiation, the outcome of such negotiation remains in doubt, although there is reason to believe that some resolution ultimately will occur.

The subjects of this chapter are the issues that will dominate trade policy discussions in the wake of the Uruguay Round. The chapter begins with a brief analysis of the conditions leading up to the 1986 Punta del Este meeting. It then considers the discussions over agriculture that have occurred during the Uruguay Round, describing the alignment of interests and key negotiating issues. The discussion then focuses on three key areas of debate likely to dominate trade policy discussions in the years ahead. The first is the role and problems of developing countries in the multilateral trading system. The second is the emergence of a North American trading bloc, which provides a microcosm of many North/South trade issues. The third is the increasing role of environmental, health, and safety regulations functioning as nontariff trade barriers. Each of these issues is likely to continue to dominate trade policy discussions in the years ahead.

THE EROSION OF THE MULTILATERAL TRADING SYSTEM: A CONCISE HISTORY

Postwar international economic relations in agriculture may be divided into three broad periods. In the 1950s and 1960s, agricultural development occurred in many parts of the world, driven especially by technological innova-

181

tions. This set the stage for the 1970s, when agricultural production and trade grew rapidly. This growth was fueled in part by substantial increases in debt in many developing countries. In part due to the burdens of accumulated debt, the gap in this growth between rich and poor countries widened. In the early 1980s, mounting debt and economic recession reduced the demand for traded agricultural commodities, yet national policies, especially in the North, continued to encourage excess production, leading to surplus disposal and falling prices in world markets. These trends affected countries differently, making broad generalizations subject to numerous exceptions.

Yet, by the mid-1980s, a consensus had emerged that world agriculture was in disarray, and that the crisis was significantly related to policies that sought to protect farmers in the North from global competition, but restricted access by poor farmers in the South from lucrative trading opportunities (Anderson and Hayami, 1986). This consensus was resisted by some of the most important players in the multilateral trading system, notably the European Community, whose Common Agricultural Policy was blamed for a large measure of global agricultural disequilibrium (von Witzke, Runge and Job, 1989). In the United States, a policy of more open trade was pursued selectively, with export subsidies and import protection continuing in critical areas of agriculture (such as sugar, dairy, and peanuts), and in textiles.

Despite these notable exceptions, the developed and many developing countries found common cause in the 1980s over general liberalization of agricultural trade, especially in grains and oilseeds. The reasons for this are relatively straightforward: it is in these sectors that the United States, as well as other net exporters such as Canada, Australia, Brazil, and Argentina, enjoy their greatest comparative advantages, and the developing countries as a whole are important markets. Far less clear was whether the United States, the European Community, and Japan were prepared to increase levels of market access to developing countries in their most heavily protected sectors, where they enjoyed far fewer advantages. This issue remained particularly difficult for the EC, whose own production advantages, even in grains and oilseeds, were generally less than in the United States and other net exporting regions.

Table 9.1 shows trends in economic growth, food production, and food imports and exports from 1965 to 1986, based on data assembled by the U.S. Congressional Budget Office from World Bank and FAO sources (U.S. Congress, 1989: 20). Developing country GDP growth per capita increased 3.9 percent from 1965 to 1980, but this growth fell to –0.5 percent from 1980 to 1985. The worst declines were in the Middle East and Africa, followed by Latin America. In Asia, growth continued to increase by 3.1 percent from 1980 to 1985, slowing in the United States and Canada from 2.0 percent from 1965 to 1980 to 1.5 percent from 1980 to 1985. In Western Europe, the decline was from 3.0 percent from 1960 to 1980 to 1.2 percent from 1980 to 1985. Growth in food production slowed by half—from 0.6 to 0.3

Table 9.1
Food Production, Consumption, and Trade Growth Rates (average annual growth rates in percent and calories)

Region[a]	GDP per Capita		Food Production per Capita		Calories Supplied per Capita[b]		Food Imports		Food Exports	
	1965–1980	1980–1985	1975–1981	1981–1986	1969–1971	1983–1985	1975–1981	1981–1986	1975–1981	1981–1986
Developing Countries										
excluding China	3.9	-0.5	0.6	0.3	2,173	2,364	9.4	0.9	6.2	0.7
including China	3.9	1.0	0.9	1.4	2,113	2,424	10.3	0.0	5.2	2.2
Selected Countries										
Latin America	4.0	-1.9	1.0	-0.5	2,517	2,700	11.9	-4.5	6.4	-0.9
Asia	3.9	3.1	1.1	1.0	2,059	2,239	2.3	3.0	7.7	5.3
Middle East	3.9	-3.4	0.4	-0.1	2,397	2,957	14.4	2.5	14.4	-0.5
Africa	3.6	-2.2	-1.8	-0.1	2,103	2,129	10.4	1.6	-1.9	-0.4
Centrally Planned Countries										
China	4.2	8.6	1.8	4.4	1,974	2,564	16.5	-5.8	-2.8	15.6
USSR/Eastern Europe	n.a.	n.a.	-0.5	2.9	3,332	3,410	11.5	-7.5	0.0	-0.2
Developed Countries										
United States/Canada	2.0	1.5	1.9	-0.9	3,456	3,632	3.8	3.2	7.8	-7.3
Western Europe	3.0	1.2	1.3	1.2	3,261	3,379	1.2	1.0	6.9	4.8
World	n.a.	n.a.	0.6	0.8	2,449	2,666	6.3	-0.4	6.4	-0.6

Sources: Congressional Budget Office, from Food and Agriculture Organization of the United Nations, *FAO Trade Yearbook 1986; FAO Production Yearbook 1986* and *FAO Trade Yearbook 1986*; World Bank, *World Development Report 1987*.

Note: n.a. = not available

[a]Regional definitions follow standard FAO groupings. China includes other Asian centrally planned economies. Asia excludes China, other Asian centrally planned economies, and Japan, as well as Middle Eastern Asian countries. The Middle East includes Egypt, Libya, and Sudan, and excludes Israel. Africa excludes South Africa, Egypt, Libya, and Sudan. Developed countries include South Africa and Israel. FAO and World Bank country group definitions can differ slightly.

[b]Calories supplied is a proxy for per capita consumption. It equals domestic food production plus food imports minus food exports, with a correction for livestock feed use. Calories supplied per capita represents the quantity of food reaching households, all of which may not be consumed because of various losses of edible food and nutrients in the household.

percent—in developing countries (excluding China) in the periods 1975 to 1981 to 1981 to 1986, although total calories supplied increased marginally.

As per capita GDP fell, so did the demand for developed countries' exports. Developing country food imports, a key variable explaining world trade frictions, plummeted from a growth rate of 9.4 percent from 1975 to 1981 to 0.9 percent from 1981 to 1986, and growth in developing country food exports also fell, from 6.2 percent in 1975 to 1981 to 0.7 percent in 1981 to 1986. In the North, the agricultural export growth rates of the United States and Canada reflected those import declines, falling from a positive rate of 7.8 percent from 1975 to 1981 to −7.3 percent from 1981 to 1986. In partial contrast, the continuing disposal of EC surpluses in world markets led Western Europe's export growth to decline only from 6.9 percent to 4.8 percent in the same periods.

These data reveal the broad outlines of trends leading to the negotiating table in the GATT: falling per capita incomes and falling food imports in developing countries, and declining agricultural exports from North America, especially relative to the European Community. These trends were manifest in increasing trade frictions, which seemed to require multilateral solutions.

The deterioration of the multilateral trading system in the 1980s can also be demonstrated by a variety of measures of protection, to which many countries resorted as markets shrank. Tyers and Anderson (1988: 201–202) calculated individual commodity price series for each major country to determine nominal rates of protection (the percentage by which producer prices in agriculture plus marketing margins exceeded border prices). They estimated that the average nominal rate of protection for grain, livestock, and sugar was 21 percent in 1965 to 1974. By 1975 to 1983, this figure was 28 percent, or one-quarter higher. These increases were concentrated in the EC-10 (an increase from 38 to 51 percent), the European Free Trade Area (EFTA) (from 62 to 89 percent), and in Japan (from 110 to 160 percent) from 1965– 1974 to 1975–1983, respectively.

The consequences of increased protection levels during the 1980s were demonstrable. Because countries in the North insulated their farmers from global market conditions, maintaining high internal prices relative to world prices, they tended to overproduce. When overproduction was dumped into world markets at subsidy, as under the export subsidies of the EC (and the retaliatory response of the United States, the Export Enhancement Program), the result was to destabilize and lower prices further. As demand weakened in developing countries due to the burdens of accumulated debts, world market prices went even lower, which further exacerbated the debt-repayment ability of countries such as Argentina and Brazil, who are primarily dependent on agricultural exports for foreign exchange.

Loans made to developing countries in the 1970s and early 1980s were predicated on expectations of continuing inflation, allowing dollar-denominated liabilities to depreciate in real value. When the opposite occurred due to the deflationary policies of the U.S. Federal Reserve Bank and a rise in the value of the dollar from 1979 to 1985, the loans increased in real value, as did the real interest levels necessary to finance them. Developing countries' combined debt in 1987 totaled more than $950 billion, of which $380 billion was concentrated in Latin America (U.S. GAO, 1988). While middle-income oil-producing countries accounted for a substantial portion of the total, more than two-thirds of the debt in 1984 was held by major importers of agricultural commodities. Most of these countries held more than 40 percent of their debt in short-term and private loans that were highly subject to interest rate swings.

After the boom lending years of the 1970s, credit tightened in the 1980s, and a major source of finance for expanded agricultural imports dissipated. By the mid-1980s, hard currency earnings in developing countries were going primarily to service existing debt, making aggressive sales of agricultural products—often at below the cost of production—one of the only means of financial survival. Per capita incomes suffered accordingly, falling as much as 50 percent in some debt-ridden developing countries in the two years from 1981 to 1983. In those countries in which agricultural export expansion has been possible, notably in Asia, the impacts of debt service were softened, but world market conditions continued to suffer.

This vicious circle, in addition to reducing the terms of trade for many developing countries, also raised the costs of export subsidies and farm programs in the United States and the European Community. In large part, it was the cost of these programs in the North (which reached $26 billion in the United States in 1987) that ultimately led the United States and the European Community to agree to open negotiations at Punta del Este in December 1986. After a near deadlock over agriculture, the EC finally agreed to formal talks under the auspices of the GATT to last four years, concluding in December 1990.

In the United States and Canada, meanwhile, discussions began concerning a possible U.S.-Canada trade agreement, which was given impetus by the Reagan/Mulroney "Shamrock summit." The U.S.-Canada free trade agreement became effective in January 1989. Yet many difficult issues of agricultural trade were deferred during the U.S.-Canada negotiations for consideration in the larger realm of the GATT. In 1990–1991, it was proposed to extend the agreement to Mexico, and negotiations began on the development of a full-scale North American Free Trade Agreement.

Some criticized the United States for "playing it both ways," seeking both multilateral and regional trade deals, but the United States maintained that the U.S.-Canada accord and proposed NAFTA demonstrated its overall willingness to move in the direction of more open markets at both levels. This position can also be interpreted as a form of diversification of trade strategy, in which U.S. policymakers prepared a North American alternative in the event the multilateral negotiations were less than successful.

Agriculture thus emerged as a key issue in the political economy of international trade in the 1980s, largely in the context of the Uruguay Round of the GATT (Runge, 1988). Because agricultural trade disputes cannot be divorced from domestic farm programs, many foreign trade officials and others in the diplomatic community were forced in the 1980s to confront complex issues of agricultural policy for the first time. In developing countries, of course, agriculture remained the central mode of production. But the problems of Third World agricultural development alone would have been insufficient to bring agriculture to the center of the multilateral trade negotiations.

It was the pernicious interaction of agricultural protectionism in the United States, the European Community, and Japan that put each of these major capitalist economies in the position of seeking to enlarge the scope and level of world trade, while continually pleading that their agricultural producers could not sustain greater trade liberalization. The consultation and dispute settlement process in the GATT was too weak to resolve successfully many trade disputes, leading parties to revert to bilateral retaliation when not satisfied with the GATT process. A notable example was the U.S. Export Enhancement Program, which, although "targeted" at the EC, caught many others in the crossfire, notably Cairns Group members such as Australia and Canada. Even the few agricultural measures that were bound under the GATT, such as the guaranteed access of soybeans and corn gluten feed shipments to Europe (the "zero duty binding"), were under steady attack by those seeking additional barriers to access.

The negotiating positions of the parties in the Uruguay Round evolved and changed over the period 1986–1991, but little compromise was achieved, especially between the principal antagonists: the United States and the European Community. This North/North division was the primary schism in the initial four-year negotiation. The second was a North/South division that was partially overcome through the negotiating efforts of the Cairns Group. A third division, along South/South lines, was also apparent throughout, reflecting the diversity of developing country interests.

The North/North division arose from the opposed positions of the United States and the European Community. These positions created the illusion of a "zero-sum game," in which the gain of the European Community was the loss of the United States, and vice versa (Runge, 1990a). An important reason for this view lay in the faulty premises under which both the United States and European Community conducted much of the Uruguay Round. The premises, which fostered the illusion that these countries were locked in a zero-sum game, were largely the creations of domestic politics on both sides of the Atlantic. In the United States, the premise was that world trade in agriculture must eventually be free and that to demand anything less than the total elimination of all trade-distorting policies would be to surrender the high ground of the negotiation. This premise caused the United States to insist until past the midpoint of the round that unless "elimination" entered the language of agreement in agriculture, there would not be one.

After the December 1988 midterm review meeting in Montreal broke up over the "elimination" issue, an agreement to pursue "substantial progressive reductions" in agricultural support was reached in April 1989 at Geneva. Prime ministers, meeting at the Houston summit in July 1990, reaffirmed a more flexible framework for negotiation built around the de Zeeuw text. This framework, authored by Art de Zeeuw, then chairman of the Agricultural Negotiating Group, appeared July 1, 1990. As discussed earlier by Moyer (see Chapter 5), the text outlined a possible agreement to reform market access through tariffication of nontariff barriers, the reduction of export subsidies, and the restraint of domestic support. The de Zeeuw text incorporated the idea that agricultural supports could be categorized into "red light," "green light," and "yellow light" policies, with differential schedules for change over time. It also provided for interpretations of what must and must not be eliminated and over what periods of time.

By October 1990, the United States had stepped back from elimination, calling instead for 90 percent reductions in border measures such as export subsidies and 75 percent reductions in domestic agricultural supports. Although clearly intended to signal a willingness to negotiate, by this point little time remained before the final scheduled meeting in December 1990 to explore fully how such reductions might be achieved. When the December meeting broke down, it was a full year before a new compromise text was put forward by GATT Director General Arthur Dunkel. And the "Dunkel text," too, failed to bridge the differences between the United States and the European Community over export subsidies, market access, and internal supports.

In contrast to that of the United States, European negotiating strategy was premised on the conviction that the Common Agricultural Policy was the centerpiece of community, and to weaken it would be to tear at the fabric of both the solidarity of the European Community and the rural culture of Europe. This premise is questionable in at least three ways. First, the increasing economic and social integration of Europe appears to be progressing rapidly, with or without the CAP. In part, this is a result of monetary union and the provisions of the Single European Act (Calingaert, 1988). This integration and harmonization, especially in terms of monetary union, does not depend on the CAP for energy or inertia. Indeed, the CAP has kept many farm assets and much capital from migrating to its highest and best uses in various parts of the EC by capitalizing its benefits into land and asset values in situ, discouraging off-farm migration of labor, and institutionalizing exchange rate adjustments for community price policies.

Second, the CAP has proven to be a far greater source of community discord than solidarity, especially in the 1980s. Its budgetary demands on scarce EC resources are well known. The very fact that the agriculture ministers cannot agree among themselves on price policies or GATT positions suggested that the CAP stands in the way of many gains from both internal and external trade reforms. These obstacles are particularly apparent in connection with exchange rates, and the tension between a European Monetary System, on the one hand, and the monetary compensatory amounts (MCAs) used to adjust CAP prices for exchange rates, on the other. As the European Community becomes more integrated, the CAP will decline in importance.

Third, the role of the CAP in preserving traditional rural culture is highly debatable. Large European farmers representing 20 percent of the total have reaped 80 percent of the benefits from the CAP. The inequity of benefits distribution is also apparent among the countries of the European Community, in which the poorest countries are not always the main beneficiaries of the CAP (Koester, 1977; Buckwell et al., 1982).

In part because of the unwillingness of the EC to concede the need for CAP reform, the United States and the EC have been largely unable to bridge the North/North division. As of summer 1992 the Dunkel text appears to be a basis for final resolution of the Uruguay Round. Whereas the EC has moved slowly in the direction of reform, strong French opposition may ultimately doom the entire negotiation.

It is doubtful that the Dunkel proposal can rescue the GATT talks before the deadline set by the U.S. Congress, which calls for retaliation against the European Community. This "GATT trigger" was made a condition of congressional reauthorization of "fast-track negotiating authority."[1] If this trigger deadline is extended or ignored, however, there remains a possibility that a compromise will emerge during 1992.

THE DEVELOPING COUNTRIES AND THE URUGUAY ROUND

The role of the South in the GATT has been problematic, as Hopkins notes in Chapter 7. What had begun in 1947 as a twenty-two-country "rich man's club" encompassed 108 negotiating parties by 1990, the bulk of which were developing countries. Yet the interests and concerns of developing countries in the GATT differ widely, and their resources are stretched to the limit as they try to stay abreast of complex and interlinked negotiating areas. In part in response to the perceived needs of developing countries, the Tokyo Round of GATT talks created important provisions for "special and differential treatment" for developing countries, allowing them to seek remedies for balance-of-payments difficulties and safeguards to protect programs of economic development. A variety of separate "codes" was also amended to the GATT articles, pertaining to subsidies and countervailing measures and other issues involving nontariff barriers to trade (Balassa, 1980; Kemper, 1980).

On the whole, however, the developing countries have had difficulty achieving their objectives in the GATT. Given the increasing number of contracting parties, the heterogeneity of countries' interests makes it difficult for a well-defined developing country agenda to emerge, and the relative influence of the rich OECD countries continues to loom large (Runge, 1990c).

Even so, the Uruguay Round was launched with a focus on agriculture in part because of the strong interests of the developing countries in gaining market access to the North. Despite a variety of special trade concessions granting access, such as the EC's Lomé Convention, in reality many competitively priced imports from the South were locked out of Northern markets by tariff and nontariff barriers. In addition to market access, some developing countries also stood to gain from reductions in the export subsidy wars conducted between the European Community and the United States, especially in grains. This interest led to a coalition of countries, the so-called Cairns Group, composed of agricultural exporters with both developed and developing country members. The Cairns Group provided critical support for liberalizing agricultural trade respecting both export subsidies and market access issues throughout the Uruguay Round. Both the Cairns Group and the United States took particular aim at reducing the distortions caused by export subsidies paid under the EC's Common Agricultural Policy (see Cooper and Higgott, Chapter 6).

As noted above, in the South the primary issues (within agriculture) were market access and, for developing countries that were net exporters, export subsidies. Because developing countries were being asked to accept terms in other areas of the Uruguay Round that were politically and economically difficult, such as textiles, services, and intellectual property, they felt strongly as a group that major market access gains were needed in agriculture as compensation. Brazil's statement to the GATT contracting parties in 1989 was typical (GATT, 1989a), emphasizing that development assistance measures should not be considered eligible for reduction under a more general program of trade reforms. Special and differential treatment for developing countries should include extended periods to implement reforms, together with fewer cuts in tariffs and nontariff measures, as well as quantitative restrictions. Higher internal supports should be tolerated in developing countries and special attention should be paid to discrimination faced by developing countries in the area of sanitary and phytosanitary measures (see Runge, 1990b).

Yet, within the developing countries, a variety of differences also existed, creating South/South fissures that made it difficult to negotiate as a bloc. Evidence of these differences emerged relatively early in the round, when a Food-Importing Group (FIG) was formed in the GATT to differentiate the needs of these countries from the main agricultural exporting countries, most of which had joined the Cairns Group. In a proposal spelling out the position of the net importers, the FIG countries called on the other GATT contracting parties to "alleviate the burden of increased prices on the import bill and balance of payments situation of net food importing developing countries," and to "enhance the capacity of these countries to increase agricultural production" (GATT, 1989b). Specifically, as will be discussed in more detail below, the proposal cited a variety of studies showing major losses to food importers from trade policy reform due to increased prices. Given such losses, the FIGs argued for compensation in the form of concessional food sales, export credits and grants, improved market access, increased food aid, and reduced levels of debt servicing.

The main South/South difference in the GATT thus occurs in large part between food importers and food exporters. This issue was linked, in turn, to debt-servicing questions. Lower world commodities prices, due to export subsidy competition between the United States and the European Community, have been a primary reason for debt-servicing problems in net exporting countries such as Argentina and Brazil. In the net importing countries, however, the situation is reversed. Because alleviation of export subsidies and internal reforms in the North are expected to raise world prices, the food bill of net importers would increase, making debt service even more difficult. As the FIG statements argued (GATT, 1989b: 3):

> The rise in import prices of food will exacerbate the debt servicing problems of net food importing developing countries and therefore we propose that international financial organizations should take the increase in import prices of food fully into account in negotiating structural adjustment programs; specifically these programs should be made more flexible.

The overall interest of developing countries in the GATT thus have two main axes: North/South and South/South. These axes are likely to remain, and the issues they involve are likely to continue as a focus of discussion beyond the Uruguay Round. From a North/South perspective, developing countries have argued in the GATT for increased market access to the industrialized countries, whether they were net food importers or exporters. But along the South/South axis, the critical issue of debt servicing divided those countries that would gain from rising international commodities prices (net exporters) from those who would lose (net importers). This South/South division turns critically on the estimated impacts of the trade reform process on prices and net welfare. It is to these estimates that we now turn.

Numerous academic and government studies have estimated the size and distribution of benefits that would result from agricultural trade reform. These estimates confront the many problems of econometric modeling and should be interpreted with caution.[2]

Tyers, one of the principal academic economists involved, has criticized the models for failing to capture important dynamic issues, including retaliation and behavior under risks, and for their tendency to treat agriculture as a small and separable sector, justifying "partial equilibrium" estimates of gains and losses. In addition, the models tend to aggregate many commodities, as if they were homogenous products. Although possibly justified when modeling OECD grain markets, these assumptions are far less appropriate for developing countries. Tyers (1990) noted:

The perception that developing countries as a group would be net losers from any reform in the industrial market economies (as suggested, for example, in Tyers, 1989) has not only increased the reticence of developing countries to support reforms in the OECD, it has also had institutional consequences in that a formal negotiating alliance has developed between net-food-importing developing countries. *Yet a more detailed examination which takes account of intersectoral and macroeconomic effects suggests that a clear majority of developing countries could benefit from such reforms* [emphasis added].

Utilizing stochastic multicommodity, partial equilibrium models of world food markets, Anderson and Tyers (1990b: 3) showed that "virtually all developing countries could benefit from global liberalization of food markets and that the vast majority of the world's poor would be better off." This differs from their earlier findings and those of other authors, which predicted major losses, especially to net food-importing developing countries, if global prices rise following liberalization. What accounts for this difference in view? The result turns critically on how realistically the reform process is described.

Four elements are introduced in the Anderson and Tyers work that provides this realism. First, while it is generally acknowledged that rising world prices of agricultural commodities would cause unambiguous improvements in the terms of trade in food-exporting countries, it is less often emphasized that some net food-importing countries would expand production and become net exporters over time. Second, this production expansion is likely to be driven by induced innovations in developing countries' technology and institutions, following the dynamic pattern predicted by Hayami and Ruttan (1985). By shifting domestic supplies out, welfare gains can exceed the losses resulting from worsened terms of trade. Third, if developing countries that have insulated consumers by subsidizing domestic food prices (thus encouraging import-dependency) instead allowed world price increases to be reflected domestically, the elimination of these distortions could more than offset the losses due to worsening terms of trade. This effect is amplified if induced innovations generate the above-mentioned supply response and increased exports. Fourth, even if a country remained a net food importer and had no domestic food subsidies, if it protected its nonfood sector (for example, through overvalued exchange rates), then eliminating these nonfood distortions would raise the relative price of food, with the same effects possible as in the first three cases above.

In short, by acknowledging that increased output, induced innovations leading to higher productivity, and distortions in existing food and nonfood sectors characterize the dynamic process of adjustment to trade reform, a different picture emerges of its impacts on food-importing countries. Negative impacts are not certain a priori and must be determined empirically.

Empirical estimates of these impacts have been made for two scenarios: (1) complete liberalization in the North only; and (2) liberalization in both the North and South. In both cases, productivity increases were first held constant and then allowed to respond to increased prices (Anderson and Tyers, 1990b: 11–25). (These productivity increases amount to an outward shift in aggregate food supply.) Food markets included in the model were grains, meats, dairy products, and sugar, accounting for about half of world food trade. The estimates for 1990 show what would have occurred in equilibrium if distortions in the North or in both North and South were eliminated. The effects of subsidized food imports in developing countries were captured by lowering the relative internal food price consistent with the 1988 calculations of Krueger, Schiff, and Valdes (1988b).

Table 9.2 shows that if the North liberalized alone, international food prices would rise (in 1985 dollars) by 24 percent compared to the reference level. Net economic welfare in developing countries would increase by $11 billion. If productivity growth is induced in response to these price increases, prices would rise by 26 percent and net economic welfare in developing

Table 9.2
Effects of Liberalizing Food Markets on
International Food Prices and Economic Welfare, 1990

	International Food Price Change (%)	Change in Net Economic Welfare (1985 US$ billion per year)		
		Industrial Countries	Developing Countries	Global Total
North liberalization of industrial country food policies with:				
exogenous productivity growth	24	40	11	50
price-responsive productivity growth	26	47	17	62
North/South liberalization of policies affecting food markets in industrial and developing countries with:				
exogenous productivity growth	−1	62	28	90
price-responsive productivity growth	−1	73	33	106

Source: Anderson and Tyers (1990b: 22).
Note: Economic welfare changes here apply only to agents in the food sector, as measured by equivalent variations in income of consumers and changes in producer surplus, in net goverment revenue from the food sector, and in net profits from food stockholding. The global total includes the (small) effect on net economic welfare of Eastern Europe and the Soviet Union.

countries would increase by $17 billion. If both the North and South liberalize, the effect on world food prices is a negligible –1 percent because these actions have offsetting effects. But welfare increases in developing countries are $28 billion with no productivity response and $33 billion with it, about twice the level that occurs if the North liberalizes alone.

The effect of these gains for different countries is detailed in Table 9.3. The welfare gains of North-only reform are widely distributed, although some developing countries still experience overall losses. These are either relatively wealthy countries (Korea, South Africa, Taiwan, and some nations in the Middle East) specializing in manufacturing and petroleum, or countries that are very heavily food-import dependent (Bangladesh and Egypt). However, no developing country is projected to face an increased food import bill.

When a joint North/South liberalization is undertaken, even fewer developing countries lose. In the South, farmers are the main beneficiaries. These policy changes not only improve net welfare, they also reduce real income inequality by raising the prices received by farmers and rural laborers.

A final dimension of these changes is shown in Table 9.4, which estimates the impacts of liberalization on the stability of international agricultural prices. When either the North or South insulate their producers from international prices, they in effect "export" domestic price instability into the international economy. This has been described as a form of "free riding," in which the international public good of price stability is eroded through protection by either producers or consumers (Runge, 1990c). Anderson and Tyers (1990b) calculated that if the North liberalized, the variation in international prices would be reduced by about one-third (from a coefficient of 0.34 to 0.23), and by about two-thirds (from 0.34 to 0.11) if a joint North/South liberalization occurred.

The implications of Anderson and Tyers's estimates are worth brief elaboration. First, they suggest that the losses due to trade liberalization predicted by net food importers such as the FIGs are probably overestimates of the welfare impacts of declining terms of trade. Conversely, earlier estimates of gains from trade policy reform, such as Tyers and Anderson's 1988 study (Tyers and Anderson, 1988), are probably underestimates. Second, the results raise questions over claims in favor of exemptions for distortionary policies in developing countries based on special and differential treatment because eliminating (downward) distortions of food prices in the South actually increases the welfare gains of liberalization in a joint North/South action. Third, the price stabilization effects of trade policy reform suggest the somewhat unorthodox view that liberalization may be a better mechanism to achieve such stability than international commodity agreements, which have often been justified as stabilization programs.

The Anderson and Tyers study also undermines arguments by apologists for the international price-depressing (and destabilizing) effects of the EC's Common Agricultural Policy, who have asserted that such effects are

Table 9.3
Effects of Completely Liberalizing Food Markets on Foreign Exchange Earnings
and Economic Welfare in Individual Developing Countries Assuming
Price-Responsive Productivity Growth, 1990 (1985 US$ billion per year)

	North Reform in Industrial Countries Only			North/South Reform in Industrial and Developing Countries		
	(1)	(2)	(3)	(1)	(2)	(3)
Bangladesh	0.2	0.7	−0.2	0.1	0.5	0.1
China	6.3	6.1	2.9	37.0	29.4	12.9
India	5.8	5.7	1.3	3.3	1.6	1.1
Indonesia	1.8	1.3	0.4	−1.3	−1.1	0.9
Korea, Republic of	0.0	0.4	−0.9	−6.8	−6.8	6.5
Pakistan	1.9	1.1	0.3	3.9	3.5	0.4
Philippines	0.1	0.1	0.0	0.3	−0.2	−0.1
Taiwan	0.1	0.4	−0.2	−1.7	−1.8	0.4
Thailand	1.0	0.6	0.5	−0.5	0.3	−0.2
Other Asia	1.8	1.4	0.5	15.3	7.5	1.7
Subtotal, Asia	20.0	17.8	4.6	49.0	32.9	23.7
Argentina	7.7	1.9	5.4	13.8	11.3	5.1
Brazil	7.9	3.8	2.9	7.8	5.8	0.8
Mexico	2.8	1.0	1.2	5.1	3.1	0.9
Other Latin America	6.4	2.3	3.2	8.6	7.4	0.8
Subtotal, Latin America	24.8	9.0	12.7	35.3	27.6	7.6
Egypt	0.0	0.2	−0.3	0.1	0.3	0.4
Nigeria	1.2	0.4	0.6	1.3	0.8	0.2
South Africa	1.1	1.3	−0.7	−1.2	−0.5	−0.2
Other Sub-Saharan Africa	3.9	1.3	2.0	12.2	7.5	2.3
Other North Africa plus Middle East	0.0	1.5	−2.3	0.8	1.3	−0.6
Subtotal, Africa and Middle East	6.2	4.7	−0.7	13.2	9.4	2.1
Total, developing countries	51.0	31.5	16.6	97.5	69.9	33.4
Total, industrial countries	−78.5	−87.0	46.5	−134.2	−160.9	73.3
World total	−20.8	−44.4	62.2	−35.2	−87.5	106.4

Source: Anderson and Tyers (1990b: 23).
Notes: (1): change in net foreign exchange earnings from food trade; (2): change in farmers' welfare; (3): change in net economic welfare. Net welfare includes the effects on food consumers, taxpayers, and food stockholders, as well as food producers. Effects on expenditures to administer and to lobby for and against food policies, not included above, would add to the net welfare gains from reform. The world total includes effects on Eastern Europe and the Soviet Union.

Table 9.4
Effects of Removing Policy Distortions to Food Markets in Industrial and
Developing Countries on the Instability of International Food Market Prices

International Price Instability	Wheat	Coarse Grain	Rice	Beef and Sheep Meat	Pork and Poultry	Dairy Products	Sugar	Weighted Average
Reference coefficient of variation	0.58	0.53	0.38	0.24	0.08	0.26	0.36	0.34
Coefficient of variation in the absence of policy distortions in:								
All industrial countries	0.33	0.47	0.28	0.07	0.08	0.11	0.25	0.23
All industrial and developing countries	0.15	0.23	0.09	0.04	0.05	0.06	0.07	0.11

Source: Anderson and Tyers (1990b: 24).
Note: The coefficient of variation is the standard deviation divided by the mean value for 100 repeated simulations with random supply shocks.

beneficial to importing countries. The estimated negative effects of these food policies on the economic welfare of developing countries is so large (as much as $17 billion in 1985 dollars) "as to effectively erode about half of the official development assistance received by developing countries from the OECD" (Anderson and Tyers, 1990b: 16).

Finally, the results have implications for the impact of liberalization in Eastern Europe, where agricultural exports are likely to be an important source of foreign exchange earnings in new democracies. Eastern Europe as well as the rest of the developing world would benefit from trade liberalization at least as much as from expanded development assistance.

A criticism applicable to Anderson and Tyers's model, as well as numerous other studies of trade reform, is that they estimate the impact of complete liberalization rather than more incremental reforms. This "first best" outcome is probably unrealistic.

A recent study conducted for UNCTAD by the United Nations World Institute for Development Economics Research of the University in Helsinki attempted to estimate the impacts of less-than-full reforms (UNCTAD, 1990b). That study estimated the impact on developing countries of four different types of trade reform undertaken by the North (Australia, Canada, the European Community, Japan, and the United States). Crop coverage included cereals (wheat, maize, rice, sorghum), meat (beef and veal), sugar, oilseeds and oils, coffee and coffee products, cocoa, tea, tobacco, and cotton. This commodity coverage is larger than that of the Anderson-Tyers study, but the methods employed are comparative static and partial equilibrium. Thus, the estimates are likely to overstate damages to net importers. However, the advantage of the UNCTAD model is that it allows comparison of different types of trade reform.

Four scenarios of trade reform were modeled, using 1984–1986 as a base. These were:

1. complete liberalization, including the elimination of all producer and consumer subsidies, all tariffs and quotas, as well as internal taxes on tropical products
2. reductions in producers price support by 20 percent
3. elimination of export subsidies
4. an increase in imports by 10 percent in five markets for tropical and other developing country products, including sugar, either through increases in quota or reductions in tariffs.

Apart from reform scenario 1, which corresponds to an unlikely first best outcome, the remaining options correspond closely to elements of the Dunkel text compromise proposal discussed earlier. Reform 2 provides an indication of the effects such cuts would have on developing countries. Reform 3 corresponds to the Cairns Group's earlier proposals, and also reflects the interests of net exporting developing countries. Reform 4 is the most important reform from the point of view of both net exporting and importing developing countries. The estimates reported below examine each of the above reforms in isolation. In reality, if a package of GATT reforms is ultimately agreed to, it will be a blend of these actions—in all likelihood some combination of 2, 3, and 4. Even so, the UNCTAD study results allow the relative importance of the reform package components to be studied in greater detail.

Table 9.5 shows the impact of the four reforms on world prices for the commodities included in the study. Reform scenarios 1 and 2 reflect a dramatic rise in rice prices, whereas reform scenario 3, export subsidy elimination, has its greatest impact on wheat, beef, and rice. For tropical products, the greatest increases in price occur under reform scenario 4, confirming the importance of even 10 percent increases in market access.

Table 9.6 shows the regional results reported in the UNCTAD (1990b) study, indicating the gains and losses in foreign exchange and welfare resulting from the price increases estimated in Table 9.5. Unlike the Anderson and Tyers study, no dynamic adjustments in production or induced shifts from imports to exports due to price increases are allowed for. Even so, the only developing region with net foreign exchange losses is Africa under either reform scenario 1 or 2. Under both complete liberalization and 20

Table 9.5
Estimated Change in World Prices of Agricultural Products (Including Tropical Products) Under Alternative Liberalization Scenarios (increase in percent)

Product	Scenario			
	Complete Liberalization (1)	20 Percent Reduction in Producer Support Price (2)	Export Subsidy (3)	10 Percent Increase in Imports (4)
Wheat	20.4	7.5	12.2	1.1
Maize	15.1	4.8	0.1	3.9
Rice	42.6	18.3	8.5	2.2
Sorghum	12.4	1.9	0.0	2.4
Soybeans	3.6	0.0	0.0	2.5
Soybean oil	1.9	0.1	0.0	0.0
Beef and veal	12.5	13.0	11.1	1.6
Sugar	26.5	10.6	0.9	4.3
Cotton	0.1	0.9	0.0	9.1
Groundnut	0.1	1.5	0.0	5.1
Groundnut oil	2.8	0.6	9.0	3.9
Copra	0.0	0.0	0.0	20.1
Palm oil	0.4	0.0	0.0	1.6
Tea	2.9	0.5	0.0	8.3
Coffee				
Green	4.4	0.4	0.0	29.9
Roasted	7.5	0.0	0.0	38.7
Extracts	7.8	1.4	0.0	1.3
Cocoa				
Beans	0.1	0.0	0.0	19.7
Butter	2.8	0.5	0.0	9.1
Powder	5.2	0.8	0.0	4.2
Chocolate, N.e.s.	9.0	1.8	0.0	1.0
Tobacco				
Leaves	2.6	0.3	0.0	12.3
Cigarettes	0.2	0.1	0.0	0.0
Cigars	3.2	0.8	0.0	0.1
N.e.s.	0.1	0.2	0.0	0.6

Source: UNCTAD (1990b: xvi).
Note: N.e.s. = Not elsewhere specified

percent reductions in support, all other regions of the South are net foreign exchange gainers. Welfare changes remain positive for Latin America and the Caribbean, but turn negative for Africa, Asia, and the Pacific. Reform scenario 3 gives the same qualitative results. Reform scenario 4 is again the most clearly beneficial, resulting in the largest gains in foreign exchange and welfare for all developing countries.

Table 9.7 shows detailed results for the countries in the UNCTAD (1990b) study. The overall results of the UNCTAD study reinforce the

Table 9.6
Estimated Foreign Exchange and Welfare Impact on Developing Countries Under
Different Scenarios: Summary by Region (millions of 1985–1987 dollars)

	Selected Agricultural Products		Selected Tropical Products		All Selected Products	
	Foreign Exhange Earnings	Welfare Change	Foreign Exchange Earnings	Welfare Change	Foreign Exchange Earnings	Welfare Change
Scenario 1						
Africa	−699	−953	219	143	−480	−810
Latin America and Caribbean	984	224	562	445	1,546	669
Asia and Pacific	428	−483	141	77	589	−406
Total	713	−1,212	922	665	1,635	−547
Scenario 2						
Africa	−280	−402	32	21	−248	−381
Latin America and Caribbean	456	152	71	31	527	203
Asia and Pacific	145	−225	18	1	163	−224
Total	321	−473	121	73	447	−402
Scenario 3						
Africa	−256	−359	0	0	−256	−359
Latin America and Caribbean	262	37	0	0	262	37
Asia and Pacific	−89	−332	0	0	−89	−332
Total	−83	−654	0	0	−83	−654
Scenario 4						
Africa	−43	−67	1,926	1,337	1,881	1,270
Latin America and Caribbean	192	87	3,446	2,769	3,638	2,856
Asia and Pacific	−19	−60	872	477	891	417
Total	166	−40	6,244	4,583	6,410	4,543

Source: UNCTAD (1990b: xvii).
Note:
    Scenario 1: Complete liberalization (elimination of all producer and
                 consumer subsidies, all tariffs and quotas, as well as internal
                 taxes on tropical products)
    Scenario 2: Reduction of producer price support (by 20 percent)
    Scenario 3: Elimination of export subsidies
    Scenario 4: Increase in imports by 10 percent

conclusion that market access is the most important element of the
negotiations for developing countries, and will remain so for the foreseeable
future. Taken in isolation, any of the scenarios 1, 2, or 3 provide fewer
benefits than 4: 10 percent increases in market access. Indeed, scenarios 1, 2,
and 3 actually impose substantial losses on some parts of the developing

Table 9.7
Major Gainers and Losers in Each Country Group
(all selected products; millions of dollars)

Country Group/ Country	Scenario 1		Scenario 2		Scenario 3		Scenario 4	
	R	W	R	W	R	W	R	W
Policy countries								
Australia	967	678	1,037	348	1,103	305	98	
Canada	730	476	866	144	1,051	231	-158	
EEC	-5,141	1,430	-2,246	455	-3,507	1,301	-3,912	
Japan	-2,819	1,345	-503	559	-208	198	-1,135	
United States	4,411	2,829	294	849	704	6,161	-769	
Other developed market economies								
Austria	36	6	21	8	23	11	-40	34
Finland	2	-12	5	0	4	0	-48	-33
New Zealand	104	59	107	56	91	57	43	-4
Norway	-16	-27	-2	-6	-2	-4	-44	-30
Sweden	32	2	19	7	23	12	-29	-90
Switzerland	3	-24	-2	-11	-4	-9	-35	-78
Eastern Europe								
Czecho- slovakia	14	-20	13	-5	-13	0	-43	-62
German Democratic Republic	-10	-36	2	-20	1	-14	-58	-32
Poland	-44	-103	-17	-42	-27	-30	-40	-67
Soviet Union	-42	-1,049	-169	-436	-166	-402	-31	-210
Central America and Mexico								
El Salvador	24	17	3	1	-1	-2	176	141
Costa Rica	35	23	13	8	8	2	155	118
Guatemala	36	28	11	8	4	5	183	138
Honduras	23	16	10	7	6	3	94	72
Nicaragua	13	9	8	8	4	2	66	44
Mexico	8	-76	-11	-22	-5	14	331	251
Caribbean								
Cuba	128	68	47	22	-9	-20	62	45
Dominican Republic	43	24	15	10	1	-1	73	55
South America								
Argentina	670	438	259	171	231	149	118	66
Brazil	431	219	114	16	6	-43	1,521	1,125
Colombia	102	86	17	12	2	-3	597	546
Ecuador	10	3	0	-2	-2	-4	93	32
Peru	0	-29	-6	-16	-9	-13	65	36

(continues)

Table 9.7 (continued)

Country Group/ Country	Scenario 1		Scenario 2		Scenario 3		Scenario 4	
	R	W	R	W	R	W	R	W
Uruguay	90	39	68	47	54	37	6	3
Venezuela	−31	−59	−12	−23	−9	−16	8	1
Sub-Saharan Africa								
Cameroon	15	10	1	0	−1	2	165	131
Côte d'Ivoire	41	6	−3	−13	−3	−12	239	408
Ethiopia	3	1	−1	−2	−3	−4	62	61
Ghana	−4	−8	−3	−4	−2	−3	99	80
Kenya	27	15	2	0	−2	−2	194	117
Madagascar	−7	−16	−6	−8	−3	−4	62	48
Magnums	−73	−80	−21	−34	−2	−3		
Nigeria	−87	−119	−39	−34	−29	−39	78	57
Uganda	33	19	3	1	0	0	252	132
United Republic of Panzara	1	−4	−2	−3	−2	−2	64	60
Zaire	3	−4	−2	−4	−3	−4	−82	64
Zimbabwe	24	16	6	3	2	1	83	65
North Africa								
Algiers	−01	−113	−33	−43	−37	−44	82	−93
Egypt	−172	−236	−69	−105	−82	−123	−16	−32
Morocco	−54	−68	−20	−25	−25	−32	−19	−24
West Asia								
Iran (Islam, Republic of)	−84	−167	−41	−81	−45	−63	−11	−19
Iraq	−85	−135	−41	−69	−41	−59	−13	−24
South Arabia	−76	−107	−37	−50	−20	−31	−24	−31
Southeast Asia								
Bangladesh	−26	−32	−12	−22	−16	−26	3	−4
India	96	21	37	9	1	−18	194	138
Indonesia	0	−61	−18	−41	−18	−34	381	266
Malaysia	−13	−69	−13	−33	−8	−18	258	31
Myanmar	109	73	44	31	20	14	6	4
Pakistan	99	88	41	18	16	44	18	
Philippines	61	20	21	4	−3	−11	52	33
Papua New Guinea	0	−3	−2	−5	−2	−3	66	53
Republic of Korea	−96	−199	−44	−88	−29	−37	−37	−77
Thailand	688	478	267	188	100	70	87	18

Source: UNCTAD (1990b: xxii).
Notes: R = revenue; W = welfare. Major gainers and losers are defined as countries for which welfare changes by more than $50 million under one of the four scenarios, as defined in the text. Welfare calculations were not made for the policy countries under the scenario of a 10 percent increase in imports because this cannot be done without specifying how the increase in imports is to be brought about.

world. It is possible to interpret the UNCTAD results to suggest that (a) complete liberalization is not only unlikely, but probably not in the interest of the developing countries; and (b) without major increases in market access, preferably greater than 10 percent, a reform package including elements of scenarios 2, 3, and 4 clearly will not be advantageous to the South. If major market access gains are achieved, however, they are likely to be so substantial as to outweigh other disadvantages.

A third major study, undertaken recently by the U.S. Department of Agriculture (Krissoff et al., 1990), offers another perspective on the impacts of trade reform. Based on the USDA SWOPSIM model, which contains 36 regions and 22 commodities, the study reconfirms the price increasing effects of liberalization, but is both less realistic and less detailed than the previous two models. The study excludes important tropical products that are included in the UNCTAD work: coffee, cocoa, and some vegetables and fruits. The SWOPSIM model is static and partial equilibrium in nature. Output increases due to increased prices following liberalization are modeled as movements along the supply curve, rather than as dynamic outward shifts, in the manner of Anderson and Tyers. Using 1986 as a base year, the model estimates what would have happened if trade distortions were eliminated and all other variables remained the same. Three scenarios are examined:

A. The North fully liberalizes and developing countries maintain their own policies so as to insulate themselves from one half of the price increases that result. A $1.00 increase in world prices thus affects them by only $0.50.
B. The North fully liberalizes and no insulation occurs in the developing countries, so that they fully absorb the price increases resulting from liberalization. Hence a $1.00 increase in world prices increases prices in developing countries by the same amount.
C. A full North/South liberalization occurs, in which all farm programs are eliminated in both developed and developing economies.

Thus, scenario C corresponds to a first best (and unrealistic) full liberalization exercise. Scenarios A and B are similar to those examined by Anderson and Tyers, although dynamic production shifts are given comparatively less leeway in the SWOPSIM model. Table 9.8 shows the price effects by commodity for all three simulations. Tables 9.9–9.11 provide summary data on supply and demand shifts, net trade, and welfare changes by country for each of the three scenarios. Table 9.8 shows world price increases of 21 percent under the first scenario and 16 percent under the second and third scenarios. Overall, the regional impacts on net welfare, shown in Table 9.9, vary widely by region, regardless of the scenario. The main conclusions are that it is clearly in the developing countries' interest to participate in the

Table 9.8
World Price Changes in Each SWOPSIM Scenario (percentages)

Commodity	A	B	C
Beef	19	16	11
Pork	14	12	11
Mutton and lamb	31	25	21
Poultry meat	18	16	16
Poultry eggs	6	5	4
Dairy milk	0	0	0
Dairy butter	99	84	85
Dairy cheese	43	37	38
Dairy products	88	81	81
Wheat	37	27	20
Corn	29	22	23
Coarse grains	22	16	15
Rice	19	11	15
Soybeans	−2	−2	−3
Soymeal	−4	−3	−5
Soy oil	5	4	8
Other oilseeds	12	8	8
Other meals	−1	1	2
Other oils	9	7	14
Cotton	12	8	4
Sugar	48	29	40
Tobacco	4	3	3
Average	21	16	16

Source: USDA (1990a: 13).
Note:

    Scenario A: North fully liberalizes and developing countries maintain their own policies.

    Scenario B: North fully liberalized and no insulation occurs in developing countries.

    Scenario C: Full North/South liberalization occurs.

process of trade reform if the industrial countries pursue such a course. Second, it would appear that Latin America will benefit most as a region from joint North/South liberalization (consistent with the UNCTAD study) and that developing countries as a whole will benefit more than they will lose, at least from scenario C. This result also underscores the enthusiasm in many Latin countries for a regional trading agreement with North America.

What general conclusions can be extracted from these estimates of the impact on developing countries of trade policy reform and trade policy debates beyond the Uruguay Round? Although interpretations may differ, four general conclusions emerge. First, although the process of trade reform is likely to be incremental, to the extent that developing countries participate in reforming their own food sectors in tandem with countries of the North, their

Table 9.9
Industrial Market Liberalization, Scenario A

Area	Supply Quantity (%)	Demand Quantity (%)	Net Trade (million $)	Producer Surplus (million $)	Consumer Surplus (million $)	Net Welfare (million $)
				Change in		
United States	-1.5	-1.2	2,832	-15,974	-4,645	8,822
Canada	-2.1	-0.4	703	-1,275	150	2,609
European Community	-5.6	2.8	-9,213	-23,466	21,510	12,059
Other Western Europe	-16.3	-1.1	-1,909	-7,146	2,184	1,293
Japan	-30.4	9.4	-6,212	-22,011	23,575	4,985
Australia	6.2	-3.6	3,151	1,543	-1,546	1,109
New Zealand	12.0	2.2	2,478	1,745	-837	1,354
South Africa	3.0	-1.6	442	503	-485	87
Eastern Europe	0.7	-0.4	1,738	2,378	-2,374	789
Soviet Union	0.4	-0.4	-588	3,507	-3,912	-1,790
China	0.7	-0.3	1,133	3,476	-3,570	-73
Mexico	2.6	-2.0	520	1,111	-1,304	-133
Central America/ Caribbean	3.3	-1.6	664	496	-306	432
Brazil	1.9	-1.5	913	1,691	-1,943	-292
Argentina	3.2	-2.0	1,730	995	-851	656
Chile	2.1	-1.7	25	60	67	9
Venezuela	2.2	-1.1	91	229	-259	-39
Other Latin America	2.6	-1.8	334	632	-684	-69
Nigeria	2.5	-1.7	12	146	-220	-62
Kenya	4.5	-2.7	28	54	-57	-4
Other Sub- Saharan Africa	1.7	-1.5	264	666	-715	-47
Egypt	1.5	-1.6	-314	511	-801	-529
Middle East/ North Africa oil producers	2.6	-1.8	-1,971	649	-1,759	-2,291
non–oil producers	2.0	-0.8	56	870	-1,032	-265
India	2.2	-2.2	2,647	4,486	-4,662	332
Pakistan	4.2	-1.9	498	528	-500	109
Bangladesh	4.4	-2.6	232	333	-359	-40
Indonesia	2.0	-1.5	302	755	-775	-84
Thailand	3.0	-0.9	534	409	-245	334
Malaysia	0.9	-1.3	157	100	-93	63
Philippines	1.5	-1.3	196	312	-322	10
South Korea	1.0	-0.9	-254	281	-485	-439
Taiwan	1.1	-1.1	-52	212	-374	-254
Other East Asia	1.7	-1.6	-251	27	-171	-293
Other Asia	1.9	-1.2	211	705	-788	-117
Rest of world	0.2	-5.8	-1,126	109	-817	-1,445
Developing country total	2.2	-1.8	5,445	16,367	-19,590	-4,476

Source: USDA (1990A: 44).

Table 9.10
Industrial Market Liberalization, Scenario B

Area	Supply Quantity (%)	Demand Quantity (%)	Net Trade (million $)	Producer Surplus (million $)	Consumer Surplus (million $)	Net Welfare (million $)
				Change in		
United States	-2.5	-0.7	191	-18,745	-1,768	8,928
Canada	-3.0	0.3	154	-1,847	596	2,483
European Community	-6.3	3.3	-10,899	-26,986	25,571	12,600
Other Western Europe	-17.2	-0.8	-2,058	-7,527	2,669	1,397
Japan	-31.5	9.9	-5,884	-22,295	24,598	5,724
Australia	4.2	-3.2	2,295	1,095	-1,369	838
New Zealand	9.9	1.9	2,041	1,457	-754	1,148
South Africa	5.0	-2.7	597	853	-802	19
Eastern Europe	0.6	-0.3	1,489	1,996	-1,978	691
Soviet Union	0.3	-0.3	-395	2,856	-3,164	-1,373
China	0.5	-0.3	879	2,563	-2,634	-69
Mexico	4.4	-3.2	1,110	1,868	-2,170	-59
Central America/ Caribbean	4.6	-2.3	550	711	-461	250
Brazil	3.2	-2.2	1,580	2,769	-3,111	-431
Argentina	5.4	-3.2	2,334	1,727	-1,420	532
Chile	3.2	-2.5	45	93	-100	-7
Venezuela	3.9	-1.7	207	404	-431	-22
Other Latin America	4.2	-2.9	625	1,048	-1,107	-59
Nigeria	3.6	-2.3	87	214	-313	-28
Kenya	6.9	-3.9	47	83	-86	-3
Other Sub-Saharan Africa	2.5	-2.0	399	971	-1,033	-61
Egypt	2.4	-2.5	-44	847	-1,304	-442
Middle East/ North Africa oil producers	4.3	-2.9	-1,144	1,084	-3,048	-1,964
non-oil producers	3.1	-1.2	301	1,386	-1,606	-220
India	3.2	-3.1	3,696	6,964	-6,931	335
Pakistan	6.0	-2.6	608	784	-734	50
Bangladesh	5.3	-3.2	295	405	-445	-40
Indonesia	2.5	-1.9	390	961	-984	-105
Thailand	4.1	-1.3	458	546	-323	195
Malaysia	1.1	-1.7	151	144	-128	12
Philippines	2.2	-1.9	254	454	-466	-27
South Korea	1.5	-1.3	-94	408	-713	-385
Taiwan	1.9	-1.6	68	329	-575	-273
Other East Asia	3.1	-2.5	-145	47	-272	-225
Other Asia	2.4	-1.4	314	907	-1,019	-112
Rest of world	0.3	-9.4	-502	218	-1,382	-1,164
Developing country total	3.3	-2.6	11,591	25,374	-30,160	-4,251

Source: USDA (1990A: 45).

Table 9.11
Industrial Market Liberalization, Scenario C

Area	Supply Quantity (%)	Demand Quantity (%)	Change in Net Trade (million $)	Change in Producer Surplus (million $)	Change in Consumer Surplus (million $)	Change in Net Welfare (million $)
United States	−3.0	−0.5	−1,207	−19,886	−771	8,784
Canada	−3.3	0.7	−103	−2,047	721	2,409
European Community	−6.6	3.4	−11,196	−27,288	26,126	12,853
Other Western Europe	−17.4	−0.6	−2,099	−7,564	2,707	1,397
Japan	−31.1	10.1	−5,810	−22,103	24,414	5,732
Australia	3.6	−2.9	1,954	985	−1,329	768
New Zealand	9.4	2.0	1,921	1,426	−750	1,122
South Africa	1.5	−2.0	368	228	−623	152
Eastern Europe	0.6	−0.3	1,493	1,924	−1,892	729
Soviet Union	0.3	−0.3	−461	2,649	−2,947	−1,341
China	0.5	−0.3	856	2,587	−2,656	−76
Mexico	2.2	−5.0	1,843	2,298	−3,337	505
Central America/ Caribbean	5.3	−2.4	740	860	−465	394
Brazil	−1.7	−2.0	1,062	−1,008	−2,930	406
Argentina	9.8	−6.6	4,601	3,626	−2,744	637
Chile	2.8	−2.5	40	87	−95	−9
Venezuela	9.7	4.1	457	158	393	400
Other Latin America	3.7	−2.7	555	983	−1,052	−69
Nigeria	4.1	−3.2	137	263	−543	24
Kenya	7.0	−4.1	45	89	−95	−6
Other Sub- Saharan Africa	3.3	−1.6	416	1,090	−1,138	−48
Egypt	−6.1	−1.4	−84	313	−1,201	−181
Middle East/ North Africa oil producers	3.9	−2.8	−1,212	989	−2,975	−1,986
non−oil producers	2.9	−0.9	220	1,229	−1,454	−225
India	2.2	−2.5	4,246	7,420	−4,139	1,746
Pakistan	16.6	−2.2	1,323	1,702	−827	317
Bangladesh	7.0	−4.1	417	549	−573	−24
Indonesia	−0.1	2.2	−157	−38	895	119
Thailand	0.6	−0.4	443	158	−235	346
Malaysia	−3.3	−0.4	328	425	38	130
Philippines	−0.8	0.7	71	−30	127	67
South Korea	−19.4	18.9	−954	−3,423	7,084	1,490
Taiwan	−1.8	3.3	−115	−268	530	−58
Other East Asia	3.1	−2.4	−139	46	−263	−217
Other Asia	3.3	−1.8	464	1,153	−1,232	−79
Rest of world	0.2	−8.8	−463	226	−1,309	−1,083
Developing country total	1.3	−1.1	14,283	18,896	−17,538	2,597

Source: USDA (1990A: 46).

benefits will substantially exceed a situation in which they attempt to insulate their economies from this process. Indeed, attempts to do so may actually cause the South to lose both foreign exchange and welfare benefits as world prices rise. Second, of the three key elements of the GATT negotiation (export subsidies, internal support, and market access), the greater the gains that can be achieved in the market access area, the more benefits will accrue to the South. Third, the negative effects on net food-importing countries attributed to rising food prices after trade reform are probably overstated. If the findings of Anderson and Tyers are valid, the majority of food importers may actually gain in welfare terms, if these price signals are transmitted and food production expands. Finally, and ironically, the emphasis that many developing countries have placed on special and differential treatment, if used to justify the continued insulation of their agriculture from world market signals, may actually deny them many of the benefits of liberalization.

Given the opportunities for developing countries from trade reform in and beyond the Uruguay Round, what kind of compromise is likely, and how could benefits to the South be maximized in the 1990s? In general, it would appear that the Dunkel text will serve as a general basis for further discussions. The exact amount of change agreed to in each of the three areas of export subsidies, internal supports, and market access remains to be seen.

On balance, the future interests of developing countries appear best served by three elements in the negotiation, in descending order of priority.

1. *Maximum gains in access to industrial country markets*, particularly in key commodities such as sugar, tropical products, and fruits and vegetables. Here the sanitary and phytosanitary discussion will also prove critical because health, safety, and environmental standards appear to be the next major growth area for nontariff barriers to developing country imports. If a true increase in market access were guaranteed, it would constitute a major victory for developing countries in the Uruguay Round and beyond.

2. *Maximum reduction in export subsidies*. The gains to exporting developing countries such as Argentina and Brazil from a cessation of North/North export subsidy wars would be substantial. Coupled with increased market access, any negative terms-of-trade effects from increased prices in food-importing countries could be largely offset by expanding export opportunities.

3. *Appropriate policy adjustments allowing transmission of increased prices to developing country domestic markets*. Although selective and continuing application of special and differential treatment will continue to be necessary in most developing countries, in order to share in the benefits of liberalization the South must be prepared to pass along the gains from higher food prices to farmers, creating incentives for expanded output and, ultimately, lower levels of import dependency. Special and differential treatment, or foreign exchange and balance-of-payments problems associated

with debt service, can become excuses for inaction in domestic policy. The critique that asserts liberalization as a cause of growing gaps between the industrial North and agrarian South can be self-fulfilling: by insulating developing country economies from global markets, adjustments are put off that, once made, would allow the South to share in opportunities for growth.

This does not imply that expanded development aid, debt relief, and other measures of technical and development assistance do not complement the process of trade reform. Indeed, to the extent that these measures help to stimulate the dynamic production response associated with higher food prices, they are a very significant part of the achievement of maximum benefits from trade reform.

If a compromise proposal in agriculture is achieved, it must be linked, of course, to agreements in other critical areas such as tropical products, services, intellectual property, and textiles. However, the better the bargain achieved in agriculture, the easier it will be to finalize agreements in these other areas. The final outcome of the Uruguay Round, if it includes the above elements in agriculture, can provide a basis for renewed growth in developing country economies.

THE NORTH AMERICAN TRADING BLOC

As the battle over multilateral trade policy reform is played out, North America has become the focus for an emerging free trade area. Whereas the politics of U.S.-Canada trade in agriculture in the 1980s has been treated extensively elsewhere (Cohn, 1990), the issue of North America as one in a set of trading blocs is likely to continue as an issue beyond the Uruguay Round. Especially when discussion over NAFTA heated up during late 1990, concerns began to be raised in both the United States and Canada. These represent, in microcosm, many of the North/South issues likely to be played out in the multilateral system.

At first, those in the United States opposed to more open trade with Mexico focused on denial of fast track negotiating authority to the president. When this effort was defeated in mid-1991, the U.S. interests opposed to extending this authority shifted their opposition to the NAFTA or a GATT deal writ large. The coalition was spearheaded by organized labor, the textile industry, sugar producers, and an assortment of environmental groups. This group of strange bedfellows was opposed by the financial services industry and, in agriculture, by most grain growers.

The interests and views of such coalition members obviously vary, although each has its stake either in continued protection or more open trade. Although the coalitions are not stable, they nonetheless reflect the outlines of trade politics in the wake of the Uruguay Round. Both the textile and sugar industries are protected from market access by the South through import quotas, and will likely remain implacable foes of liberalization. Organized labor primarily fears a U.S.-Mexico deal, largely on the basis of wage rates and scanty benefits paid to Mexican workers. The environmental groups fear that polluting practices or methods of production barred in the United States (such as some insecticide spraying), which are permitted in the South, will open the United States to imports tainted by these practices or methods—the so-called "circle of poison."

Those favoring more open trade, both regionally and in the GATT, are major export industries. Financial services and corn, wheat, and soybean producers would all gain large markets from more open trade, both regionally and globally. A few commodities producers, such as dairy, would benefit from NAFTA, but fear reductions in import quotas under the GATT. From a Canadian perspective, concerns over a U.S.-Mexico accord, even if it included Canada, reflect the influence of many of the same interests opposing the scheme in the United States: labor, together with commodities protected by quotas and tariffs, form a core of opposition. Conversely, Canadian wheat and oilseed producers and financial services would be likely to gain new markets from a regional deal with Mexico.

Although some analysts and numerous protectionist political interests have interpreted NAFTA as an alternative to broader multilateral trade liberalization in the GATT, a different outcome is likely. Assuming a multilateral deal in the GATT occurs eventually, negotiations over a regional trading arrangement are also likely to be aggressively pursued in the 1990s, roughly in parallel with the European schedule of integration under the Single European Act.

This simultaneous bilateral and multilateral effort, criticized by some as inconsistent, is nonetheless likely because it allows diversification of the risk of failure on either the bilateral or multilateral front. It also allows each front to be used as a threat vis-à-vis the other, so that if progress is stalled in one arena, it can be moved ahead in the other.

In addition, the president and the U.S. trade representative will be under continuing pressure from Congress to utilize unilateral trade actions, such as Section 301 of the 1988 Trade Act, especially against Japan. In an attempt to fight against such a Congress-dominated policy, the president and trade representative will seek to pursue both bilateral and multilateral gains to blunt the critics who advocate such unilateral retaliation.

Even if they do, there are reasons to expect that protectionism will reappear in other guises. In the 1990s, perhaps the most important will be the growing use of environmental, health, and safety standards in developed countries as nontariff trade barriers. This problem is not new, but will present itself with new force in the 1990s. In part, this is because of the growing constituency favoring "eco-protectionism," a group fearful of food contaminated by chemical residues, meat tainted by hormones, and products manufactured in any manner defined as "environmentally unsound." The sanitary and phytosanitary negotiations in the GATT have considered a subset of these issues, notably the food and kindred products covered by the FAO's *Codex Alimentarius*, but the issues extend beyond food and agriculture to include almost any trade goods affected by EHS standards.

THE RISE OF ECOPROTECTIONISM

Because EHS standards have a growing national constituency, they are especially attractive candidates for disguised protectionism in the wake of the Uruguay Round. International distinctions in the tolerable level of environmental risks are created because the weight attached to environmental standards tends to vary with the income levels of different countries. Incentives are created to move restricted product and processes into areas of lax regulation, notably developing countries, while denying import access to countries that may not subscribe to the regulatory policies of the developed countries. Without multilateral action, environmental standards become sources of trade tension.

Indeed, there has been long-standing recognition of the possibility for conflicts between national environmental policy and more liberal international trade. The GATT articles explicitly recognize the possibility that domestic health, safety, and environmental policies might override general attempts to lower trade barriers (Jackson, 1969, 1989). GATT Article XI, headed "General Elimination of Quantitative Restrictions," states in paragraph (1):

> No prohibitions or restrictions other than duties, taxes or other changes, whether made effective through quotas, import or export licenses or other measures, shall be instituted or maintained by any contracting party on the importation of any product of the territory of any contracting party or on the exportation or sale for export of any product destined for the territory of any other contracting party.

Yet Article XX, headed "General Exceptions," provides that

> nothing in the Agreement shall be construed to prevent the adoption or enforcement by any contacting party of measures: . . . (g) relating to the conservation of exhaustible natural resources if such measures are made effective in conjunction with restrictions on domestic production or consumption; provided that such measures: . . . are not applied in a manner which would constitute a means of arbitrary or unjustifiable discrimination between countries where the same conditions prevail, or a disguised restriction on international trade.

A similar set of exceptions was applied to health-related measures under Article XX(b). GATT law emphasizes that any restrictions imposed on foreign practices for environmental or health reasons must also reflect a domestic commitment, so that the exception cannot be misused as a disguised form of protection.

The Tokyo Round of Multilateral Trade Negotiations promulgated a "standards code" that has tried (also largely without success) to grapple with the balance between health, safety, and environmental standards and trade liberalization (GATT, 1982). This 1979 code supplemented the GATT rules that require "national treatment" (no less favorable to importers than to domestic parties) and prohibit the "nullification or impairment" of trade concessions through the back-door device of nontariff barriers (Jackson, 1969). One purpose of the code was to prevent any product, technical, health, safety, or environmental standard from creating "unnecessary obstacles to international trade" (Rubin and Graham, 1982: 8).

Despite an additional decade of discussions, including substantial attention to both technical standards and nontariff barriers in the Uruguay Round, it is still unclear when and where such standards constitute an "unnecessary obstacle to international trade." If anything, the temptation to use environmental and health standards to deny access to home markets is stronger now than it was in the 1980s. As the European Community moves toward its goal of market integration in 1992, it will have strong incentives to create common regulations for internal purposes, but to impose restrictions vis-à-vis the rest of the world. Even if national standards can be harmonized, moreover, there is every reason to expect subnational jurisdictions to utilize various health and environmental standards to protect certain markets.

Underlying the development of these trade tensions are fundamental differences in the views of developed and developing countries concerning the appropriate level and extent of environmental regulation. Differences in the domestic policy response to these problems are well represented in the food systems of the North and South. In the developed countries of North America and Western Europe, the "food problem" arises not from too little food and land in production, but generally too much. As predicted by Engels' Law, the incomes of developed countries have increased, the share of this income spent has increased, and the share of this income spent on food has fallen in proportion to other goods and services. This characteristic makes food an "inferior good" in economics jargon. In contrast, environmental quality and health concerns have grown in importance with increasing income levels. They are what economists call "superior goods" in the sense that they play a larger role in the national budget as national incomes increase (see Runge, 1987).

In low-income developing countries, whereas the share of national resources devoted to food and agriculture remains large, environmental quality and occupational health risks are widely perceived as concerns of the rich. Even if environmental and health risks are acknowledged, the income levels of most developing countries do not permit a structure of environmental regulation comparable to that in the North. This two-tiered structure of international environmental regulation, with stricter regulatory regimes in developed countries paired with lax or nonexistent regulations in developing countries, increases the North-South flow of environmental risks. A kind of "environmental arbitrage" results, in which profits are gained by exploiting the differential in regulations. This environmental arbitrage results from conscious policy choices that reveal differences in the value attached to environmental quality by rich and poor countries. As these paths of institutional innovation increasingly diverge, so will the differential impact of environmental constraints on producers in the North and competitors in the South, such as Argentina and Brazil (Runge et al., 1988).

The competitiveness implications of these trends are not lost on Northern producers. They have been quick to see the trade relevance of environmental and health standards. Growing consumer concerns with the health and environmental impacts of agriculture create a natural (and much larger) constituency for nontariff barriers to trade, justified in the name of health and safety. As between countries in the North, obvious differences in values also exist, although the regulatory gap is less yawning.

Given the tension separating North and South, and the lesser differences between countries in the North, it would appear that a single set of standards is unlikely to be successful. The Subsidies Code adopted during the Tokyo Round is at least a necessary starting point, but some mechanism must be found to accommodate differences in national priorities linked to levels of economic development and cultural factors.

In view of differences in levels of economic development and national priorities, it is clear that standards cannot be wholly uniform. James (1982: 260) has contended that, despite valid arguments for improved health and environmental regulations in the South, "it does not follow from this that countries of the Third World should adopt either the same *number* or the same *level* of standards as developed countries." James suggested what may be called intermediate standards, "in the same sense and for the same basic reason as that which underlies the widespread advocacy of intermediate technology in the Third World" (James, 1982: 265). This does not imply a "downgrading" of developed countries' regulations, but an "upgrading" of developing countries' norms, together with the recognition that the social costs of regulation are relative to national income.

Unfortunately, despite recent attempts to deal with these issues in forums such as the GATT, the linkages from environmental regulation to international trade have not been clearly recognized. The Food and Agriculture Organization of the United Nations has worked to develop comprehensive rules affecting food and agriculture in the *Codex Alimentarius* (FAO, 1987). A special technical working group at the GATT Secretariat in Geneva is attempting to use this code as the basis for harmonizing member countries' regulations. But there are only a few agreed-upon standards, and none are regarded as binding in law. With the exception of the GATT working group, the issue has not been given priority by international institutions.

Beyond environmental considerations are the large problems of trade distortion and market access discussed above. These distortions threaten more liberal international trade in ways that are damaging to both developed and developing country interests. In addition to the development of carefully reasoned legal arguments determining when environmental and health standards are in fact trade barriers, an international accord on environmental and health regulations would be appropriate. Similar in nature to the 1988 Montreal Protocol agreed to by forty nations to reduce emissions shown harmful to the ozone layer, its purpose would be to call for the rights, duties, and liabilities that define national regulations on environment and health, which can then be brought more nearly into accord. In the absence of such an agreement, groups within nations will continue to advocate the use of regulations as disguised protectionism, or loosening standards of environmental quality in the name of greater competitiveness.

SUMMARY

This chapter has examined three issues likely to dominate agricultural trade policy discussions after the Uruguay Round: (1) the role of developing countries within the GATT; (2) the North American Free Trade Agreement and similar trade blocs; and (3) the potential for environmental, health, and safety standards to become new barriers to trade.

Although the problems of developing countries in the multilateral trading system probably will not be resolved in the Uruguay Round, they stand to gain from agricultural trade reform. Future interests of developing countries will be served best by three aspects of the trade negotiations: (1) increased access to industrial countries' markets in key commodities such as sugar, tropical products, and fruits and vegetables; (2) reduction in export subsidies; and (3) policy adjustments allowing transmission of increased prices to developing country domestic markets. Debt relief, aid, and other forms of assistance will be important complements to trade reform. Developing countries that use the various forms of assistance to help stimulate the production response associated with higher food prices will find them to be important in achieving maximum benefits from trade reform.

As the Uruguay Round winds down, the possibility of a free trade agreement for North America is receiving increased attention. Whether or not its purpose is to provide an alternative to broader trade liberalization within the GATT, it and similar arrangements will be among the major issues for the multilateral trading system in the 1990s. For the United States, the simultaneous bilateral and multilateral negotiations serve the dual purpose of diversifying the risk of failure in either negotiation and in enabling negotiators to use each as threats against the other. In any event, North American free trade very likely will be aggressively pursued, roughly in tandem with the European schedule for market integration.

Environmental, health, and safety standards are increasingly attractive candidates for disguised protectionism in world trade. Strong domestic constituencies are emerging, especially within developed industrial states, in support of tough national environmental laws. Developing countries are concerned that these laws will be used to deny their food exports access to the markets of developed countries. So far, there are very few agreed-upon multilateral standards, and none are regarded as legally binding. More important, however, the issue has received little of the much-needed international attention within appropriate institutions.

However these issues ultimately play out in future agricultural trade discussions, there can be little doubt that they will form a significant part of the international trade agenda over the next several years.

NOTES

1. "Fast-track" authority for trade agreements dates to 1974. U.S. law provides that, if the procedural requirements of the statute are met, Congress will give fast-track treatment to legislation proposed by the president that implements multilateral or bilateral trade agreements. The two key elements are: (1) time-limited consideration in Congress of the president's implementing legislation; and (2) no amendments permitted to the legislation. With the fast-track authority in place, once the president submits legislation implementing a trade agreement, to reject a portion of the legislation, one must vote against the entire package. A two-year extension of the fast-track authority was made as of June 1, 1991. The statute provides a procedure, itself on the fast track, for one house of Congress to disapprove such extension requests.

2. The leading studies cited by the FIG as of 1989 were:
   a. Organization of Economic Cooperation and Development (OECD, 1987). This study presents several scenarios. The scenario selected here assumes a 10 percent across-the-board reduction in support from 1979–1981 levels: the results have been multiplied by 10 to yield approximate price changes consistent with the "full liberalization" assumptions of the other studies reported here.
   b. Roningen, Dixit, and Seeley (1988). The results are derived from the SWOPSIM model of the Economic Research Service of the USDA. The price changes simulate the effect of free trade in OECD countries in the year 2000 compared with a reference scenario in which policies are held at their 1984–1985 levels.
   c. International Agricultural Trade Research Consortium (IATRC, 1988). The reported scenario simulates the effects of the elimination of existing agricultural policies of OECD countries, using 1986 as the base period.
   d. Tyers and Anderson (1988).
   e. Parikh et al. (1986).

References

Aggarwal, V. K. (1981) *Hanging by a Thread: International Regime Change in the Textile/Apparel System, 1950–1979.* Stanford, Calif.: Stanford University.
——— (1985) *Liberal Protectionism: The International Politics of Organized Textile Trade.* Berkeley, Calif.: University of California Press.
Agra Europe, various issues, 1990–1992.
Allison, G. T. (1971) *Essence of Decision.* Boston, Mass.: Little, Brown.
Anderson, H. (1990) "Canada's Position on Agricultural Trade Hurts its Stature as a Middlepower." *Montreal Gazette* (August 2), p. D1.
Anderson, K., and Y. Hayami, eds. (1986) *The Political Economy of Agricultural Protection: East Asia in International Perspective.* Sydney: Allen & Unwin.
Anderson, K., and R. Tyers (1988) "Japan's Agricultural Policy in International Perspective." *Pacific Economic Papers* (July), No. 161. Canberra: Australia-Japan Research Centre.
——— (1990a) "How Developing Countries Could Gain From Food Trade Liberalization in the Uruguay Round." In I. Goldin and O. Knudsen, eds., *Agricultural Trade Liberalization: Implications for Developing Countries*, ch. 2. Paris: Organization of Economic Cooperation and Development (OECD).
——— (1990b) "Welfare Gains to Developing Countries From Food Trade Liberalization Following the Uruguay Round." Department of Economics and Centre for International Economic Studies, University of Adelaide, Adelaide, Australia.
Australian Bureau of Agricultural and Resource Economics (1985) *Agricultural Policies in the European Community: The Origins, Nature and Effects on Production and Trade.* Policy Monograph No. 2. Canberra: Australian Government Publishing Service.
——— (1988a) *Japanese Agricultural Policies: A Time of Change.* Policy Monograph No. 3. Canberra: Australian Government Publishing Service.
——— (1988b) *Japanese Beef Policies: Implications for Trade, Prices and Market Shares.* Occasional Paper No. 102. Canberra: Australian Bureau of Agricultural and Resource Economics.
——— (1989) *U.S. Grain Policies and the World Market.* Policy Monograph No. 4. Canberra: Australian Bureau of Agricultural and Resource Economics.
Australian (The), April 6, 1983, 7.
Australian Financial Review, August 15, 1986; August 28, 1986.

Balassa, B. (1980) "The Tokyo Round and the Developing Countries." *World Bank Staff Working Paper No. 370*, February. Washington, D.C.: World Bank.

Bergsten, C. F. (1988) "Reforming World Agricultural Trade: A Policy Statement by Twenty-nine Professionals from Seventeen Countries." In W. M. Miner and D. E. Hathaway, eds., *World Agricultural Trade: Building a Consensus*, pp. 3–31. Halifax, Nova Scotia: The Institute for Research on Public Policy.

Bertin, O. (1986) "Canadian Farmers Face Heavy Losses in World Trade War." *Globe and Mail (Toronto)*, July 3: B1.

Bhagwati, J. (1988) *Protectionism*. Cambridge, Mass.: MIT Press.

Block, F. (1977) *The Origins of International Economic Disorder*. Berkeley, Calif.: University of California Press.

Buckley, A. (1986) "Aust Hopes to Help Found Group to Counter Protectionist Traders." *Australian Financial Review* (August 25): 10.

Buckwell, A. E., D. R. Harvey, K. J. Thomson, and K. A. Parton (1982) *The Costs of the Common Agricultural Policy*. London: Croom-Helm.

Butler, N. (1983) "The Ploughshares War Between Europe and America." *Foreign Affairs* 62 (Fall): 105–122.

Calder, K. E. (1988) "Japanese Foreign Economic Policy Formation: Explaining the Reactive State." *World Politics* 40, 4 (July): 517–541.

Calingaert, M. (1988) *The 1992 Challenge from Europe: Development of the European Community's Internal Market*, No. 237. Washington, D.C.: National Planning Association.

Canadian House of Commons (1987) *Debates*: 5357.

Canadian Wheat Board, *Annual Report*, various years. Winnipeg: CWB.

Carey, M. J. (1981) "Introduction: The Political Economy of Food—The Regional Approach." In D. N. Balaam and M. J. Carey, eds., *Food Politics: The Regional Conflict*, pp. 1–8. Totowa, N.J.: Allanheld, Osmun.

Chenery, H., and T. N. Srinivasan (1988) *The Handbook of Developmental Economics*, 2 vols. New York: North Holland.

Choices, fourth quarter, 1986.

Cohn, T. H. (1979–1980) "The 1978-9 Negotiations for an International Wheat Agreement: An Opportunity Lost?" *International Journal* 35: 132–149.

——— (1990) *The International Politics of Agricultural Trade: Canadian-American Relations in a Global Agricultural Context*. Vancouver: University of British Columbia Press.

——— (forthcoming) "Canada and the Ongoing Impasse over Agricultural Protectionism." In A. C. Cutler and M. W. Zacher, eds., *Canadian Foreign Policy and International Economic Regimes*. Vancouver: University of British Columbia Press.

Coleman, W. D. (1988) *Business and Politics: A Study of Collective Action*. Kingston and Montreal: McGill–Queen's University Press.

Commission of the European Communities (1987) *Agricultural Situation in the Community: 1986 Report*. Brussels: Commission of the European Communities.

Conybeare, J. (1985) *Trade Wars: The Theory and Practice of International Commercial Policy*. New York: Columbia University Press.

Cooper, A. F. (1990) "Australia: Domestic Political Management and International Trade Reform." In G. Skogstad and A. F. Cooper, eds., *Agricultural Trade: Domestic Pressures and International Tensions*, pp. 11–133. Halifax, N.S.: The Institute for Research on Public Policy.

——— (1990) "Exporters versus Importers: LDCs, Agricultural Trade and the Uruguay Round." *Intereconomics* 25 (Winter): 13–17.

———— (1991) "Between Integration and a Way of Life: Trade Liberalization and the Political Economy of Agriculture." In L. A. Pal and Rainer-Olaf Schultze, eds., *The Nation-State Versus Continental Integration: Canada in North America—Germany in Europe*, pp. 115–130. Bochum: Universitatverlag: Dr. N. Brockmeyer.

————(1992) "Like-Minded Nations/Contrasting Diplomatic Styles: Australian and Canadian Approaches to Agricultural Trade." *Canadian Journal of Political Science* 25 (June): 349–379.

Cooper, A. F., R. A. Higgott, and K. R. Nossal (1991) "Bound to Follow?: Leadership and Followership in the Gulf Conflict." *Political Science Quarterly* 106 (Fall): 391–410.

Cowhey, P. F., and E. Long (1983) "Testing Theories of Regime Change: Hegemonic Decline or Surplus Capacity?" *International Organization* 37: 157–188.

Cribb, J. (1987) "Bushwacked by Labor." *The Weekend Australian*, August 1–2, 8B.

Critchley, B. (1986) "Fair Traders Taking Aim at Agricultural Subsidies." *Financial Post (Toronto)*, August 23, p. 7.

Curtis, T. B., and J. R. Vastine, Jr. (1971) *The Kennedy Round and the Future of American Trade*. New York: Praeger.

Destler, I. M. (1986) *American Trade Politics: System Under Stress*. Washington, D.C.: Institute for International Economics.

Dewitt, D. B., and J. Kirton (1983) *Canada as a Principal Power*. Toronto: John Wiley.

Donnelly, M. W. (1984) "Conflict over Government Authority and Markets: Japan's Rice Economy." In E. S. Krauss, T. P. Rohlen, and P. G. Steinhoff, eds., *Conflict in Japan*, pp. 335–374. Honolulu: University of Hawaii Press.

Drohan, M. (1990) "Canada at Odds with Trade Group." *Globe and Mail (Toronto)*, October 24.

Drohan, M., and D. Fagan (1991) "Canada Makes Last-Ditch Bid to Save Marketing Boards." *Globe and Mail (Toronto)*, November 26.

Evans, G. (1988) "Australia in the Asia-Pacific Region." Address by the minister for foreign affairs and trade before the World Trade Affairs Council and Asia Society, October 7.

Evans, J. W. (1971) *The Kennedy Round in American Trade Policy: The Twilight of the GATT?* Cambridge, Mass.: Harvard University Press.

Finlayson, J. A., and M. W. Zacher (1981) "The GATT and the Regulation of Trade Barriers: Regime Dynamics and Functions." *International Organization* 35: 561–601.

————(1983) "The GATT and the Regulation of Trade Barriers: Regime Dynamics and Functions." In S. D. Krasner, ed., *International Regimes*, pp. 273–314. Ithaca, N.Y.: Cornell University Press.

Food and Agriculture Organization (FAO) (1980) *Principles of Surplus Disposal and Consultative Obligations of Member Nations*, 2nd ed. Rome: FAO.

———— (1987) *Introducing Codex Alimentarius*. Rome: FAO/WHO Food Standards Program.

———— (1990) *Country Tables*. Rome, Italy: FAO.

Food and Fiber Letter (The), vol. 8, no. 43, November 7, 1988.

Fox, A. B. (1980) "The Range of Choice for Middle Powers: Australia and Canada Compared." *The Australian Journal of Politics and History* 26: 193.

Fukui, H. (1987) "The Policy Research Council of Japan's Liberal Democratic Party: Policy Making Role and Practice." *Asian Thought and Society* 11, 34 (March): 3–30.

Funabashi, Y. (1992) "Globalize Asia." *New Perspectives Quarterly* 9, 1 (Winter): 23–27.

Gallagher, P. W. (1988) "Setting the Agenda for Trade Negotiations: Australia and the Cairns Group." *Australian Outlook: The Australian Journal of International Affairs* 42, 1 (April): 3–8.

Garnaut, R. (1989) *Australia and the North East Asian Ascendancy*. Canberra: Australian Government Publishing Service.

George, A. (1988) "Rice Politics in Japan." *Pacific Economic Papers*, no. 159 (May). Canberra: Australia-Japan Research Centre.

——— (1990) "The Politics of Liberalization in Japan: The Case of Rice." *Pacific Economic Papers*, no. 188 (October). Canberra: Australia-Japan Research Centre.

——— (1991) "Japan's America Problem." *Washington Quarterly* 14, 3 (Summer): 5–19.

George, A., and E. Saxon (1986) "The Politics of Agricultural Protection in Japan." In K. Anderson and Y. Hayami, eds., *The Political Economiy of Agricultural Protection: East Asia in International Perspective*, pp. 91–110. Sydney: Allen & Unwin.

General Agreement on Tariffs and Trade (GATT) (1982) *Code of Conduct for Preventing Technical Barriers to Trade*, GATT Multilateral Trade Negotiations, Doc. MTN/NTM/W1192/Rev. 5. Cited in S. J. Rubin and T. R. Graham, eds. (1989) *Factors Influencing Trends in World Agricultural Production and Trade*. Washington, D.C.: General Accounting Office (GAO/RCED-89-1).

——— (1986) Text of the General Agreement. Geneva: GATT.

——— (1988) "News of the Uruguay Round," No. 18, August 2.

——— (1989a) "Special and Differential Treatment: Brazilian Statement," Geneva: GATT.

——— (1989b) "Ways to Take Account of the Negative Effects of the Agriculture Reform Process on Net Food Importing Developing Countries by Group W/74," in conjunction with MTN. GNG/NG5/W/74. Submitted to the Negotiating Group on Agriculture, General Agreement on Tariffs and Trade, Geneva, Switzerland, October 25, 1989.

——— (various years) *International Trade*. Geneva: GATT.

Gill, S., and D. Law (1988) *Global Political Economy*. Baltimore, Md.: Johns Hopkins University Press.

Gilpin, R. (1987) *The Political Economy of International Relations*. Princeton, N.J.: Princeton University Press.

Goldin, I., and O. Knudsen, eds. (1990) *Agricultural Trade Liberalization: Implications for Developing Countries*. Paris: Organization of Economic Cooperation and Development (OECD).

Goldstein, J. (1988) "Ideas, Institutions, and American Trade Policy." *International Organization* 42 (Winter 1988): 179–217.

Goldstein, J., and R. Keohane (1990) "Ideas and Foreign Policy." Unpublished manuscript, October 18.

Gosovic B., and J. Ruggie (1976) "On the Creation of a New International Economic Order." *International Organization* 30 (Spring): 2.

Gourevitch, P. (1986) *Politics in Hard Times: Responses to International Economic Crises*. Ithaca, N.Y.: Cornell University Press.

Government of Canada (1989) "Government Expresses Disappointment over GATT Ruling on Ice Cream and Yoghurt." News release no. 218, September 15.

Grunberg, I. (1990) "Exploring the 'Myth' of Hegemonic Stability." *International Organization* 44: 431–477.

Haas, E. B. (1982) "Words Can Hurt You; or, Who Said What to Whom About Regimes." *International Organization* 36: 207–243.

Harris, S. F. (1989) "Regional Economic Cooperation, Trading Blocs and Australia's Prospects." *Australian Outlook: The Australian Journal of International Affairs* 43 (August): 16–25.

Hathaway, D. E. (1983) "Agricultural Trade Policy for the 1980s." In W. R. Cline, ed., *Trade Policy in the 1980s*, pp. 435–453. Washington, D.C.: Institute for International Economics.

———— (1987) *Agriculture and the GATT: Rewriting the Rules*. Policy Analysis in International Economics, No. 20. Washington, D.C.: Institute for International Economics.

Hausner, U. (1992) "Determinants of Corn and Wheat Price Policy in the United States," Department of Agricultural and Applied Economics, University of Minnesota.

Hayami, Y. (1988) *Japanese Agriculture Under Siege: The Political Economy of Agricultural Policies*. London: MacMillan.

Hayami, Y., and V. W. Ruttan (1985) *Agricultural Development: An International Perspective*, 2nd ed. Baltimore, Md.: Johns Hopkins University Press.

Hemmi, K. (1982) "Agriculture and Politics in Japan." In E. N. Castle and K. Hemmi, with S. A. Skillings, eds., *U.S. Agricultural Trade Relations*, pp. 219–268. Washington, D.C.: Resources for the Future.

Higgott, R. A. (1987a) "Australia and the New International Division of Labor in the Asia Pacific Region." In J. Caporaso, ed., *A Changing International Division of Labor*, pp. 147–185. Boulder, Colo.: Lynne Rienner.

———— (1987b) "Australia: Economic Crisis and the Politics of Regional Economic Adjustment." In R. Robison et al., eds., *East Asia in the 1980s*, pp. 177–217. Sydney: Allen & Unwin.

———— (1987c) *The World Economic Order and the Trade Crisis: Implications for Australia*. Canberra: Australian Institute of International Affairs.

———— (1989) "From High Politics to Low Politics: The Ascendancy of the Economic Dimension in Australian-American Relations." In J. Ravenhill, ed., *No Longer an American Lake: Alliance Politics in the Pacific*. Berkeley: University of California, Institute of International Studies.

———— (1991) "The Politics of Australia's International Economic Relations: Adjustment and Two-Level Games." *Australian Journal of Political Science* 26 (March): 2–28.

———— (forthcoming) "International Constraints on Labor's Economic Policy." In B. Galligan and G. Singleton, eds., *How Labor Governs: The Hawke Government and Business*. Melbourne: Longmans.

Higgott, R. A., and A. F. Cooper (1990) "Middle Power Leadership and Coalition Building: Australia, the Cairns Group, and the Uruguay Round of Trade Negotiations." *International Organization* 44: 589–632.

Higgott, R. A., et al. (1990) "Asia-Pacific Economic Cooperation: An Evolving Case Study of Leadership and Cooperation Building." *International Journal* 45 (Autumn): 823–866.

Hill, J. T. (1977) "Changes in United States Agriculture Policy and the Implications for Canada." *Agriculture Abroad* 32: 29–33.

Hillman, J. S., and R. A. Rothenberg (1985) "Wider Implications of Protecting Japan's Rice Farmers." *The World Economy* 8, 1 (March): 43–62.

Holmes, J. (1976) *The Shaping of Peace: Canada and the Search for World Order, 1943–1957*. Vol. 1. Toronto, Canada: University of Toronto Press.

Honma, M., and Y. Hayami (1986) "Structure of Agricultural Protection in Industrial Countries." *Journal of International Economics* 20: 115–129.

Hopkins, R. F., and D. J. Puchala, eds. (1978) *The Global Political Economy of Food*. Madison: University of Wisconsin Press.

Houck, J. P. (1980) "U.S. Agricultural Trade and the Tokyo Round." *Law and Policy in International Business* 12: 265–295.

Hudec, R. E. (1975) *The GATT Legal System and World Trade Diplomacy*. New York: Praeger.

——— (1988) "Dispute Settlement in Agricultural Trade Matters: The Lessons of the GATT Experience." In K. Allen and K. Macmillan, eds., *U.S.-Canadian Agricultural Trade Challenges: Developing Common Approaches*, pp. 145–153. Washington, D.C.: Resources for the Future.

Hufbauer, G. C., and J. J. Schott (1985) *Trading for Growth: The Next Round of Trade Negotiations*. Policy Analyses in International Economics, no. 11 (September).Washington: Institute for International Economics.

Hughes, H. (1989) *Australian Export Performance, Obstacles and Issues of Assistance: Report of the Committee for Review of Export Market Development Assistance* Canberra: Australian Government Publishing Service.

Ikenberry, G. J. (1986) "The State and Strategies of International Adjustment." *World Politics* 39 (October): 53–77.

——— (1992) "A World Economy Restored: Expert Consensus and the Anglo-American Postwar Settlement." *International Organization* 46: 1 (Winter): 289–321.

International Agricultural Trade Research Consortium (IATRC) (1988) *Assessing the Benefits of Trade Liberalization*. Annapolis, Md.: IATRC.

International Monetary Fund (IMF) (1990) *International Financial Statistics Yearbook*. Washington, D.C.: IMF.

Jackson, J. H. (1969) *World Trade and the Law of GATT*. Indianapolis: The Bobbs-Merrill Co.

——— (1989) *The World Trading System: Law and Policy of International Economic Relations*. Cambridge, Mass.: MIT Press.

James, J. (1982) "Product Standards in Developing Countries." In F. Stewart and J. James, eds. *Economies of New Technology in Developing Countries*. Boulder, Colo: Westview: 256–271.

Japan Economic Almanac, Nihon Keizai Shinbun, Tokyo, 1990.

Johnson, D. G. (1984) "Domestic Agricultural Policy in an International Environment: Effects of Other Countries' Policies on the United States." *American Journal of Agricultural Economics* 66: 735–744.

Junz, H. B. and C. Boonekamp (1991) "What is at Stake in the Uruguay Round"? *Finance & Development* 28, 2 (June): 11–15.

Katzenstein, P., ed. (1978) *Between Power and Plenty: Foreign Economic Policies of Advanced Industrial States*. Madison: University of Wisconsin Press.

Kemper, R. (1980) "The Tokyo Round: Results and Implications for Developing Countries." *World Bank Staff Working Paper* No. 372, February. Washington, D.C.: World Bank.

Keohane, R. O. (1984) *After Hegemony: Cooperation and Discord in the World Political Economy*. Princeton, N.J.: Princeton University Press.

Knudsen, O., and J. Nash (with contributions by J. Bovard, B. Gardner, and L. A. Winters) (1990) *Redefining the Role of Government in Agriculture for the 1990s*. Discussion Paper No. 105. Washington, D.C.: World Bank.

Knutson, R. D., J. B. Penn, and W. T. Boehm (1983) *Agricultural and Food Policy*. Englewood Cliffs, N.J.: Prentice-Hall.

Koester, U. (1977) "The Redistributional Effects of the Common Agricultural Policy." *European Review of Agricultural Economics* 4: 321–345.

———— (1982) *Policy Options for the Grain Economy of the European Community: Implications for Developing Countries.* Washington, D.C.: IFPRI Research Report 35.

Krasner, S. D. (1982) "Structural Causes and Regime Consequences: Regimes as Intervening Variables." *International Organization* 36: 185–205.

———— (1988) *Asymmetries in Japanese-American Trade: The Case for Specific Reciprocity.* Policy Paper in International Affairs, No. 32. Berkeley: University of California, Institute for International Studies.

Krause, L. B. (1984) "Australia's Comparative Advantage in International Trade." In R. E. Caves and L. B. Krause, eds., *The Australian Economy: The View from the North.* Sydney: Allen & Unwin for the Brookings Institution.

Krissoff, B., J. Sullivan, J. Wainio, and B. Johnston (1990) *Agricultural Trade Liberalization and Developing Countries.* Staff Report No. AGES 9042. Washington, D.C.: U.S. Department of Agriculture, Economic Research Service.

Krueger, A., M. Schiff, and A. Valdes (1988a) "Agricultural Incentives in Developing Countries." *World Bank Economic Review* (September 2): 255–272.

———— (1988b) "Measuring the Impact of Sector-specific and Economy-wide Policies on Agricultural Incentives in LDCs." *World Bank Economic Review* 2:2 (September): 255–272.

Krugman, P., ed. (1986) *Strategic Trade Policy and the New International Economics.* Cambridge, Mass.: MIT Press.

Lake, D. A. (1983) "International Economic Structures and American Foreign Economy Policy, 1887–1934." *World Politics* 35 (July): 517–543.

Lipson, C. (1982) "The Transformation of Trade: The Sources and Effects of Regime Change." *International Organization* 36: 417–455.

Maier, G. (1977) "The Politics of Productivity: Foundations of American International Economic Policy After World War II." *International Organization* 31 (Summer): 607–634.

McCallum, B. T. (1976) "Rational Expectations and the Estimation of Econometric Models: An Alternative Procedure." *International Economic Review* 17: 484–490.

McDonald, B. J. (1990) "Agricultural Negotiations in the Uruguay Round." *The World Economy* 13: 299–327.

McLin, J. (1979) "Surrogate International Organization and the Case of World Food Security, 1949–1969." *International Organization* 33: 35–55.

Mendelowitz, A. I. (1989) Statement before several subcommittees of the U.S. House of Representatives, Committee on Agriculture, Washington, D.C., GAO/T-NSIAD-90-12, November 16.

Miller, G. (1989) *The Political Economy of International Agricultural Policy Reform.* Canberra: Department of Primary Industries, Australia, Government Publishing Service.

Milner, H. V. (1988) *Resisting Protectionism: Global Industries and the Politics of International Trade.* Princeton, N.J.: Princeton University Press.

Ministerial Declaration on the Uruguay Round (1986) Punta del Este, Uruguay (September).

Moore, L. (1985) *The Growth and Structure of International Trade Since the Second World War.* Sussex: Wheatsheaf Books.

Moyer, H. W., and T. E. Josling (1990) *Agricultural Policy Reform: Politics and Process in the EC and USA.* New York and London: Harvester Wheatsheaf.

Murphy, A. (1990) *The European Community and the International Trading*

System, vols. 1 and 2. Brussels: Centre for European Policy Studies.

Nam, C. H. (1987) "Export-Promoting Subsidies, Countervailing Threats, and the General Agreement on Tariffs and Trade." *The World Bank Economic Review* 1: 727–743.

Nelson, C. R. (1975) "Rational Expectations and the Estimation of Econometric Models." *International Economic Review* 16: 555–561.

Nerlove, M. (1958) *The Dynamics of Supply: Estimation of Farmers' Response to Price*. Baltimore, Md.: Johns Hopkins University Press.

Nossal, K. R. (1989) *The Politics of Canadian Foreign Policy*. Scarborough, Ont.: Prentice-Hall Canada.

Nye, J. S. (1990) *Bound to Lead: The Changing Nature of American Power*. New York: Basic Books.

Odell, J. (1982) *U.S. International Monetary Policy*. Princeton, N.J.: Princeton University Press.

Olson, M. (1965) *The Logic of Collective Action*. Cambridge, Mass.: Harvard University Press.

——— (1986) "The Exploitation and Subsidization of Agriculture in Developing and Developed Countries." In A. Maunder and U. Renborg, eds., *Agriculture in a Turbulent World Economy*. Brookfield, Vt.: Gower.

Ono, N. (1991) "Canada, Japan Ally on Farm Tariff Issue." *Nikkei Weekly*, November 2.

Organization of Economic Cooperation and Development (OECD) (1987) *National Policies and Agricultural Trade*. Paris: OECD.

Oxley, A. (1990) *The Challenge of Free Trade*. New York: Harvester Wheatsheaf.

Oye, K. (1992) *The World Political Economy of the 1930s and 1980s*. Princeton, N.J.: Princeton University Press.

Paarlberg, R. L. (1982) "Three Political Explanations for Crisis in the World Grain Market." In W. P. Avery and D. P. Rapkin, eds., *America in a Changing World Political Economy*, pp. 119–146. New York: Longman.

——— (1988) *Fixing Farm Trade: Options for the United States*. Cambridge: Ballinger for the Council on Foreign Relations.

——— (1989a) "Agricultural Policy and Trade Reforms in Developed Countries: Projected Consequences for Developing Countries." Paper presented at the Center for Agriculture and Rural Development (CARD), Iowa State University, Ames, Iowa.

——— (1989b) "Is There Anything American About American Agricultural Policy?" In C. S. Kramer ed., *The Political Economy of U.S. Agriculture*, pp. 37–55. Washington, D.C.: Resources for the Future.

——— (1990a) "The Mysterious Popularity of EEP." *Choices* 5: 14–17.

——— (1990b) "The Upside Down World of U.S.-Japanese Agricultural Trade." *Washington Quarterly* (Autumn): 131–143.

Palmeter, N. D. (1989) "Agriculture and Trade Regulation: Selected Issues in the Application of U.S. Antidumping and Countervailing Duty Laws." *Journal of World Trade* 23: 47–68.

Pappas et al. (1989) *The Global Challenge, Australian Manufacturing in the 1990s: What Part Will Manufacturing Play in Australia's Future?* Interim report. Melbourne: Australian Manufacturing Council.

Parikh, K. S., et al. (1986) *Towards Free Trade in Agriculture*. Dordrecht, Netherlands: Martinus Nijhoff Publishers.

Pastor, R. (1983) "The Cry-and-Sigh Syndrome: Congress and Trade Policy." In A. Schick, ed., *Making Economic Policy in Congress*, pp. 158–195. Washington, D.C.: American Enterprise Institute for Public Policy Research.

Petit, M. et al. (1987) *Agricultural Policy Formulation in the European Community: The Birth of Milk Quotas and CAP Reform*. Amsterdam: Elsevier Science.

Pomfret, R. W. (1988) *Unequal Trade: The Economics of Discriminatory International Trade Politics*. Oxford: Basil Blackwell.

Porter, M. E. (1991) *Canada at the Crossroads: The Reality of a New Competitive Environment*. Ottawa: Business Council on National Issues and Ministry of Supply and Services, Government of Canada.

Porter, J. M., and D. E. Bowers (1989) *A Short History of U.S. Agricultural Trade Negotiations*. Washington, D.C.: U.S. Department of Agriculture, Economic Research Service.

Puchala, D. J., and R. F. Hopkins (1982) "International Regimes: Lessons from Inductive Analysis." *International Organization* 36: 245–275.

Putnam, R. D. (1988) "Diplomacy and Domestic Politics: The Logic of Two-Level Games." *International Organization* 42, 3 (Summer): 427–460.

Rapp, D. (1988) *How the U.S. Got into Agriculture and Why It Can't Get Out*. Washington, D.C.: Congressional Quarterly.

Randall, K. (1985) "Caught in the Cross-Current." *Business Review Weekly (Australian)*, July 19, pp. 15–22.

Reich, M. R., Y. Endo, and C. P. Timmer (1985) "Agriculture: The Political Economy of Structural Change." In T. K. McGraw, ed., *America versus Japan*, pp. 151–192. Boston, Mass.: Harvard Business School Press.

Resources for the Future (1988) *Mutual Disarmament in World Agriculture*. Washington, D.C.: Resources for the Future.

Riethmuller, P., and T. L. Roe (1986) "Government Intervention in Commodity Markets: The Case of Japanese Rice and Wheat Policy." *Journal of Policy Modelling* 8: 327–349.

Roningen, V. O., P. M. Dixit, and R. Seeley (1988) "Agricultural Outlook for the Year 2000: Some Alternatives," unpublished manuscript.

Rosenau, J. N. (1976) "Capabilities and Control in an Interdependent World." *International Security* 1: 32–49.

Rothacher, A. (1989) *Japan's Agro-Food Sector: The Politics and Economics of Excess Protection*. London: MacMillan.

Rothstein, R. (1979) *Global Bargaining*. Princeton, N.J.: Princeton University Press.

Rubin, S. J., and T. R. Graham, eds. (1982) *Environment and Trade*. Totowa, N.J.: Allanheld, Osmun.

Ruggie, J. G. (1982) "International Regimes, Transactions, and Change: Imbedded Liberalism in the Postwar Economic Order." *International Organization* 36: 379–415.

Runge, C. F. (1987) "Induced Agricultural Innovation and Environmental Quality: The Case of Groundwater Regulation," *Land Economics*: 249–258.

——— (1988) "The Assault on Agricultural Protectionism." *Foreign Affairs* (Fall): 133–150.

——— (1990a) "Illusion and Reality in International Agricultural Trade Negotiations." Paper presented at conference, "The World Field Crops Economy: Scope and Limits of Liberalization of Agricultural Policies," Paris, December. Reprinted as Staff Paper P90-67, Center for International Food and Agricultural Policy, Department of Agricultural and Applied Economics, University of Minnesota.

——— (1990b) "International Public Goods, Export Subsidies and the Harmonization of Environmental Regulations." Staff paper P90-77, Center for International Food and Agricultural Policy, Department of Agricultural and Applied Economics, University of Minnesota.

——— (1990c) "Trade Protectionism and Environmental Regulations: The New Nontariff Barriers." *Northwestern Journal of International Law and Business*, 11, 1 (Fall).

Runge, C. F., J. P. Houck, and D. W. Halback (1988) "Implications of Environmental Regulations for Competitiveness in Agricultural Trade." In J. D. Sutton, ed., *Agricultural Trade and Natural Resources: Discovering the Critical Linkages*, ch. 4. Boulder and London: Lynne Rienner.

Runge, C. F., and H. von Witzke (1987) "Institutional Change in the Common Agricultural Policy of the European Community." *American Journal of Agricultural and Economics*, 69, 2 (May): 213–222.

Runge, C. F., H. von Witzke, and S. J. Thompson (1989) "International Agricultural and Trade Policy: A Political Economic Coordination Game." In H. von Witzke, C. F. Runge, and B. Job, eds., *Policy Coordination in World Agriculture*, pp. 89–116. Kiel, Germany: Wissenschaftsverlag Vauk.

Ruttan, V. W., and H. von Witzke (1990) "Toward a Global Agricultural System." *Interdisciplinary Science Review* 15: 57–63.

Sanger, C. (1987) *Ordering the Oceans: The Making of the Law of the Sea.* Toronto, Canada: University of Toronto Press.

Sarris, A. H., and J. Freebairn (1983) "Endogenous Price Policies and International Wheat Prices." *American Journal of Agricultural Economics* 65: 214–224.

Schnittker Associates (1979) *Multilateral Trade Negotiations: Results for U.S. Agriculture.* Report prepared for the Congressional Research Service. Washington, D.C.: U.S. Government Printing Office.

Schott, J. J. (1988) "Implications for the Uruguay Round." In J. J. Schott and M. G. Smith, eds., *The Canada–United States Free Trade Agreement: The Global Impact.* Washington, D.C.: Institute for International Economics and Institute for Research on Public Policy.

Shefrin, F. (1966) "World Agricultural Production and Trade." In Economic Council of Canada and Agricultural Economics Research Council of Canada, eds., *Conference on International Trade and Canadian Agriculture*, pp. 33–75. Ottawa: Queen's Printer.

Skogstad, G. (1990a) "Canada: Conflicting Domestic Interests and the MTN." In G. Skogstad and A. F. Cooper, eds., *Agricultural Trade: Domestic Pressures and International Tensions.* Halifax, N.S.: The Institute for Research on Public Policy.

——— (1990b) "The Farm Policy Community and Public Policy in Ontario and Quebec." In W. D. Coleman and G. Skogstad, eds., *Policy Communities and Public Policy in Canada: A Structural Approach.* Mississauga, Ont.: Copp Clark.

Smith, P. (1991) "Letter from Tokyo." *The New Yorker* (October 14): 105–118.

Snape, R. (1986) *Should Australia Seek a Free Trade Agreement with the USA?* Discussion Paper 86/01. Canberra: Economic Planning Advisory Council and the Department of Trade.

Steger, D. P. (1988) "Canadian-U.S. Agricultural Trade: A Proposal for Resolving Disputes." In K. Allen and K. Macmillan, eds., *U.S.-Canadian Agricultural Trade Challenges: Developing Common Approaches*, pp. 161–167. Washington, D.C.: Resources for the Future.

Stewart, F., and J. James, eds. (1982) *The Economics of New Technology in Developing Countries.* Boulder, Colo.: Westview.

Strange, S. (1979) "The Management of Surplus Capacity: Or, How Does Theory

Stand Up to Protectionism 1970s Style?" *International Organization* 33: 303–334.

—— (1987) "The Persistent Myth of Lost Hegemony." *International Organization* 41: 551–574.

—— (1988) *States and Markets*. London: Frances Pinter.

"Survey: World Trade" (1990) *The Economist*, September 22, pp. 29–30.

Tracy, M. (1989) *Government and Agriculture in Western Europe 1880–1988*, 3rd ed. London: Harvester Wheatsheaf.

—— (1990) "The Political Economy of Agriculture in the European Community." Paper for conference, "The Political Economy of European-North American Agricultural Policy and Trade," Saskatoon, Canada, March.

Tyers, R. (1989) "Developing Country Interests in Agricultural Trade Reform." *Agricultural Economics* 3: 169–186.

—— (1990) "Searching Under the Light: The Neglect of General Equilibrium, Dynamics and Risk in the Analysis of Food Trade Reforms." Lecture presented to the Center for International Food and Agricultural Policy, February 22. Reprinted as Staff Paper P90-66, Center for International Food and Agricultural Policy, Department of Agricultural and Applied Economics, University of Minnesota.

—— (forthcoming) "The Role and Interest of the Cairns Group in the Uruguay Round." In R. C. Hine et al., eds., *Agriculture in the Uruguay Round: Reform Objectives and Outcome*. Nottingham: Nottingham University Press.

Tyers, R., and K. Anderson (1988) "Liberalizing OECD Agricultural Policies in the Uruguay Round: Effects on Trade and Welfare." *Journal of Agricultural Economics* 39 (May): 197–216.

United Nations Conference on Trade and Development (UNCTAD) (1990a) "Agricultural Trade Liberalization in the Uruguay Round: Implications for Developing Countries." UNDP/UNCTAD Projects of Technical Assistance to Developing Countries for Multilateral Trade Negotiations. UNCTAD/ITP/48. New York: United Nations.

—— (1990b) *Effects of Agricultural Trade Liberalization on Developing Countries*. New York: United Nations.

U.S. Congress, Budget Office (1989) *Agricultural Progress in the Third World and Its Effect on U.S. Farm Exports*. Washington, D.C.: U.S. Government Printing Office.

U.S. Department of Agriculture (USDA) (1984) *Background for 1985 Farm Legislation*, various volumes. Washington, D.C.: Economic Research Service–NASS.

—— (1989a) *Economic Implications of Agricultural Policy Reform in Industrial Market Economies*. Washington, D.C.: Economic Research Service.

—— (1989b) *Western Europe: Agriculture and Trade Report*. Washington, D.C.: Economic Research Service, RS-89-2.

—— (1990a) *Agricultural Outlook*. Washington, D.C.: Economic Research Service.

—— (1990b) *The Basic Mechanisms of U.S. Farm Policy: How They Work, With Examples and Illustration*. Washington, D.C.: Economic Research Service, Miscellaneous Publication No. 1479.

—— (1990c) *Agricultural Trade Liberalization and Developing Countries*. Washington, D.C.: Economic Research Service.

U.S. General Accounting Office (GAO) (1987) *Implementation of the Agricultural Export Enhancement Program*. Washington, D.C.: U.S. Government Printing Office, GAO/NSIAD-87-74BR.

———— (1988) *Agricultural Trade Negotiations: Initial Phase of the Uruguay Round*. Washington, D.C.: U.S. Government Printing Office, GAO/NSIAD-88-144BR.

Vogt, D. (1989) *Addressing Unfair Trade: Agricultural Cases Under Section 301 of the Trade Act of 1974*. Washington, D.C.: Congressional Research Service, 89-552 ENR.

von Witzke, H. (1986) "Endogenous Supranational Policy Decisions: The Common Agricultural Policy of the European Community." *Public Choice* 48: 157–174.

———— (1990) "Determinants of the U.S. Wheat Producer Support Price: Do Presidential Elections Matter?" *Public Choice* 64: 155–165.

von Witzke, H., and U. Hausner (1990) "International Agriculture and Trade Policy Interdependence: The Case of U.S. and EC Price Support. *Jahrbuch für Neue Politische Ekonomie* 9: 93–107.

von Witzke, H., C. F. Runge, and B. Job, eds. (1989) *Policy Coordination in World Agriculture*. Kiel, Germany: Wissenschaftsverlag Vauk.

Wallis, K. (1980) "Econometric Implications of the Rational Expectation Hypothesis." *Econometrica* 48: 49–73.

Warley, T. K. (1976) "Western Trade in Agricultural Products." In A. Shonfield, ed., *International Economic Relations of the Western World 1959–1971*, pp. 287–402. London: Oxford University Press for the Royal Institute of International Affairs.

———— (1989) "Agriculture in the GATT: A Historical Perspective." In *Agriculture in the Uruguay Round of GATT Negotiations: Implications for Canada's and Ontario's Agrifood Systems*, pp. 1–26. Guelph, Ont.: University of Guelph, Department of Agricultural Economics and Business.

———— (forthcoming) "Agriculture in the Uruguay Round: Canada's Position." In R. C. Hine et al., eds., *Agriculture in the Uruguay Round: Reform Objectives and Outcome*. Nottingham: Nottingham University Press.

Webb, M. C., and S. D. Krasner (1989) "Hegemonic Stability Theory: An Empirical Assessment." *Review of International Studies* 15: 183–198.

Weber, M. (1958) "The Social Psychology of the World's Religions." Translated and published in H. H. Gerth and C. W. Mills, eds., *From Max Weber: Essays in Sociology*. New York: Oxford University Press.

Weekend Australian (The), August 16–17, 1986.

Whalley, J. (1986) "Canada-United States Relations and the Global Trading System." In D. H. Flaherty and W. H. McKercher, eds., *Southern Exposure: Canadian Perspectives on the United States*, pp. 83–94. Toronto: McGraw-Hill Ryerson.

———— (1988) "Commentary." In J. J. Schott and M. G. Smith, eds., *The Canada–United States Free Trade Agreement: The Global Impact*, pp. 173–177. Washington, D.C.: Institute for International Economics and the Institute for Research on Public Policy.

Winham, G. R. (1986) *International Trade and the Tokyo Round Negotiation*. Princeton, N.J.: Princeton University Press.

———— (1989) "The Pre-Negotiation Phase of the Uruguay Round." *International Journal* 44: 290.

Winters, L. A. (1990) "Digging for Victory: Agricultural Policy and National Security." *The World Economy* 13, 2 (June): 170–190.

Wilson, B., and P. Finkle (1990) "Is Agriculture Different? Another Round in the Battle Between Theory and Practice." In C. Skogstad and A. F. Cooper, eds., *Agricultural Trade: Domestic Pressures and International Tensions*, pp. 3–12. Halifax, N.S.: Institute for Research on Public Policy.

World Bank (1990) *World Development Report, 1990: Poverty.* Washington, D.C.: World Bank.

———— (1991) *World Development Report, 1991: The Challenge of Development.* Washington: World Bank.

Yoshino, B. (1989) "Japan and the Uruguay Round." In H. R. Nau, ed., *Domestic Trade Politics and the Uruguay Round,* pp. 111–135. New York: Columbia University Press.

Yoshioka, Y. (1982) "The Personal View of a Japanese Negotiator." In E. N. Castle and K. Hemmi, with S. A. Skillings, eds., *U.S. Agricultural Trade Relations,* pp. 341–367. Washington, D.C.: Resources for the Future.

Young, O. R. (1991) "Political Leadership and Regime Reform: On the Development of Institutions in International Society." *International Organization* 45 (Summer): 281–308.

Zacher, M. W. (1987) "Trade Gaps, Analytical Gaps: Regime Analysis and International Commodity Trade Regulation." *International Organization* 41: 173–202.

Index

About the Book

Agriculture—central to the interests of both the rich industrialized countries, where it is heavily subsidized, and the poor nonindustrialized countries, where it is often the principal source of export earnings—has posed a problem for the global-free-trade regime since the beginning of the GATT. Multilateral trade negotiations have continually failed to bring agriculture into the free-trade system. And the most recent negotiations, the Uruguay Round, collapsed in December 1990 because of lack of agreement on terms to liberalize agricultural trade. Resumed in 1991, those talks continue to deadlock over this issue.

This book examines the role of agriculture in global free-trade, the competing interests of the United States, Europe, Japan, and the LDCs, the tension between states' domestic agricultural and international trade interests, and the particular impact of agriculture on the Uruguay Round.